IMAGES of America

MOUNT WHITNEY

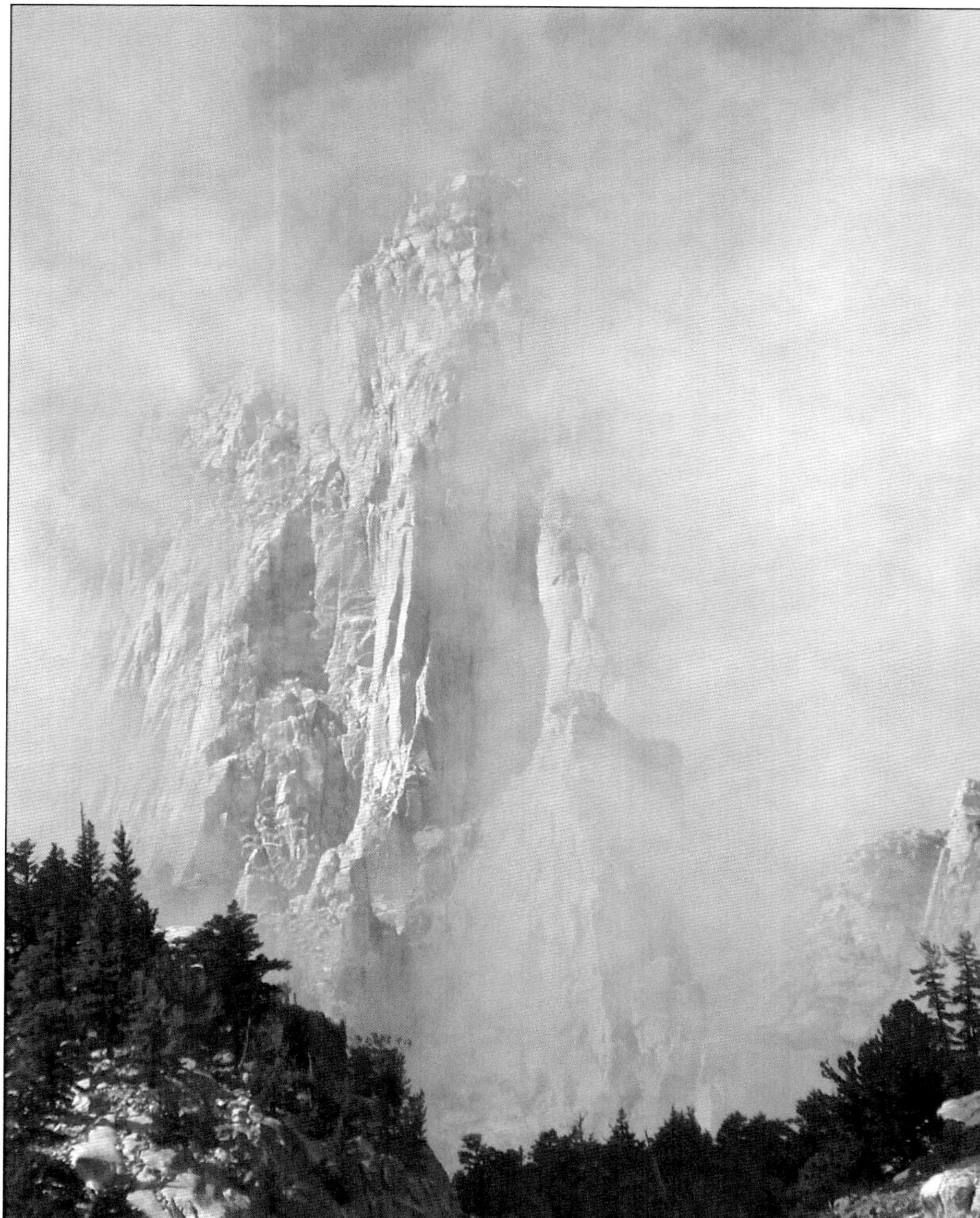

Mount Whitney stands veiled in mists as the morning light illuminates her face. Known as "a shy mountain," Whitney has called to indigenous peoples, pioneers, geologists, mountaineers, and tourists for thousands of years.

ON THE COVER: Easter Sunday morning was a special time at the Civilian Conservation Corps camp at the foot of Mount Whitney. Besides the CCC boys, families and people from Lone Pine also attended the services. This picture is from the mid-1930s.

IMAGES
of America

MOUNT WHITNEY

Christopher Langley and Michael Prather

ARCADIA
PUBLISHING

ISBN 978-0-7385-9536-8

Published by Arcadia Publishing
Charleston, South Carolina

Printed in the United States of America

Library of Congress Control Number: 2011942098

For all general information, please contact Arcadia Publishing:
Telephone 843-853-2070
Fax 843-853-0044
E-mail sales@arcadiapublishing.com
For customer service and orders:
Toll-Free 1-888-313-2665

Visit us on the Internet at www.arcadiapublishing.com

To Sandy and Nancy, our wives, who supported us through the long hours of research and exploration.

Contents

Acknowledgments

We would like to thank the following people and institutions: Jon Klusmire and Roberta Harlan, Eastern California Museum; Rob Barron, The Beverly and Jim Rogers Museum of Lone Pine Film History; Alison Sheehey, Audubon Kern River Preserve; K.C. Wiley, director, Interagency Visitors Center; Dave Kirk; Kevin Mazzu; Doug Thompson, owner, Mount Whitney Store and Hostel; Bruce Branson photograph collection; Mildred Langston; Relles Amick; Alabama Hills Stewardship Group; the Bureau of Land Management; www.owensvalleyhistory.com; George Marsh; and Amy Perryman, who kept us on track.

Unless otherwise noted, photographs are from the Eastern California Museum. LPFHM refers to the Beverly and Jim Rogers Museum of Lone Pine Film History.

INTRODUCTION

The story of a mountain includes formation, discovery, naming, conquest, adventures, stories, images, challenge, and human imagination. Mount Whitney is as much made of granite and surrounded by other tall peaks as in the minds of those who see it, hike it, and then experience it throughout the rest of their lives.

Although Paiute and other indigenous people undoubtedly first climbed it, the mountain was first identified by the California Geological Survey of 1864. Like good employees, surveyors named it for their boss, J.D. Whitney. Although one of these men, Clarence King, had to try four times before he made the summit, it was three fishermen from Lone Pine, the tiny town at the foot of Mount Whitney, who climbed it first. They wanted to call it Fishermen's Peak, a local name that became quite popular. However, the name was finally made official as Mount Whitney.

John Muir climbed "the rock" several times, and as the decades went on, more and more people made the scramble up to the top. Scientist S.P. Langley of the Allegheny Observatory set up a lab to study solar energy, and he began campaigning for a formal trail and an official observatory at the summit. Gustave Marsh of Lone Pine managed the project of creating a trail, which was completed in 1904. He then set about fulfilling Langley's dream (Langley was by then director of the Smithsonian), and the Smithsonian Observatory was built by 1909.

The next project was to build a road from Lone Pine to a location once called Hunter Flat, but which had been renamed Whitney Portal. The road was a project undertaken by the Civilian Conservation Corps that existed during the Depression. The CCC boys were young and enthusiastic, and the engineering feat was accomplished. More work was done on the trail in the mid-1940s, when the amazing 99 switchbacks were put in place. Later, the Whitney Portal Store was opened, and the Whitney Pack Station was located at the Portal as well.

As access increased, so did rescues. Writers, artists, and moviemakers all began to record their experiences on Whitney. Muir, King, and LeConte all wrote factual, literary accounts of their experiences on the mountain and achieving the summit. Both scientists and academicians wrote carefully about various aspects of the physical world found at different elevations. Many poets began to create their own responses to the mountains. Gary Snyder brought Jack Kerouac to the mountain, and the most famous beat writer captured the moment in his novel *The Dharma Burns*. W.R. Burnett wrote *High Sierra*, which became a famous movie whose thrilling conclusion happened on Whitney.

Hollywood came several times to the Portal area, although a crew never filmed on the summit. Tom Mix, Hopalong Cassidy, Tyrone Power, Richard Boone, and Randolph Scott appear in beautiful scenes shot on the mountain or at its base.

Photographers such as Ansel Adams, Galen Rowell, and David Muench all made personal images of the mountain. Painters including Albert Bierstadt and modernist Dave Kirk have created lasting interpretations of the mountain.

Mount Whitney is a mecca for tourists and vacationers. As you read, you are invited to leave your easy chair and drive, fly, or hike to Lone Pine and engage the mountain firsthand. There are many routes to take. Simply hike up and up and up. Test your ropes and mountaineering skills on the east face. Spend a leisurely few hours along the trail, looking for various plants and flowers, meeting a marmot or a bear. Fishing is good, but the high altitudes will tax your respiratory system, especially if you have not taken time to acclimate.

More so, the weather can turn suddenly; the temperatures can drop to a frigid level though you were in short sleeves a few hours before. Don't be on summit when a summer thunderstorm breaks or when an early winter storm starts to howl. Mount Whitney is not for the faint of heart or the unprepared, and many have paid a terrible price.

For some, it is the timelessness of the mountain that illuminates their souls and challenges their minds. It is a dynamic changing landscape. Great forces are at work here in the Sierra Nevada. They have been for eons. Glaciers have come and gone, and it is not an accident that the lowest and the highest areas are about 80 miles apart in this place of extremes.

This book is not a climber's manual. It does not tell how to climb Whitney, what routes are best or worst, what maps will help guide you, and what supplies and equipment you will need. This book is a cultural and natural history of the mountain. It opens doors to the work of artists, writers, and even just everyday people who create poetry, movies, and Internet expressions in trying to capture their Mount Whitney experiences. We believe this book will enrich one's own personal encounter with the mountain, and that will enrich a personal life to the end of one's days.

One

Icon of a Dynamic Landscape

Geologic landmarks such as California's Mount Whitney are often created by distant forces that are removed in time and space. Crustal plates cover the Earth's surface, fitting together like puzzle pieces. Here in California, the Pacific Plate and the North American Plate collide and slide past each other. Along the infamous San Andreas Fault, the Pacific Plate moves north while the North American Plate travels south. This collision has resulted in the buckling of the Earth's crust, forming wrinkled mountain ranges from the Pacific coast all the way to the Rocky Mountains.

The scarp of the Sierra Nevada in the Mount Whitney region is known as the range front. It has been exposed by the uplifting of 400 miles of the east side of the Sierra Nevada. The scarp is sheer and dramatically precipitous as it rises nearly 11,000 feet above Lone Pine on the floor of the Owens Valley. This uplift has been within the last 10 million years, geologically recent, and is still rising at roughly one foot per century. The 1872 Lone Pine earthquake demonstrated how suddenly uplift could occur when, in minutes, the earth's crust rose 15 to 20 feet vertically and slid horizontally an equal distance. The adobe village of Lone Pine suffered complete destruction and several dozen deaths.

But how did the Sierran granite, a volcanic (igneous) rock formed miles below the Earth's surface, rise to nearly three miles above sea level today? Three distinct sequences faraway in time and space led to the current form of the Whitney Crest area. First, around 150 million years ago, the Pacific Plate began diving under the North American Plate. Its ocean sediments were melted as they slid deep below the crust resulting in massive molten magma chambers, which formed the Sierra Nevada Batholith and became today's granite. The Sierra Nevada Batholith is an enormous body of granite, extending the length of the Sierra Nevada and beyond. As the plate subducted (dived) beneath the North American Plate, some of the molten material rose to the surface as volcanic eruptions and formed a mountain range nearly 15,000 feet high that predated the Sierra Nevada. Second, over tens of millions of years after the subduction, the range that preceded the Sierra Nevada eroded away until the area became rolling hills with extensive exposed granite. The eroded sediment flowed into the Central Valley and the Owens Lake Basin. Third, starting roughly 10 million years ago, the Sierra, especially the Southern Sierra, began to be uplifted. Most of this rise took place in the last 700,000 years, resulting in granitic Mount Whitney, which was 14,495 feet above sea level.

While the Mount Whitney Crest rose, it was shaped by weathering, erosion, and glaciation. It continues to be shaped today. Chemical weathering by the natural acidity of rain slowly percolates into granite and separates its grains. Chemicals created by decaying vegetation leach into rock and soil and hasten their breakdown into simpler forms. The shaping of the current Mount Whitney Crest began in earnest around two and a half million years ago. Geologists label this period the Pleistocene, more commonly known as the Ice Ages. Ample snow accumulated, and summers cooled enough for glaciers to form. In total, there were three to four major glacial advances. At its greatest expanse, the ice field was 275 miles long and 20 to 40 miles wide. The thickness of the ice was measured in thousands of feet.

The Eastern Sierra glaciers were shorter due to lower precipitation, but they were able to carve the classic U-shaped drainages, such as Meysan Creek, which can be seen to the southwest as Whitney Portal is approached. They left behind large boulders called erratics and cirques or small bowls, often with a small lake or tarn at the top of watersheds where the glaciers began. Glacial polish or glass-like rock surfaces were created by the movement of the glaciers. Walking up the Mount Whitney Trail, one can switchback up steep slopes and then walk into relatively gentler flats. This is a glacial staircase that was carved as the glacier moved down the Lone Pine Creek Canyon.

The High Sierra in the Mount Whitney area has become many things to many people. For John Muir, it was his "Range of Light." For Los Angeles, it is a dream catcher that captures the moisture of winter storms. For climbers and hikers, it is a challenge surrounded by awesome beauty and natural quiet. For ranchers and the Paiute, it is where one lives and secures food.

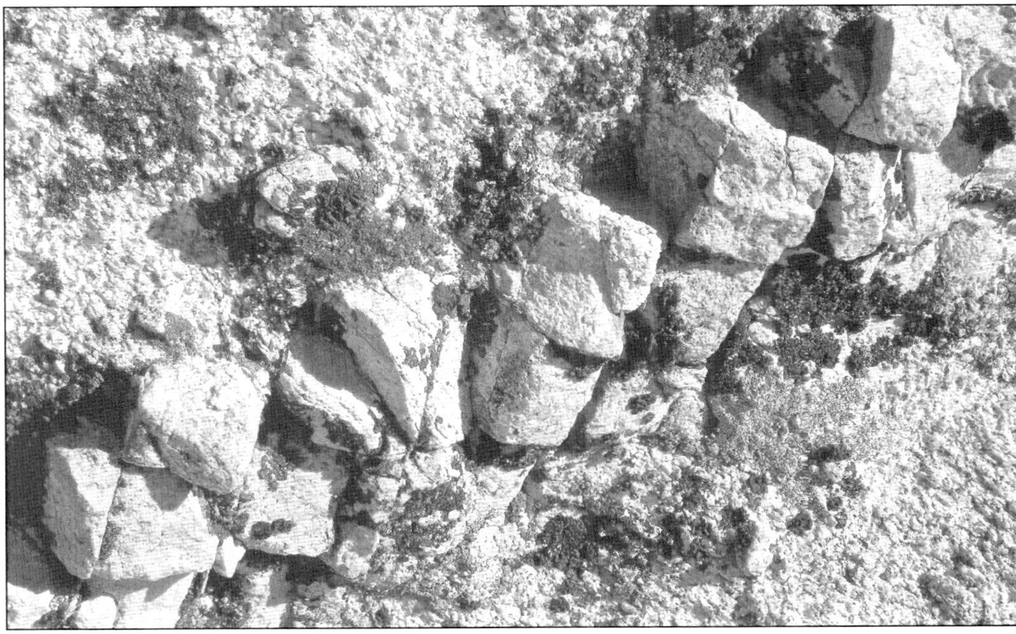

Seen here is an intrusion, or dike, of feldspar crystals in a matrix of granite. Slow cooling deep below the Earth's surface allows large crystals to form. The word *feldspar* is derived from the German *feld*, meaning "field," and *spath*, meaning "rock that does not contain ore." The rectangular crystals are often found imbedded in granite boulders. (Mike Prather.)

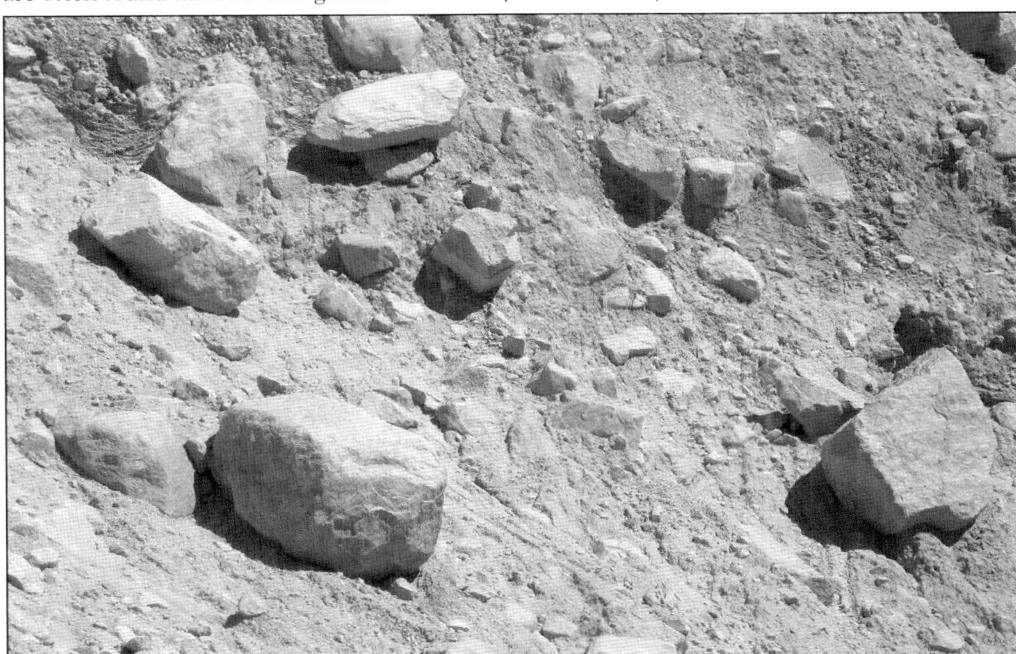

This is a photograph of glacial till along the Whitney Portal Road. This mix of rock and sediments is left over from the glacial periods. Glaciers pushed material around as they advanced and retreated. (Mike Prather.)

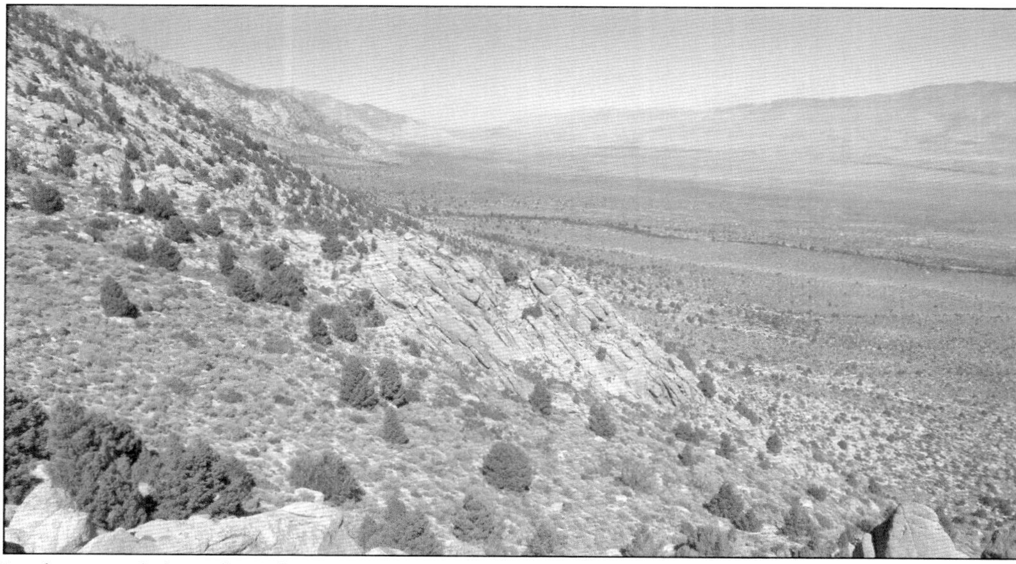

Looking north from the Whitney Portal Road, the steep range front slopes down to meet the gentler sloping bajada. Bajadas are formed when alluvial fans join and blend into each other, forming a continuous gentle slope from the base of the mountains to the valley floor. (Mike Prather.)

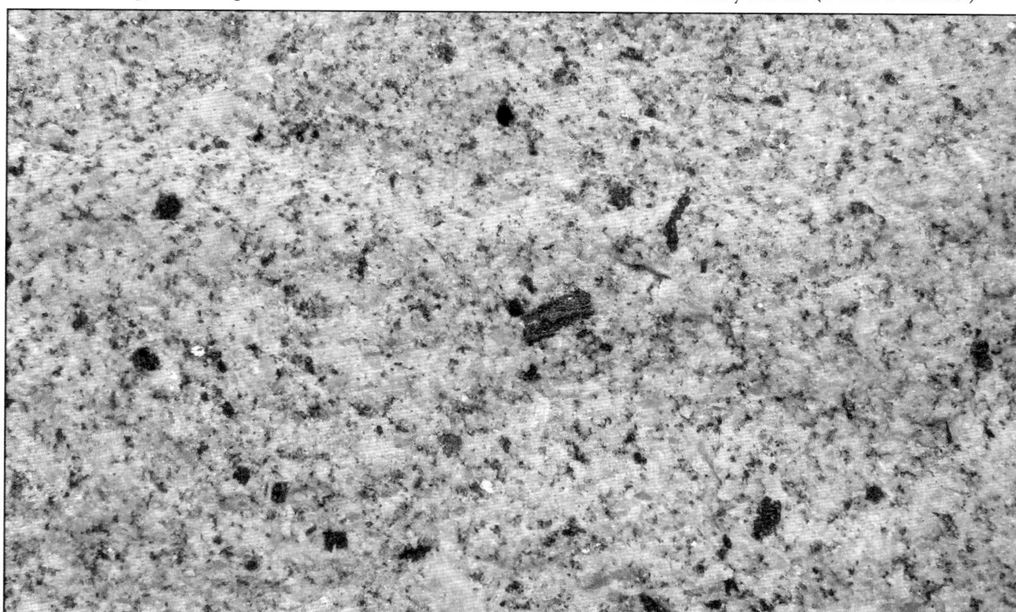

Granite in general has a basic recipe of quartz, feldspar, and dark iron/manganese compounds. In large pockets of molten rock located miles below the surface called magma chambers, granite began crystallizing as it cooled over many years. The separate minerals in the mix had different melting temperatures; therefore, during millions of years of cooling, they crystallized in a sequence beginning with the darker iron/manganese crystals with the highest melting point, followed by feldspar, and lastly quartz with the lowest melting point. The rate of magma cooling influenced crystal formation. Rapid cooling resulted in micrograntes, or rock with nearly imperceptible crystals. Slower cooling allows larger crystals to form. (Mike Prather.)

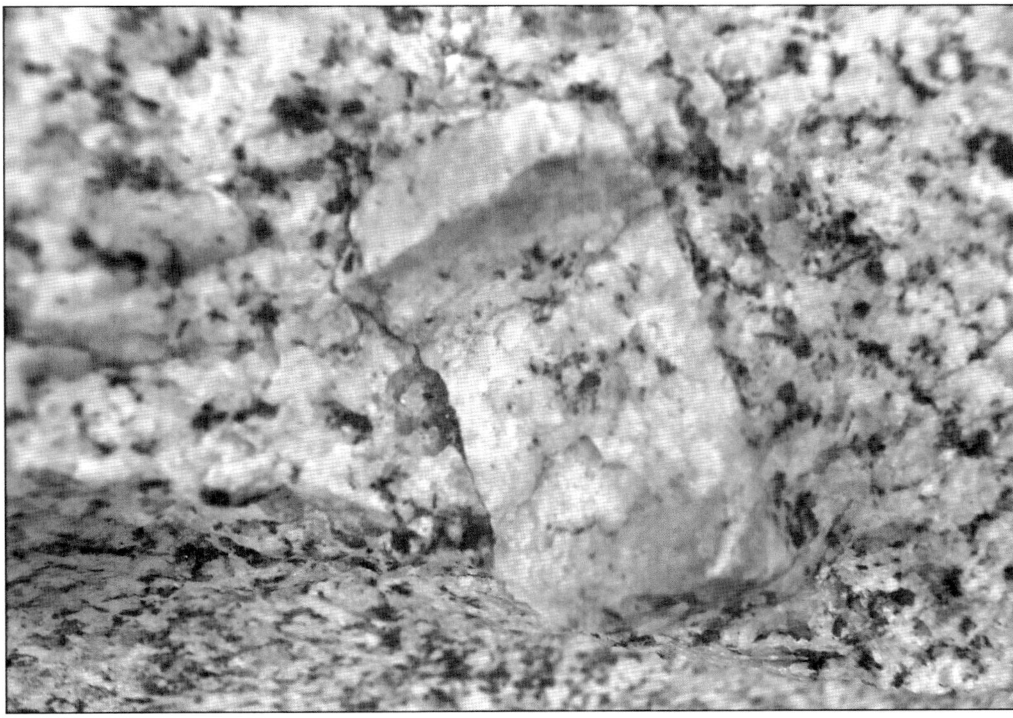

This is a typical feldspar crystal, one and a half inches by three-fourths of an inch. Slow cooling resulted in large crystals of pinkish and white feldspar. The rectangular crystals can be seen embedded in the matrix. (Mike Prather.)

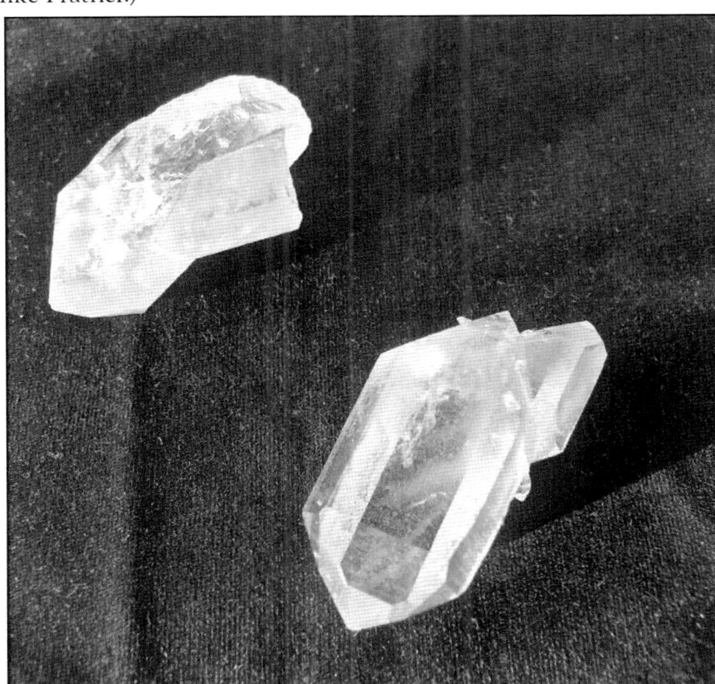

Silicon dioxide, or quartz, has the lowest melting point of the granite soup mix. Therefore, it crystallizes or solidifies last. Slow cooling grows finger-like quartz crystals. (Mike Prather.)

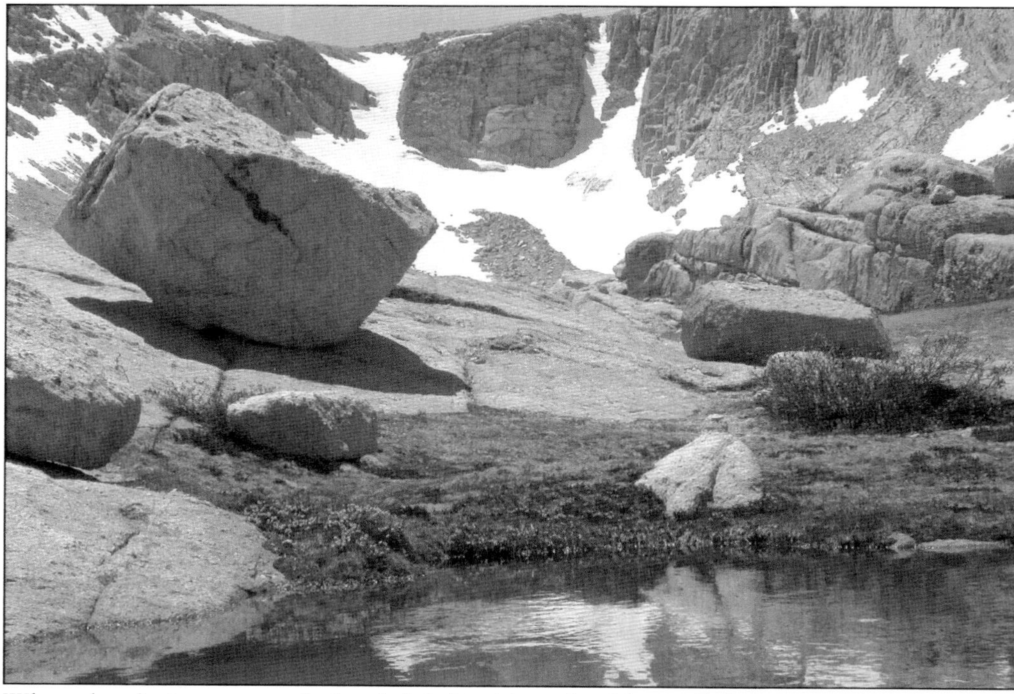

When the glaciers retreated, they left behind large boulders called erratics. The size of these erratics teaches the power of glaciers. (Mike Prather.)

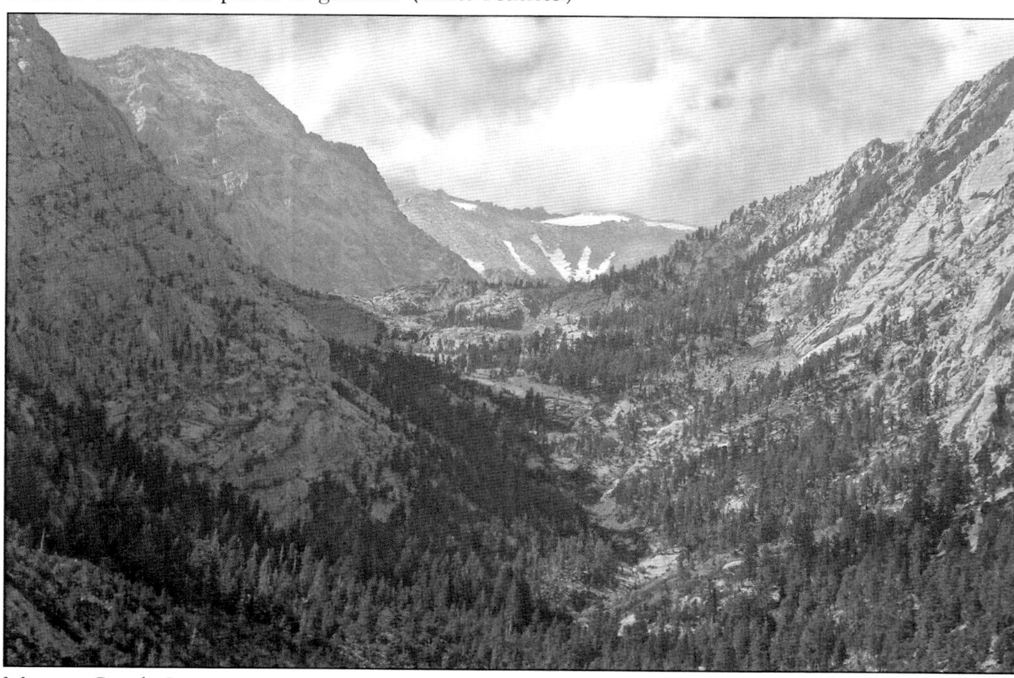

Meysan Creek Canyon is an example of a U-shaped drainage that was carved by a glacier. Stream-carved canyons have a V-shape. This canyon is south across Lone Pine Creek Canyon above the summer cabins as one nears Whitney Portal. (Mike Prather.)

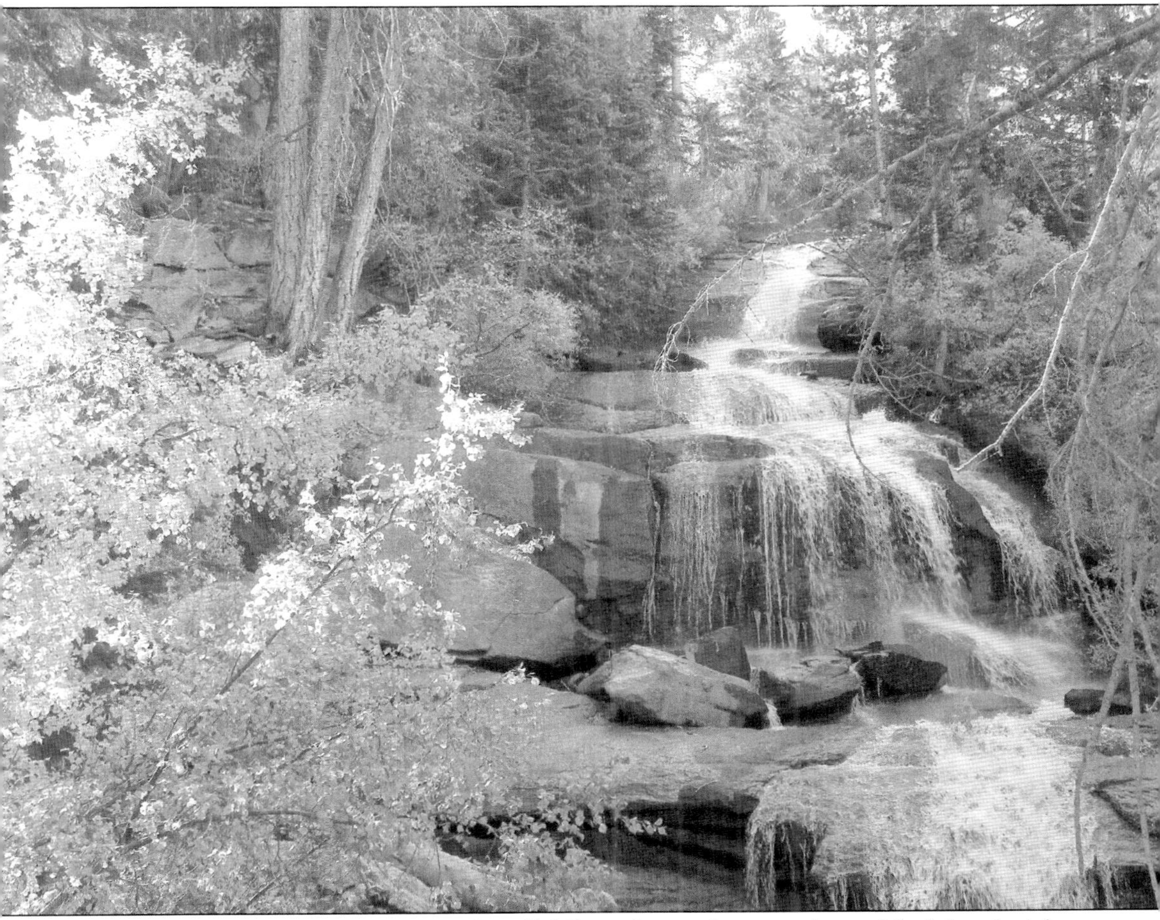

The Whitney Portal cascade is a series of small falls and steps. It is a scale model of the glacial staircase that the Mount Whitney Trail follows. For those hiking the Mount Whitney Trail from Whitney Portal, both Outpost Camp and Trail Camp are steps on the staircase to the summit. (Mike Prather.)

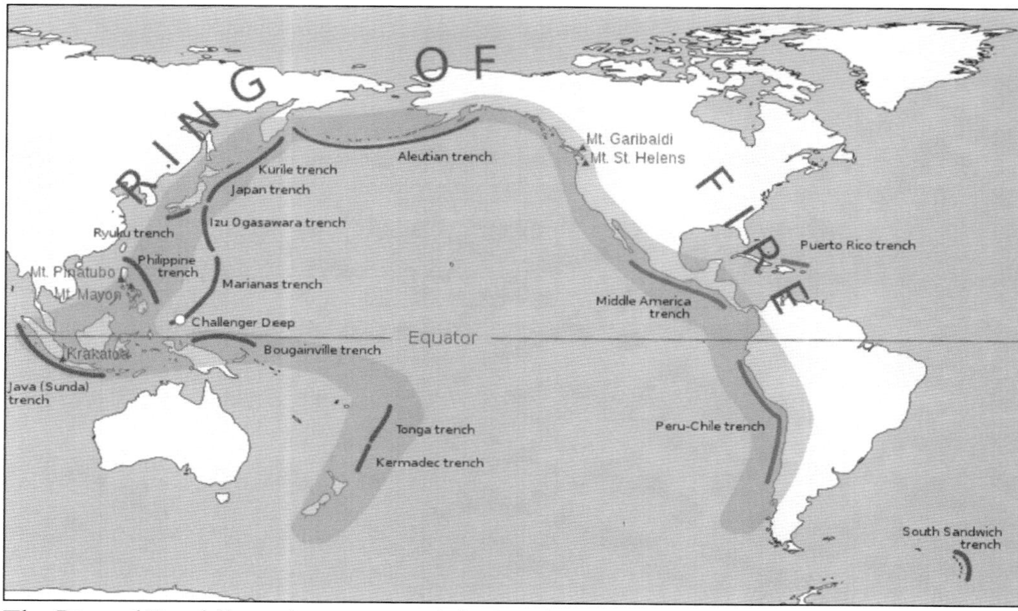

The Ring of Fire follows the margins of the Pacific Ocean from Alaska's Aleutian Islands to South America's Tierra del Fuego and through Polynesia to Japan and on to far eastern Russia. It is a zone of complex and vigorous geologic activity in the form of earthquakes and volcanoes. Volcanoes spew out new islands and mountains, while deep trenches in the ocean's floor swallow oceanic crustal plates. Three-fourths of the earth's volcanoes and earthquakes occur in these regions. The outer skin of Earth wears a crust of plates floating on molten material extending miles below the surface. These rafts of crust vary in size and may be on the scale of continents or even larger. Over millions of years, these tectonic plates have slid by, collided with, and dived under each other creating zones of earthquake and volcanic mayhem. (Mike Prather.)

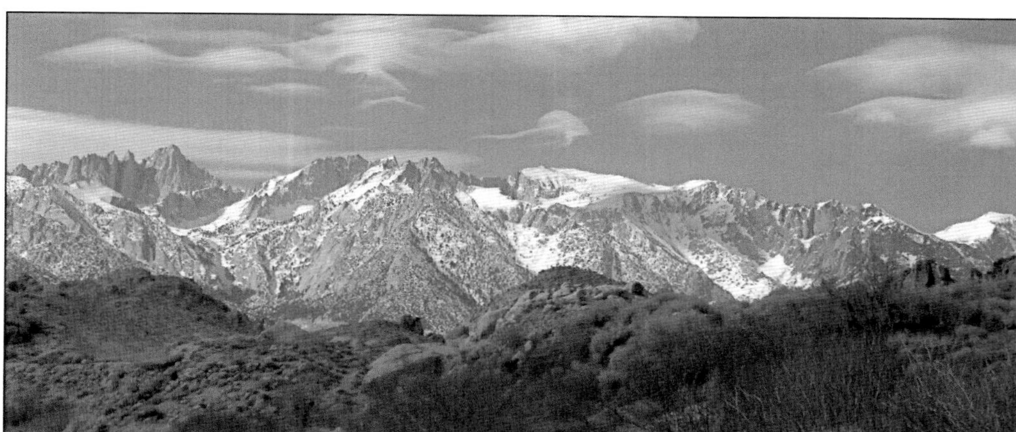

Westerly winds and mountain ranges that run primarily north and south create a unique atmospheric phenomenon known as wave clouds or lenticular clouds. The Sierra Nevada forces west winds to flow upward over the crest and to form ripples or wavelets of air to the east. As air travels up, it cools and moisture condenses forming lines of clouds parallel to the range. At times, these clouds form in layer upon layer. They signal high winds aloft and often predict wind increases at the surface as well. (Mike Prather.)

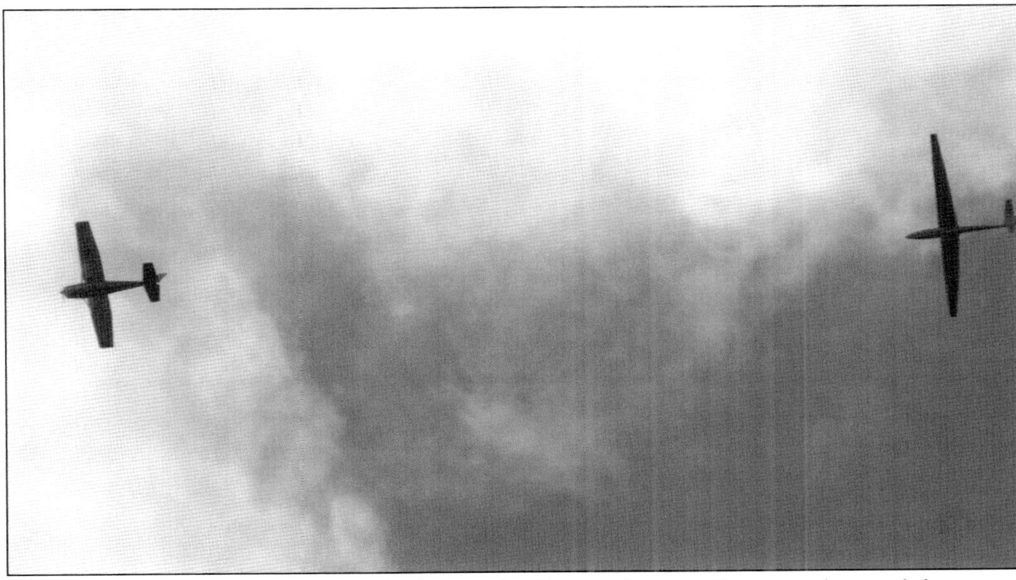

In the 1950s, extensive research took place in the Eastern Sierra to better understand the nature of wave clouds. This was the Sierra Wave Project, which set out using sailplanes to measure the forces in wave clouds and their threat to aviation. The data collected showed ascent and descent rates of over 2,500 feet per minute and 15 g's of acceleration. These are forces beyond the design limits of commercial and private aircraft.

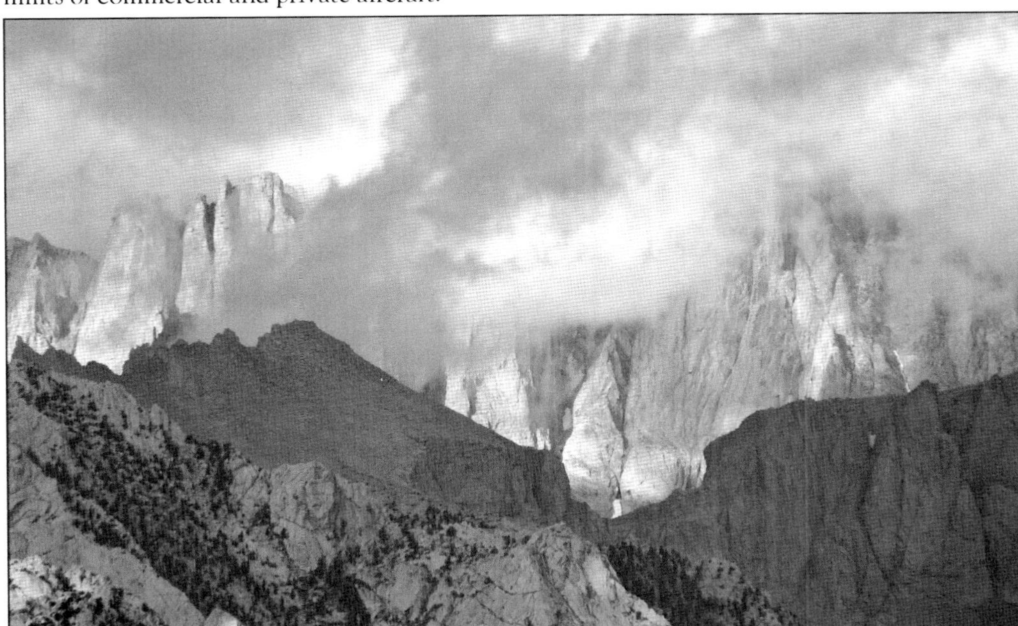

Hypothermia can threaten life as easily and often as accidents in the back country. A windy wet day or night with temperatures in the 40s and 50s can be deadly if a hiker is not prepared. Once clothes become wet, the body's core temperature begins to drop. Shivering, delirium, and death can follow in a surprisingly short time. Conditions in the mountains can change in minutes, so proper protection against cold and moisture is critical. (Mike Prather.)

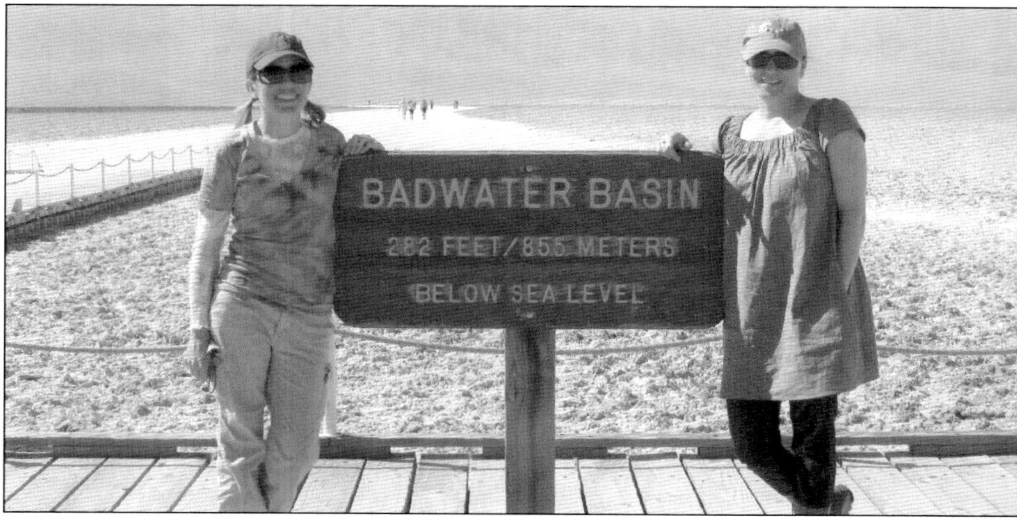

Badwater in Death Valley National Park is the lowest place on land in the western hemisphere. It is 282 feet below sea level and is only 90 miles away from Mount Whitney, the highest point in the Lower 48 states. Due to its latitude, the Sierra Nevada experiences prevailing westerly winds. These winds deliver moisture from the Pacific Ocean in the form of rain and snow. Most of the precipitation is captured on the western slope of the Sierra, and little moisture is able to reach east of the high crest. A rain shadow of aridity extends east of the Mount Whitney Crest. The Owens Valley's annual precipitation averages four to six inches, and Death Valley averages one and a half inches per year. (Mike Prather.)

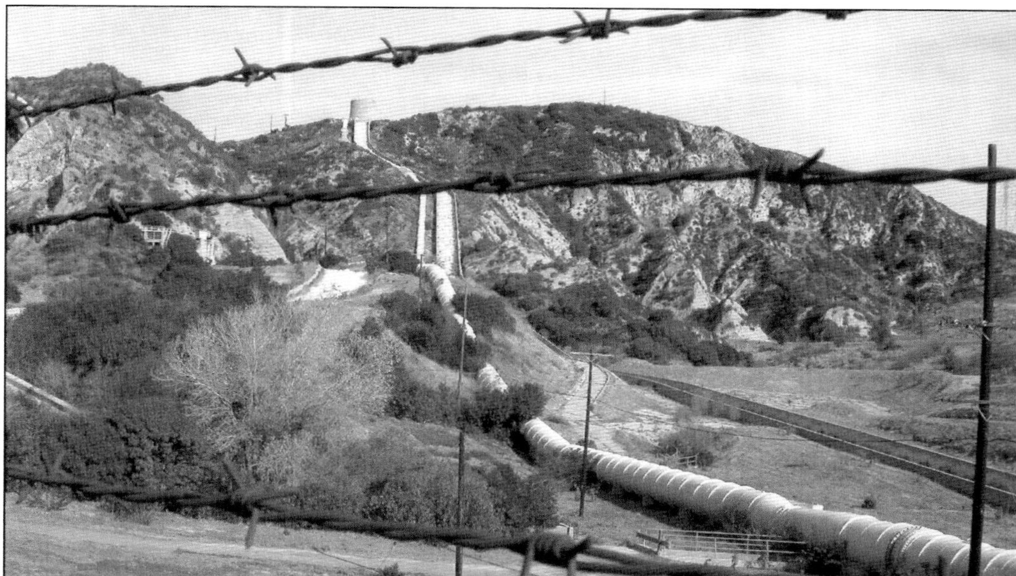

The completion of the first Los Angeles Aqueduct in 1913 led to the capture of all streams flowing out of the Sierra Nevada into the Owens Valley. The lower Owens River dried up and was soon followed by Owens Lake. This photograph shows the aqueduct water flowing down the cascade in Sylmar as it arrives in Los Angeles after its 238-mile trip from the Owens Valley. (Mike Prather.)

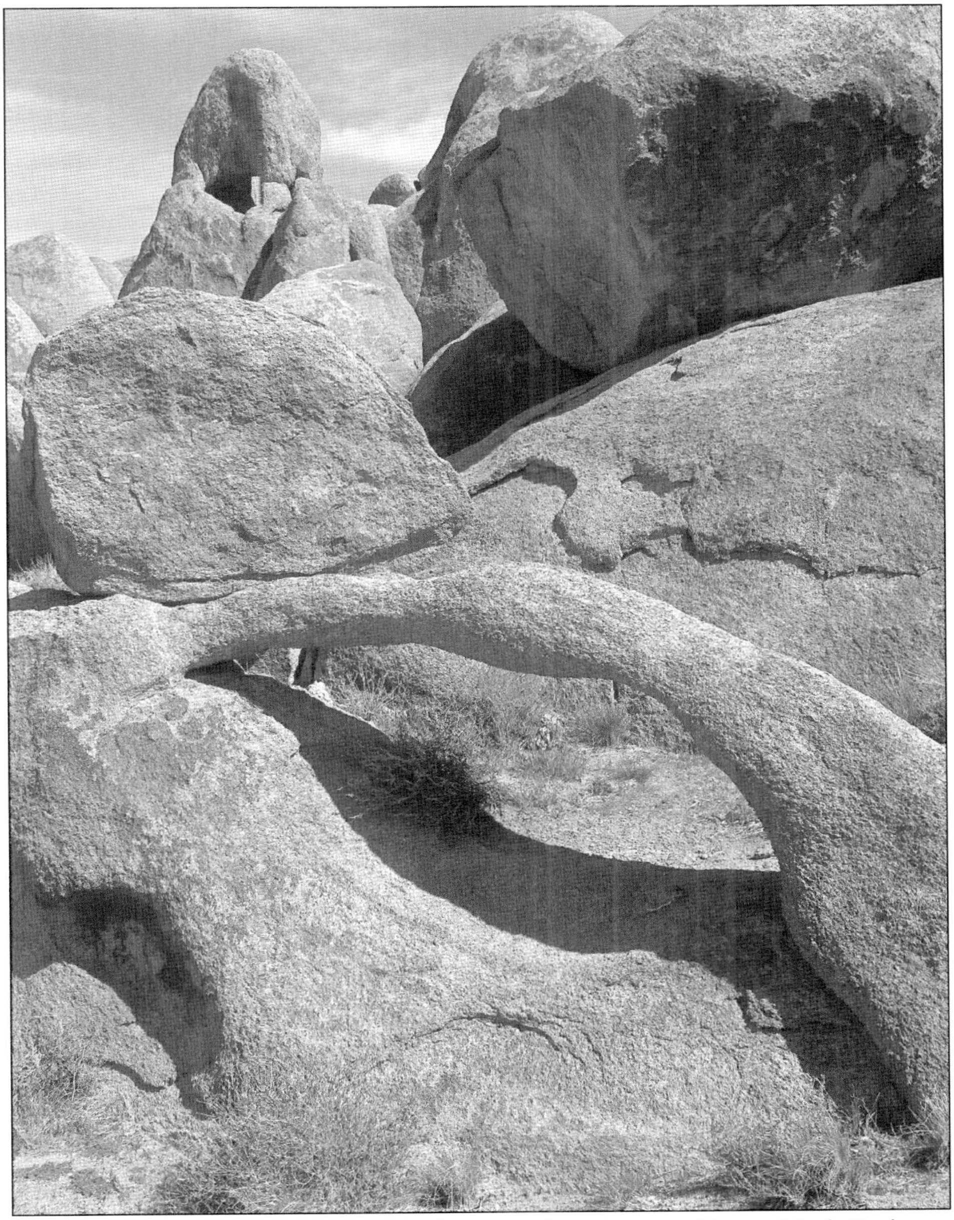

The fault block of the Alabama Hills has broken away from the main Sierran block. Faults on the western and eastern edge of the Alabama Hills have allowed this movement. The rhombohedral corners of the granite have been rounded off through chemical weathering while the granite was underground prior to its emerging. Looking up to Mount Whitney's summit from Lone Pine on the floor of the Owens Valley, one would be surprised that under his or her feet is 6,000 to 8,000 feet of sediment eroded from the Sierra Nevada and the mountain range that preceded it. If the vertical distance were calculated from Mount Whitney's summit, 11,000 feet above Lone Pine, to the bedrock far below, the distance would be nearly 19,000 vertical feet. In addition, the bedrock far below Lone Pine is roughly 4,000 feet below sea level. That is far below the elevation of Badwater in Death Valley National Park at 282 below sea level. (Mike Prather.)

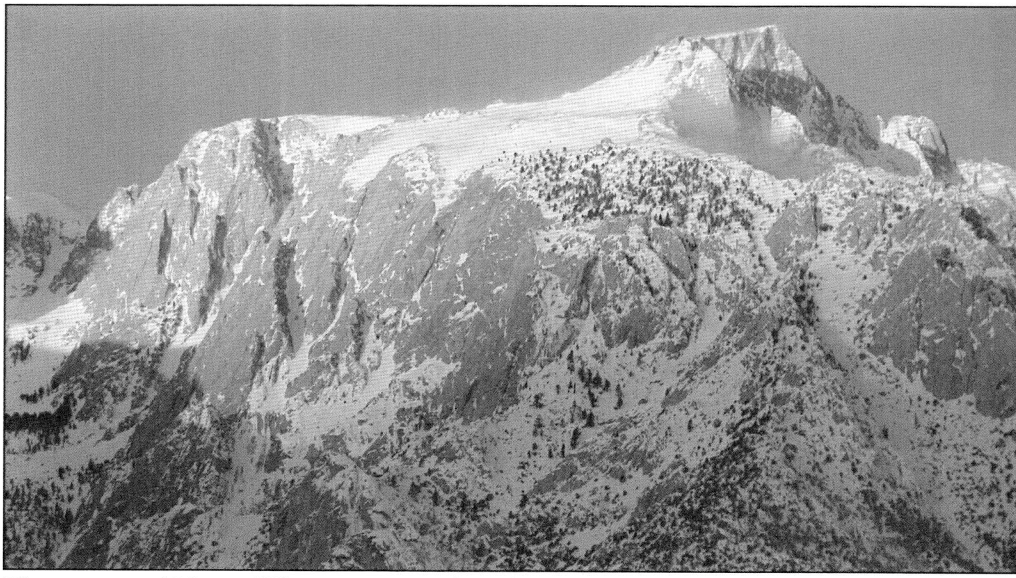

The summit of Mount Whitney is part of a ridge of tall peaks, many of which are 14,000 feet or higher. This is the true High Sierra, the land above the trees. Below the bright granite of the High Sierra is the dark coniferous forest. Visitors to the Owens Valley often mistake Lone Pine Peak (seen here), which is 12,944 feet, for Mount Whitney. They fail to notice that Mount Whitney is part of a crest that is set back from Lone Pine Peak and therefore appears shorter. (Mike Prather.)

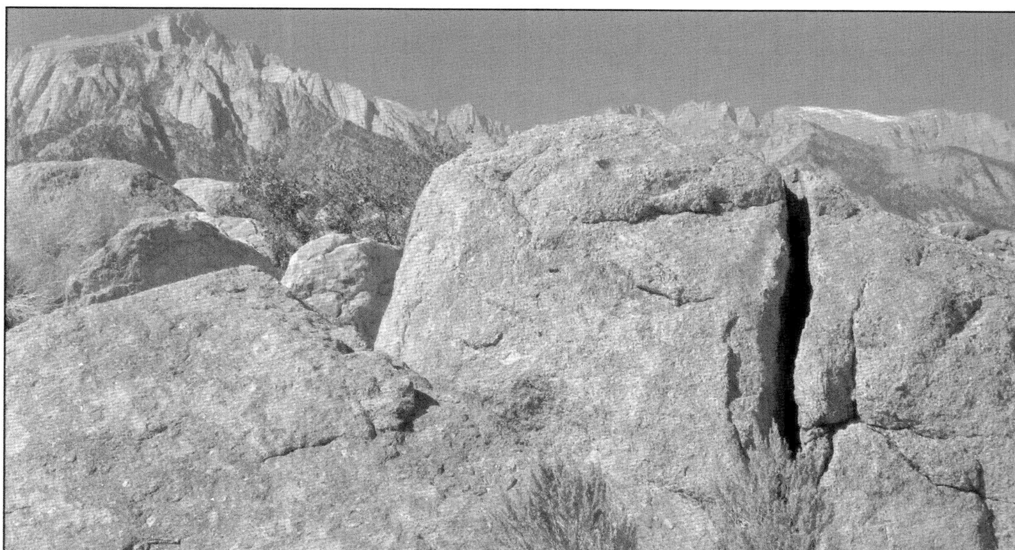

Frost wedging uses the power of the expansion of water as it turns to ice. Snowmelt or rain seeps down inside the joints in the rock. When the water freezes and expands with a force of around 1,000 pounds per square inch, it can pry apart solid rock. Gravity moves weathered material downslope as the mountains disintegrate. (Mike Prather.)

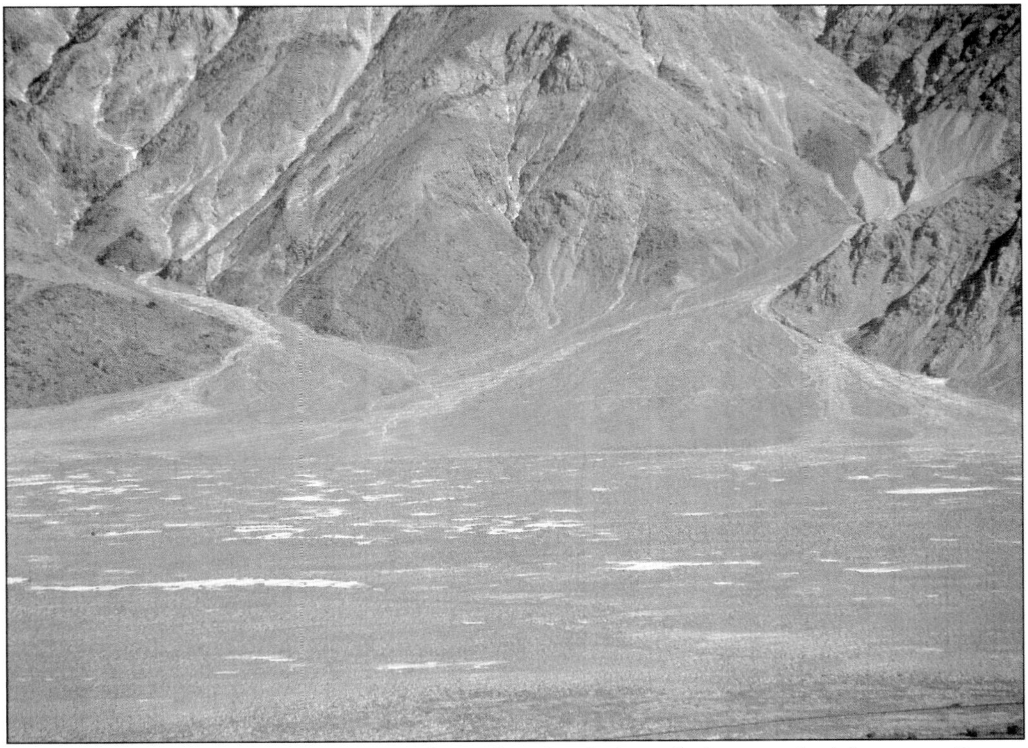

Lone Pine Creek's flowing water carries silt, sand, and rock through the watershed down into Owens Valley. Historically, its water flowed into the Owens River and on to Owens Lake. However, since the 1913 completion of the Los Angeles Aqueduct, this water now flows to the City of Angels. Owens Lake was dry by the mid-1920s. Historically, when Lone Pine Creek ran free, it spread rock and sediment over what is called an alluvial fan, or fan-shaped outflow from its canyon. The alluvial fans from the Inyo Mountains are shown here. (Mike Prather.)

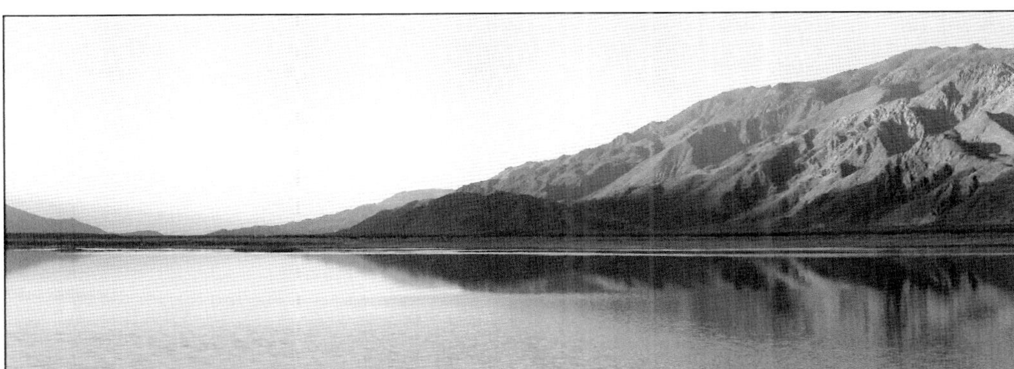

Owens Lake was an ancient lake with important habitat for thousands of migrating waterfowl and shorebirds. Recent dust-control efforts by Los Angeles are resulting in a welcome return of those heritage wildlife populations. (Mike Prather.)

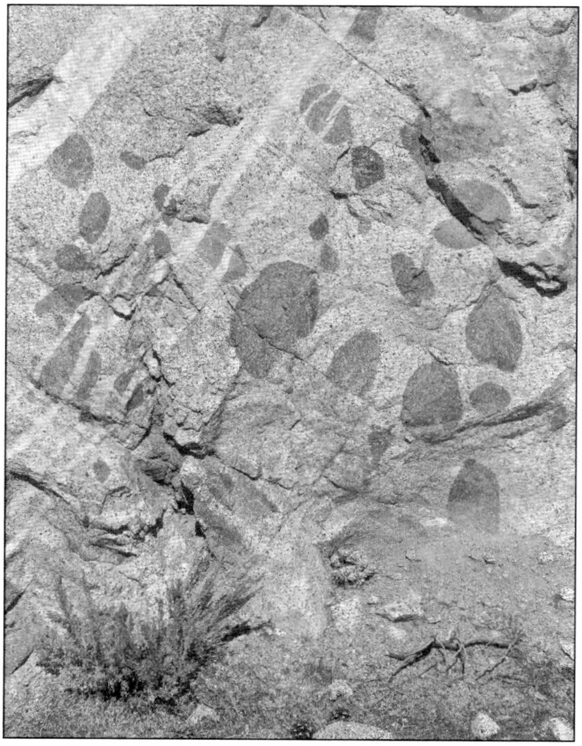

Magma chambers often rose and melted into the surrounding rock, which sometimes broke off and floated into the mix. These dark rounded xenoliths (from the Greek *xenos*, meaning "foreign"; and *lithos*, meaning "rock") are seen in the otherwise pure granite rock. (Mike Prather.)

After the granite crystallized, it often fractured. Molten intrusions of other minerals spread through the fractured spaces and cooled to form thick dikes. Various metals, such as gold, silver, and lead were concentrated in these veins. "Boom and bust" miners have searched for the mother lode following these intrusions throughout history. (Mike Prather.)

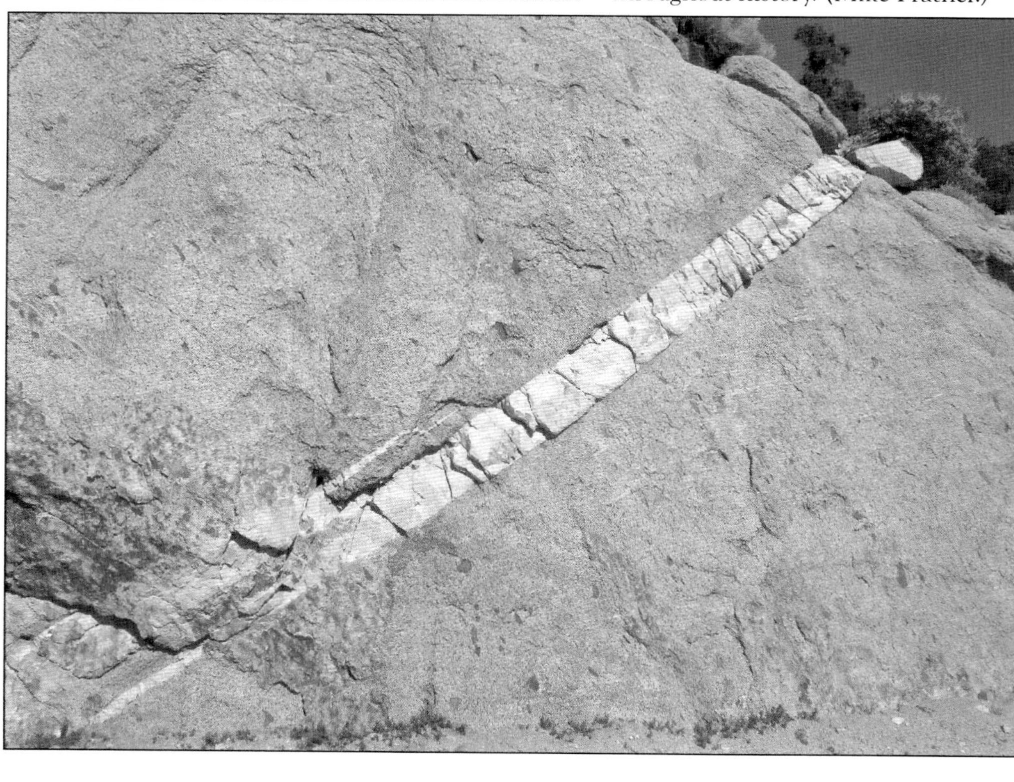

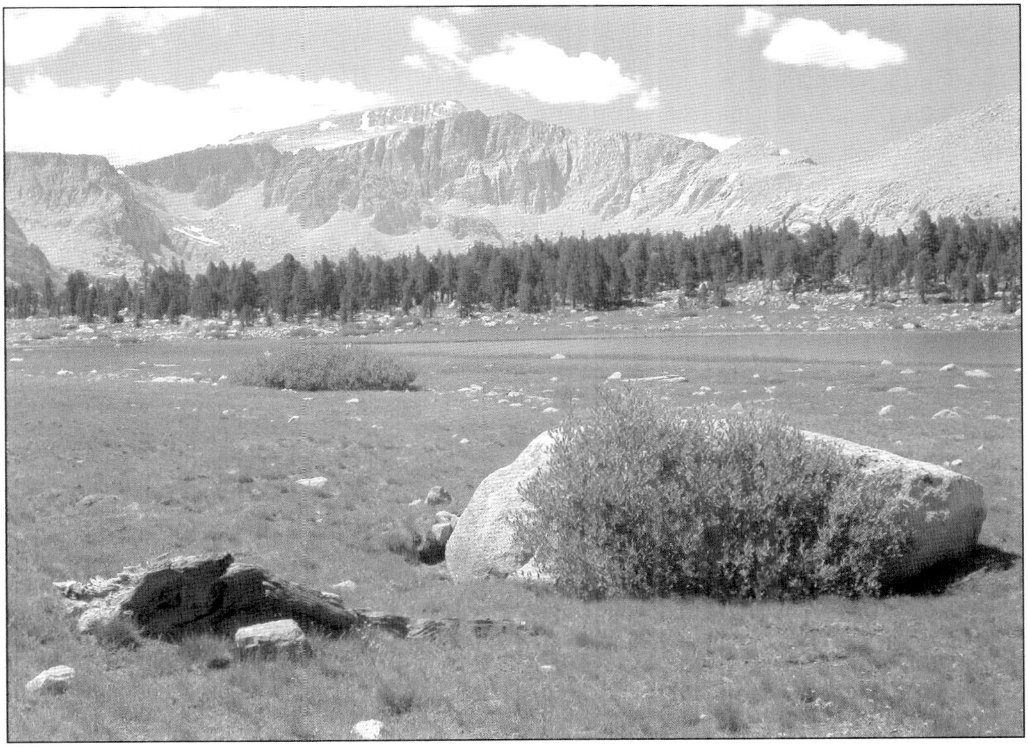

Mount Langley, at 14,027 feet, is seen from the Cottonwood Lakes Basin. It is an example of a tabular peak, with a gentler west slope and a precipitous east face. Mount Whitney is also a tabular peak. These summits were snow-free during the glacial periods due to prevailing winds and therefore less sculpted by ice. Glacier formation requires abundant snow, which can accumulate and persist through cooler summers. (Mike Prather.)

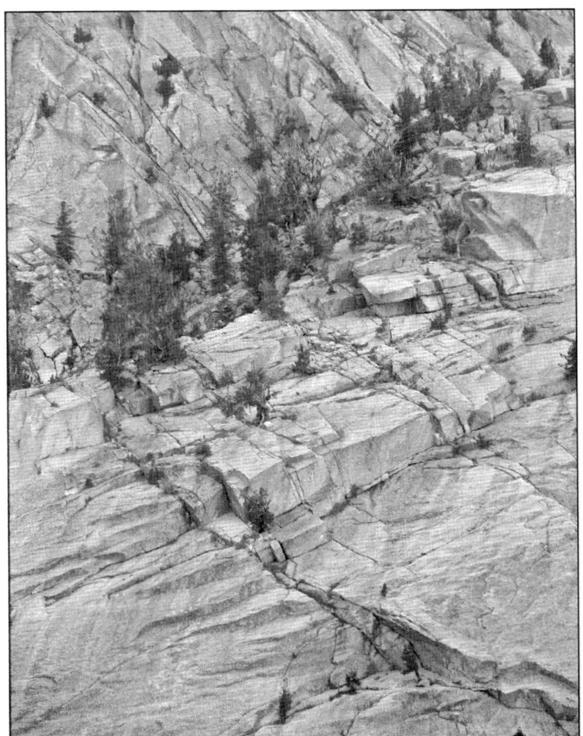

Granite breaks apart along joints. The fewer joints, the more solid and resistant is the rock. Large, well-spaced joints are evident in this photograph. (Mike Prather.)

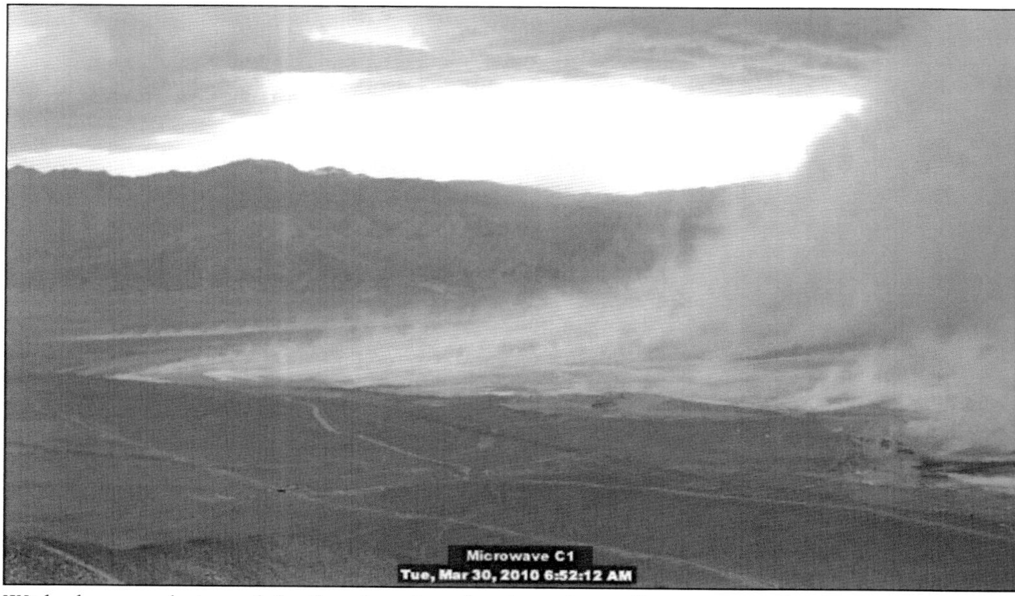

With the completion of the first Los Angeles Aqueduct, all streams in the Owens Valley were captured and sent south. The lower Owens River dried up and within 10 years, Owens Lake was gone. For 80 years, Owens Lake was the largest dust-pollution source in the United States and a regional public health hazard. (Mike Prather.)

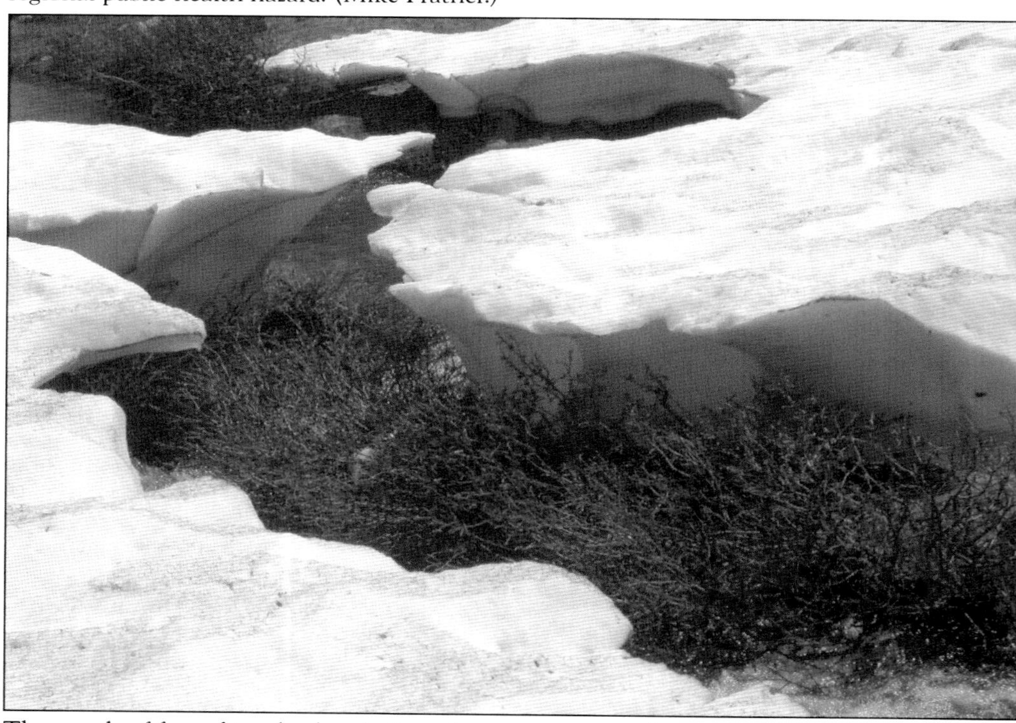

Thousands of feet of ice slowly grinding along can carve and smooth the hardest granite. John Muir won his debate with Josiah Whitney over what force shaped the Sierra Nevada. It was glaciers. (Mike Prather.)

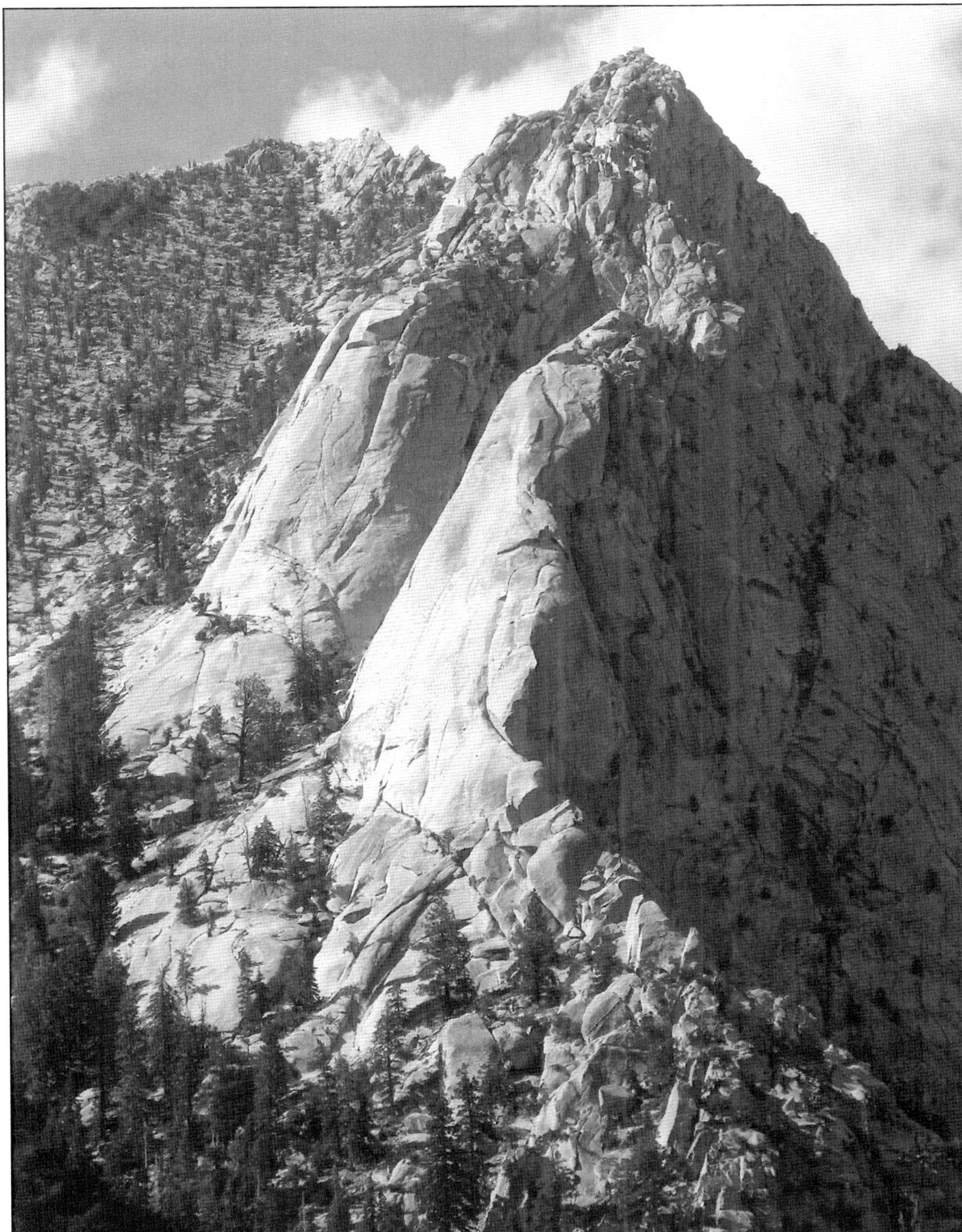

Melting snow runoff peaks in May and June and provides eastern-slope water for the city of Los Angeles, 220 miles to the south. (Mike Prather.)

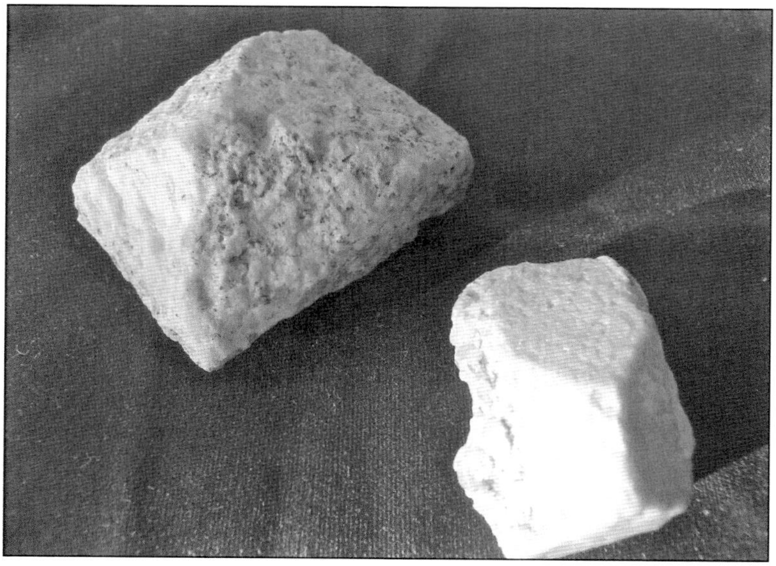

Feldspar crystals can be found scattered over the ground where granite rock is decomposing. Keep a sharp eye out. Don't just "take it for granite" anymore. (Mike Prather.)

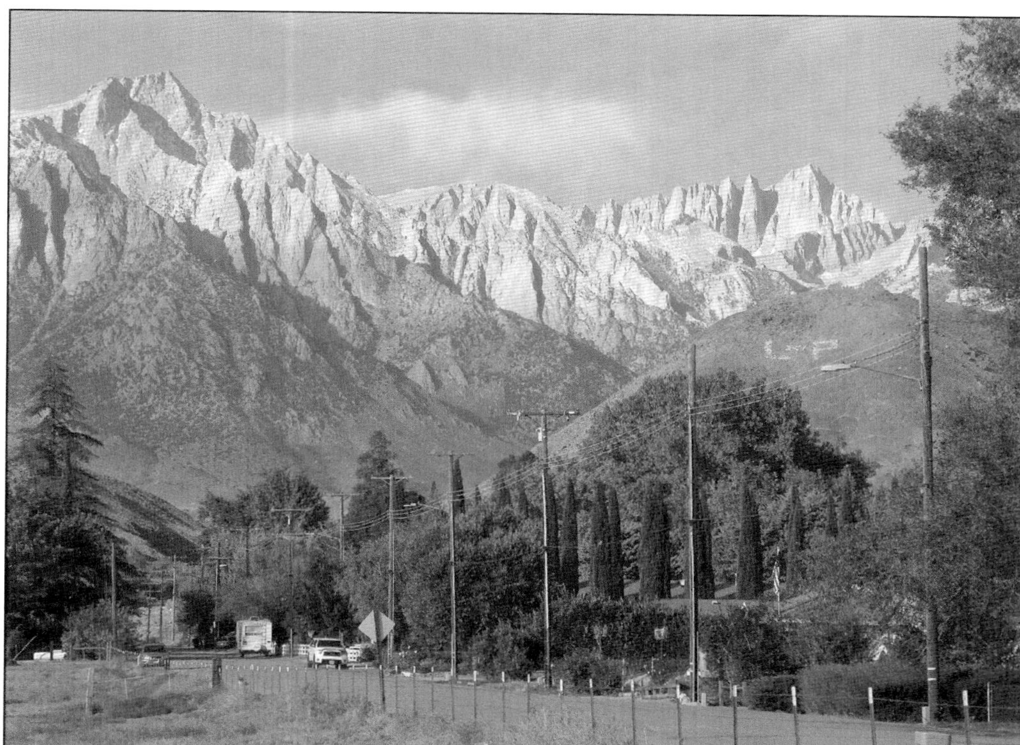

Lone Pine Peak is mistaken for Mount Whitney by many visitors to the Owens Valley. It is closer to the observer, while the higher Mount Whitney is farther back along the crest. (Mike Prather.)

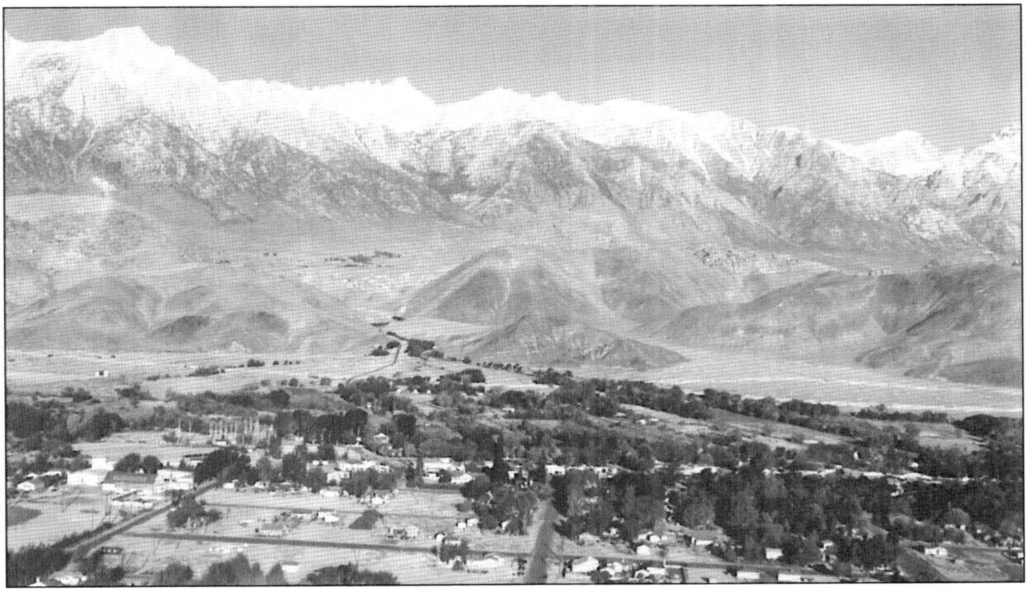

Mount Whitney stands back from the Owens Valley spread at her feet.

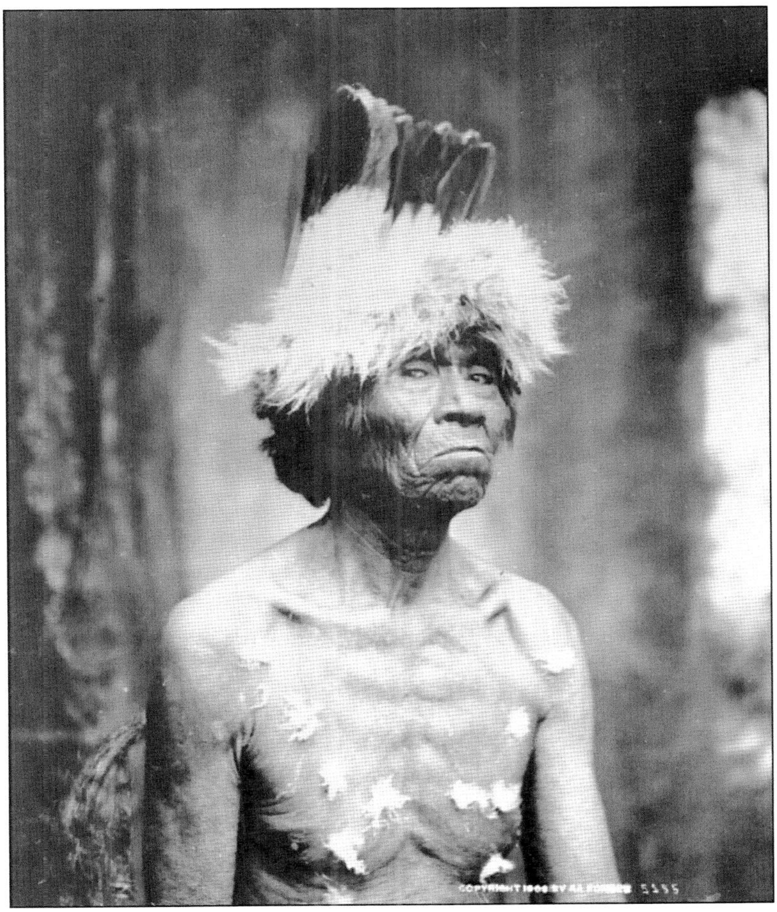

Paiute tribes have lived in the area for thousands of years, and it is reasonable to believe that members were the first to climb Mount Whitney. They may have started out hunting or gathering pine nuts and just kept on climbing to the top. This magnificent portrait is of Captain Jack.

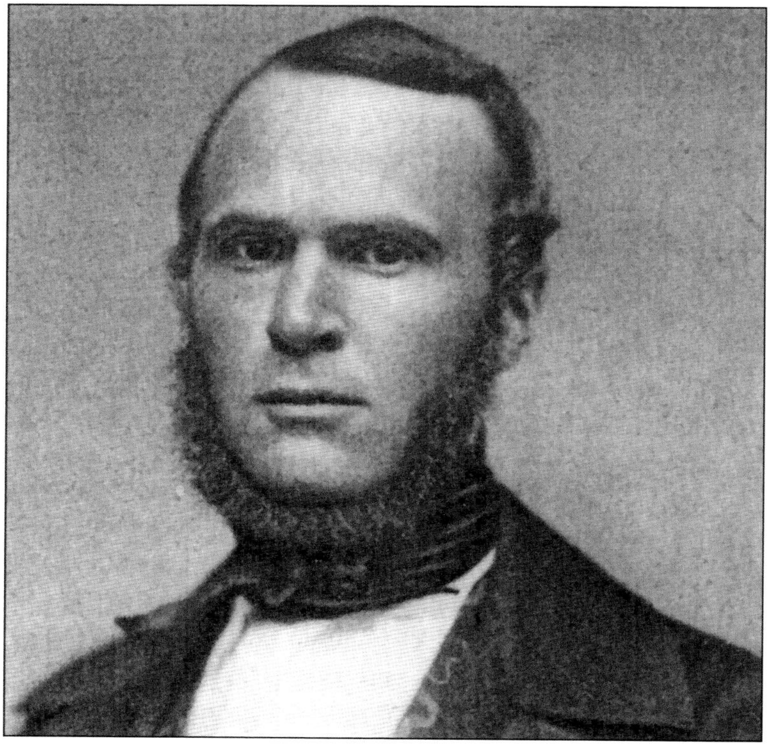

J.D. Whitney spent his early career in the East but was selected to head up the California Geological Survey which was set up by the California Legislature in 1860. He never climbed the mountain named after him.

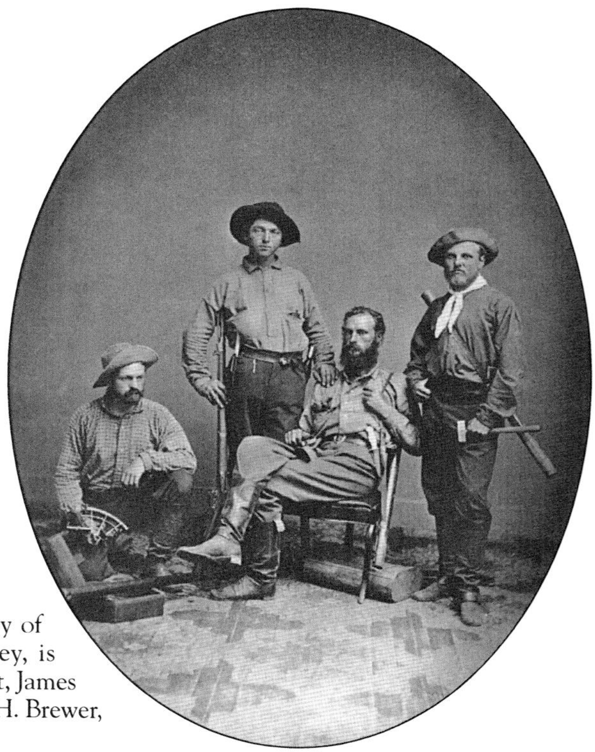

The California Geological Field Survey of 1864, which identified Mount Whitney, is shown here. Pictured are, from left to right, James T. Gardiner, Richard D. Cotter, William H. Brewer, and Clarence King.

Two

Which Peak is Whitney?

Local Lone Pine residents characterize Mount Whitney as a shy mountain. When clouds obscure the upper areas, which they often do, they say, half jokingly, "She has pulled her veil over her face."

Perhaps it was this shyness that made for all the confusion about which peak was actually Whitney as identified by the survey team in 1864. Mountaineers, such as Clarence King, failed to climb the correct mountain a few times before local fisherman from Lone Pine finally succeeded. Charles Begole, J.P. Johnson, and J.J. Lucas are often credited as the first men to climb Whitney, but that is totally forgetting that the Southern Paiute regulars crossed the Sierra for trade. Is it so unlikely that at some point they climbed the peak?

A Paiute story, recorded by Julian Steward, ethnologist of the Owens Valley Paiute, indicates that they were certainly well aware of the peak that finally came to be called Whitney. It is titled "Tuhu'ni and Mount Whitney" and goes as follows: "A community of people lived up in the mountains by Monache. Bear, Coyote, and others were there, with Fox as their leader." The story records all of the animals being killed by the Bees, except for Hawk, who only survives near the end of the story. After awhile, Hawk got tired. He came to Mount Whitney, and thought of making a trap there. He took a long feather from each wing and placed them on the south side of Mount Whitney. When the bee came through he was caught in his trap, and Hawk killed him. Then Hawk went on and stopped at a hill near Black Rock, which is now called Tuhu'mni Mountain." This explains how what today is called the Keeler Needle came to be located south of Mount Whitney.

The legislature of California passed the act establishing the Geological Survey of California on April 21, 1860. This enactment set up the department, with J.D. Whitney being appointed the state geologist.

It was in the summer of 1864 that the survey team first caught sight of the set of magnificent peaks. On this trip were William H. Brewer, assisted by topographer Charles F. Hoffman, Clarence King, and his friend James T. Gardiner, with Dick Cotter coming on board as a packer. After climbing a cone, Brewer recorded what he and Hoffman saw, which is included in Robert Leonard Reid's *A Treasury of the Sierra Nevada*. "The view was wilder than any we had seen before. Such a landscape! A hundred peaks in sight over 13,000 feet–many very sharp—deep canyons, cliffs in every direction, sharp ridges almost inaccessible to man on which human foot has never trod—all combine to produce a view the sublimity of which is rarely equaled, one which few are privileged to behold." This "so far as known the culminating peak of the Sierra" was named Mount Whitney. King and Cotter set out to climb "Whitney."

The final ascent is captured beautifully in King's *Mountaineering the Sierra Nevada* and concludes, "The summit was reached without serious difficulty, after some risky climbing." Unfortunately, it was immediately clear that they were not on the highest peak in the range. "That which looked highest of all was a cleanly cut helmet of granite, lying about six miles south . . . The summit looks glorious but inaccessible."

It would take three more attempts before King summited. In the meantime, three local Lone Pine fishermen had gotten there. As W.A. Chalfant reports in his history of Inyo County, A.H Johnson, J.J. Lucas, and C.D. Begole accomplished the first ascent of the real Whitney on August 18, 1873. James Gregory Moore reports the three men approached the challenge from the west, as they were apparently on a fishing trip, and they named the mountain Fisherman's Peak. Chalfant is of the opinion, it seems, that locals had several more regional names for the mountain than Whitney—for a man who had not climbed it.

Then, two more successful ascents happened the same year. William Crapo and Abe Leyda climbed the mountain, and on September 6, a third ascent was made by William Crapo, William L. Hunter, Tom McDonough, and Carl Rabe.

In his third attempt to climb Whitney, King assumed he had been successful and reported a monument and an arrow, which he just assumed was placed there by Indians. King also left an inscribed half-dollar. Using Hoffman's map published with the incorrect location of Whitney from a mistake in triangulation, King had climbed "Whitney" only to discover it was, in fact, Sheep Mountain instead. Later, the mountain was renamed as Mount Langley because of scientist Samuel Pierpont Langley's work in the area a decade after King climbed the mountain.

When he finally climbed the true Whitney, King writes in *Mountaineering in the Sierra Nevada*, "This is the true Whitney, the one we named in 1864, and upon which the name of our chief is forever to rest. It stands, not like white Shasta, in grandeur of solitude, but about it gather companies of crag and spire, piercing the blue or wrapped in monkish raiment of snowstorm and mist."

A graduate of Yale, Clarence King worked for the California Geological Survey and was on the team to first identify and name Whitney. He established the Geological Expedition of the 40th Parallel and wrote the classic book *Mountaineering in the Sierra Nevada*.

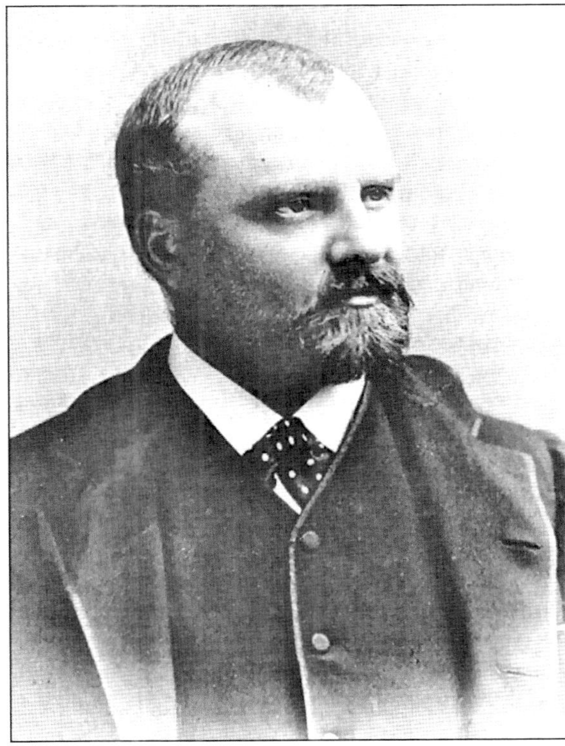

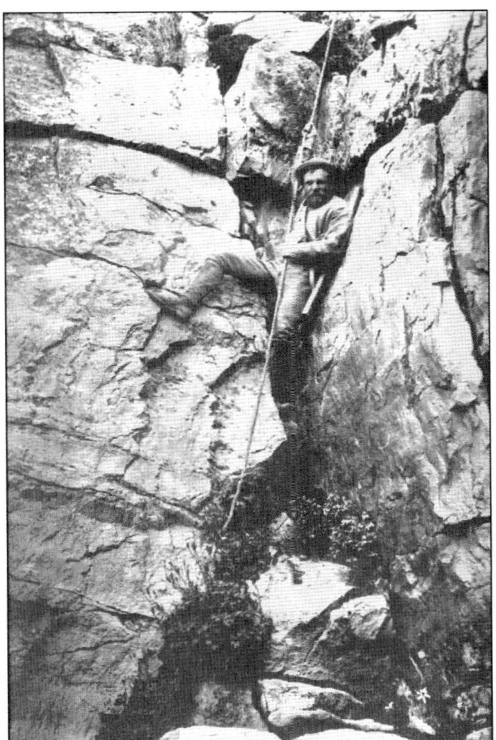

Clarence King made several attempts to climb Whitney. He climbed Langley by mistake; he stopped only a few hundred feet the third time; and only succeeded on his fourth attempt—after three fishermen from Lone Pine had succeeded.

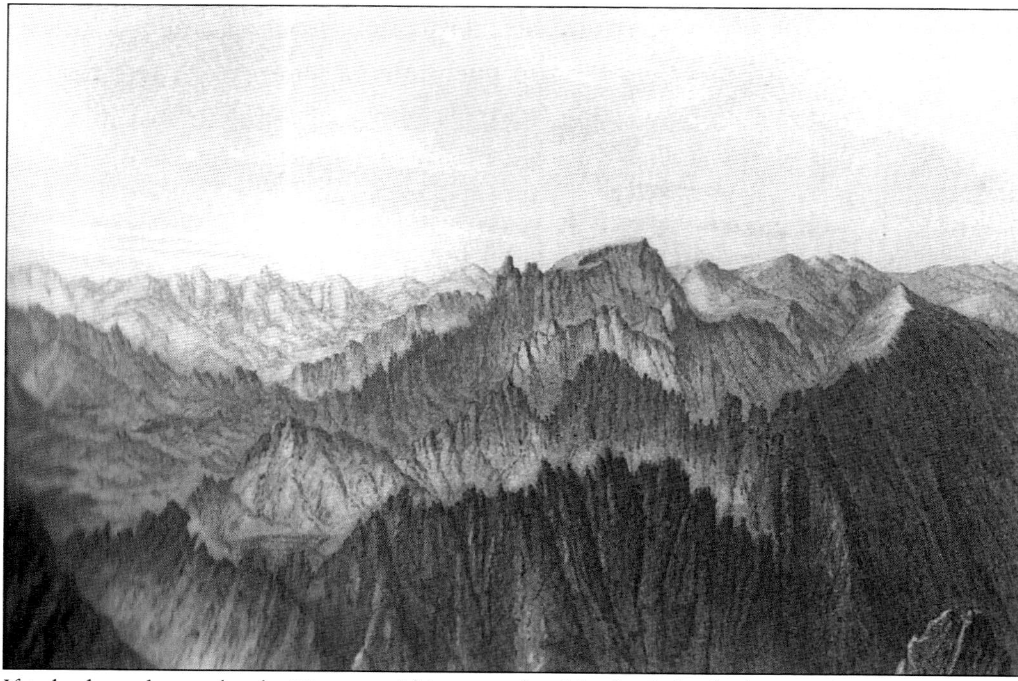

If it had not been cloudy, King would have realized he had climbed not Whitney but Sheep Mountain (later called Langley), as seen in this sketch made in 1875 by William A. Cowles on the Wheeler Expedition.

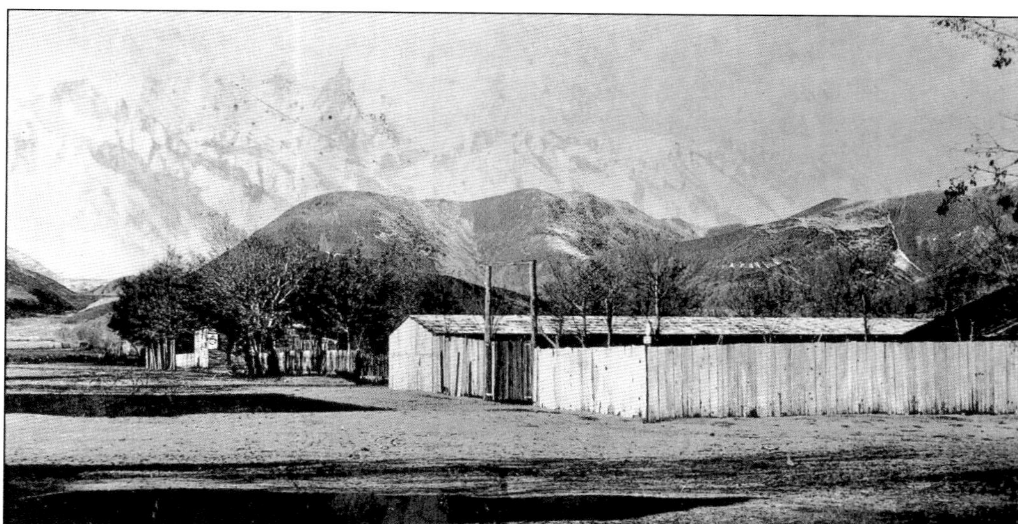

In one of the earliest photographs of Lone Pine, the Dodge livery stables on Bush and Main Streets are seen. This photograph was taken soon after Lone Pine was rebuilt after the earthquake, this time using all wood.

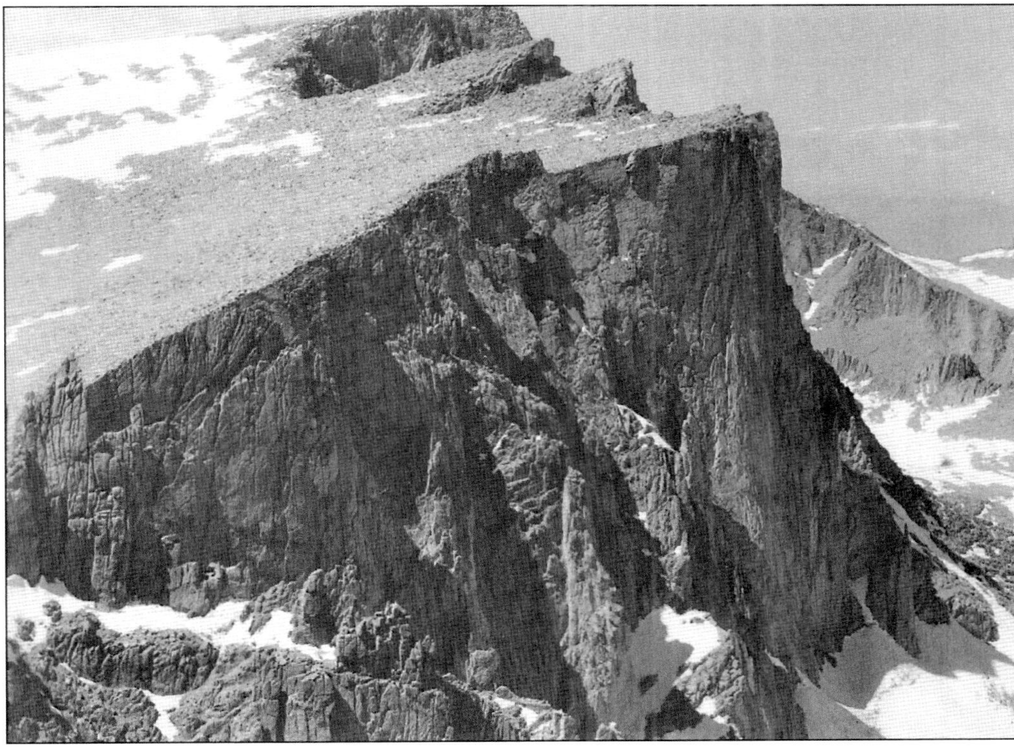

Whitney is seen from the east, and from left to right are Day and Keeler Needle, then the main peak. Day has since been renamed for climber Hulda Crooks. A Southern Paiute story explains the origins of the Keeler Needle.

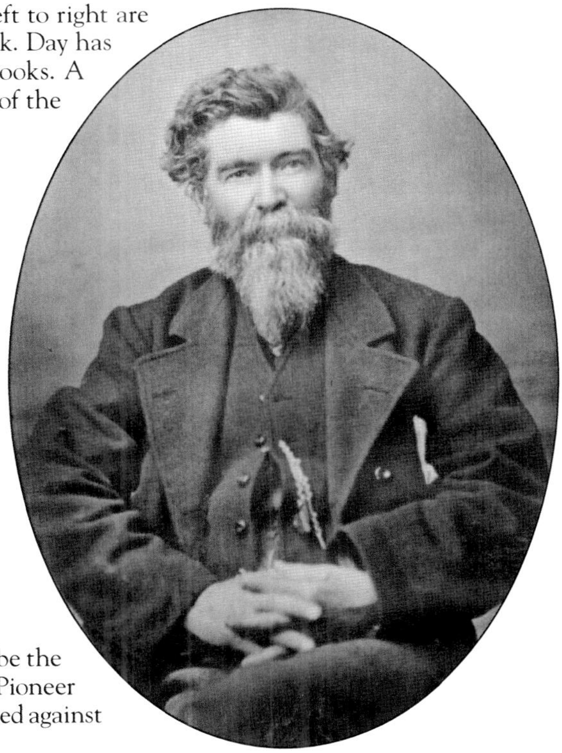

Charles Begole was considered by many to be the founder of Lone Pine. He is buried in the Pioneer Cemetery, where his tall grave marker is viewed against Mount Whitney.

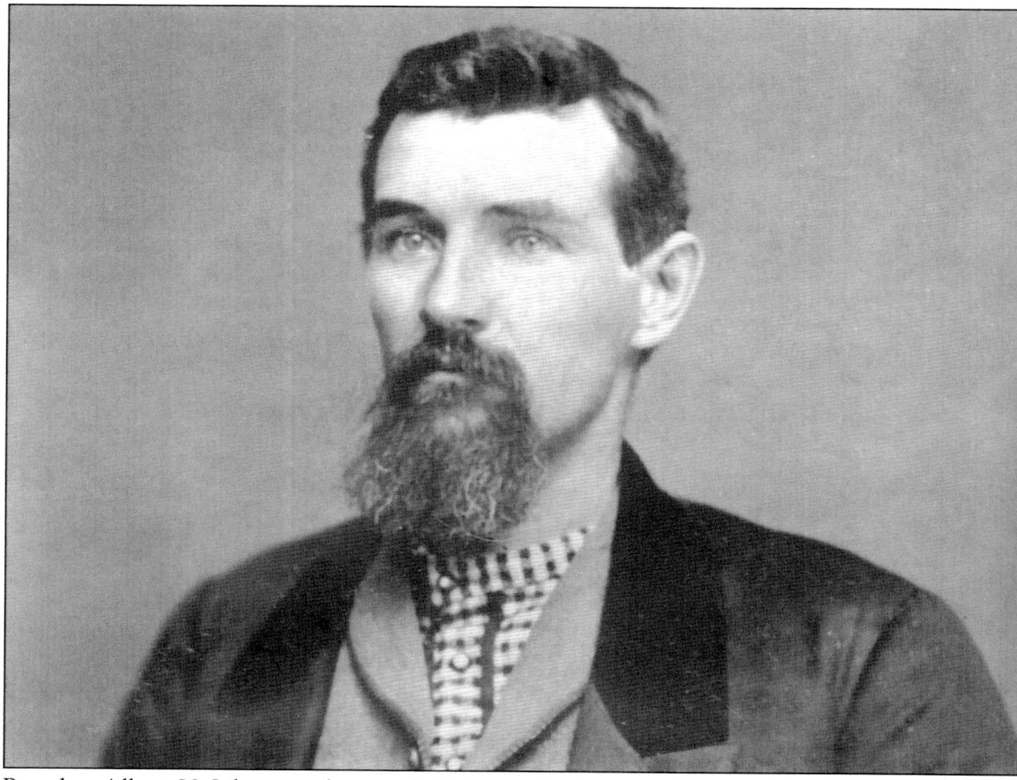

Rancher Albert H. Johnson, along with J.J. Lucas (no known photograph), accompanied Begole and summited Whitney on August 18, 1873.

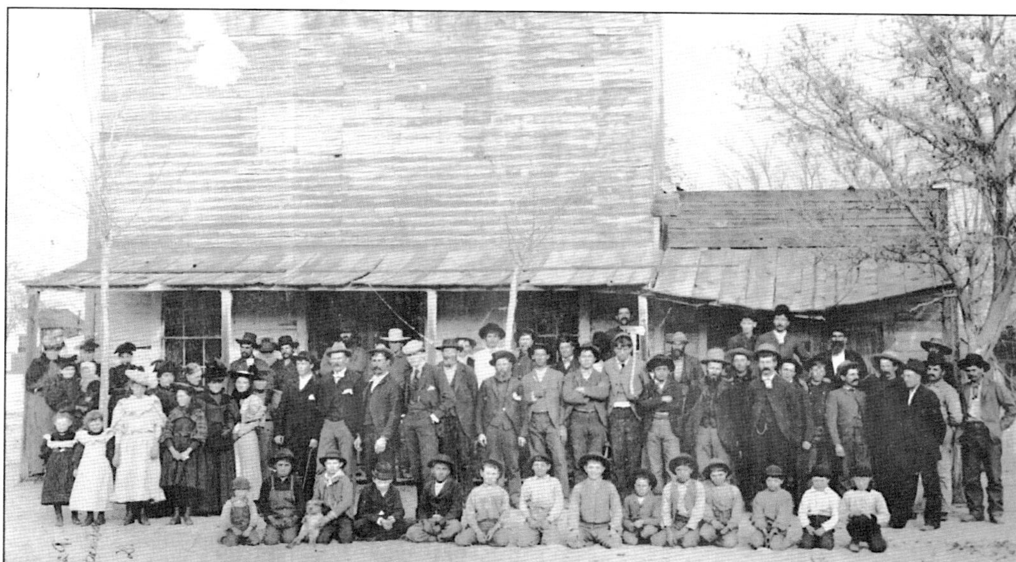

Begole was one of the town leaders. Here is his place of commerce, located in the town of Lone Pine. Begole was responsible for laying out the broad streets of the town, which remain one of its charms today.

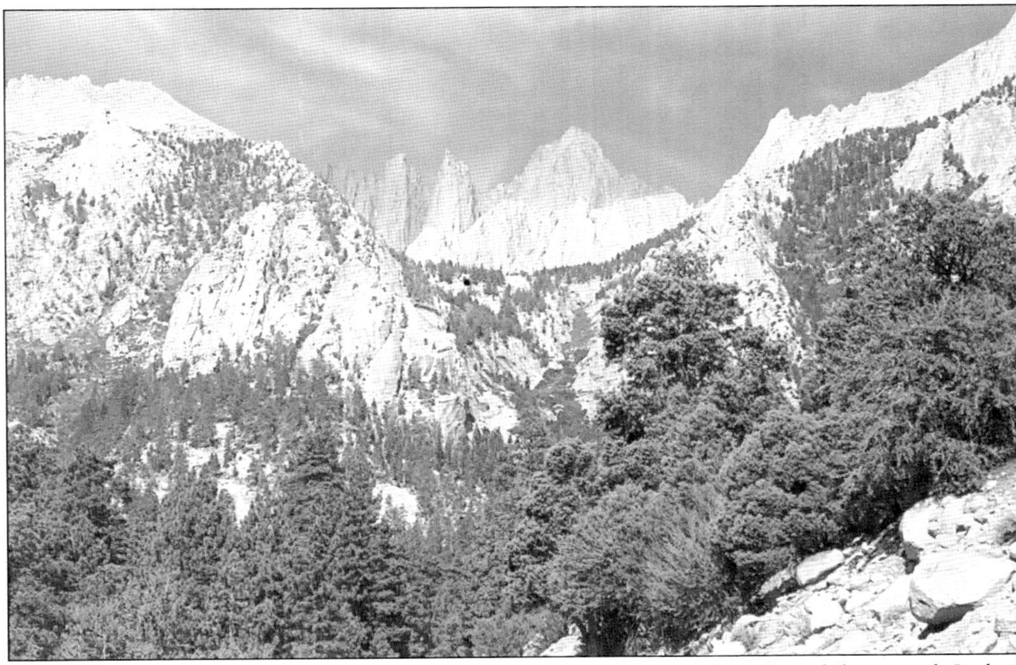

While set back from view from the east, Mount Whitney sits at the edge of the portal. It does not appear as the tallest from this angle, captured from the Portal Road, which might explain ongoing misidentification of the peak by visitors. (Langley.)

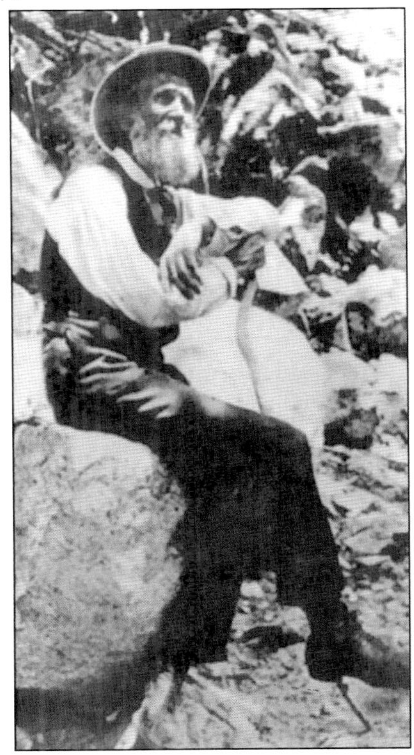

John Muir hiked from Independence and climbed what he thought was Whitney, only to discover it was Sheep (later Langley.) He hiked back to Independence, rested a day, and made a successful attempt on the real Whitney. He did not recommend his east face ascent to the "soft and succulent."

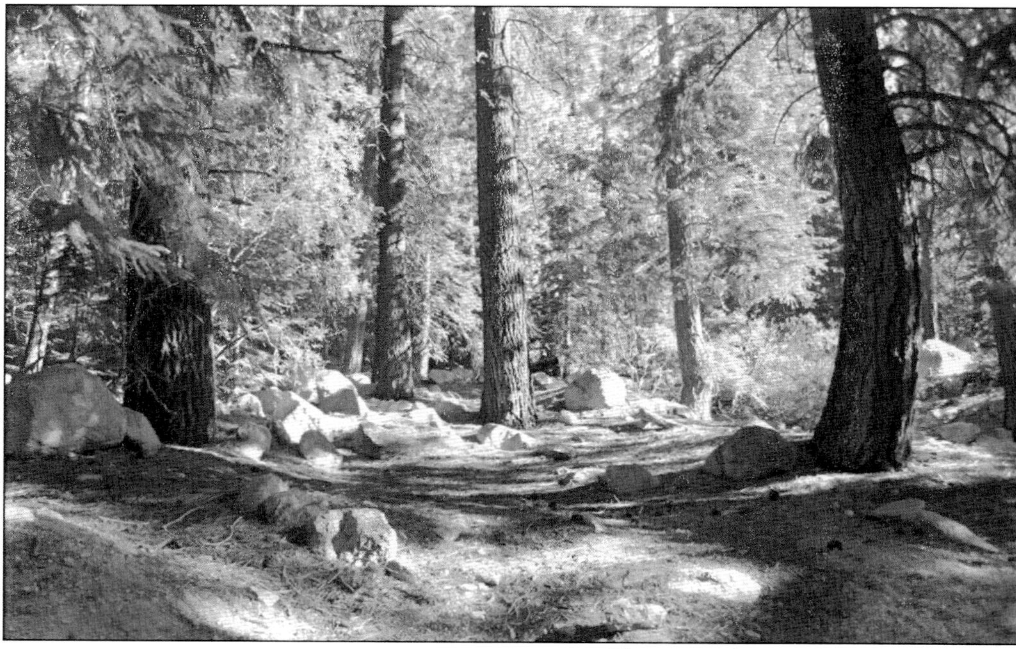

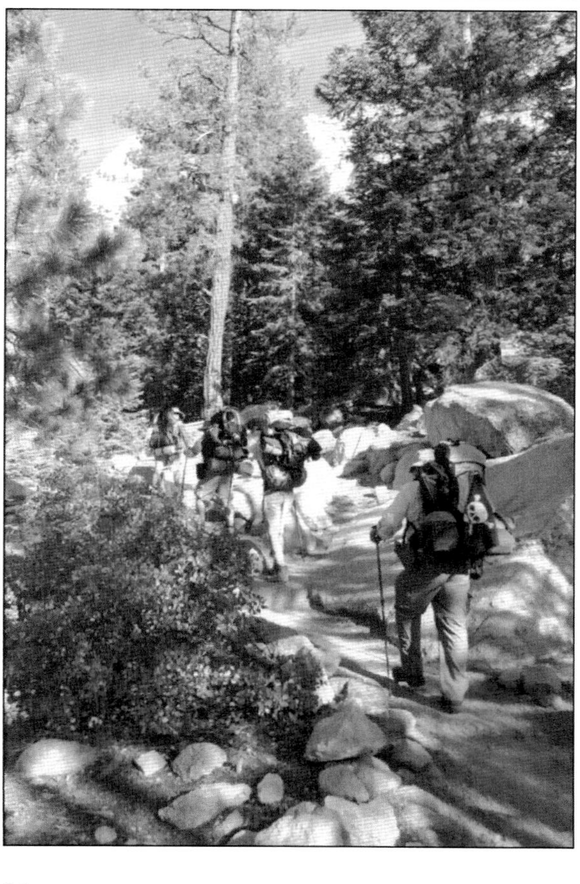

The original name for the Whitney Portal area was Hunter Flat. The bowl-like area has a small pond, a waterfall, and lots of lodgepole pine trees. Now mostly in a wilderness area, the portals were once famous for hunting. (Langley.)

Climbers and hikers begin the trail at the Whitney Portal Trailhead. The earliest climbers had no trail to follow, but much work and courage resulted in a very fine trail used by many today. In 1951, more than 6,500 attempted the hike. (Langley.)

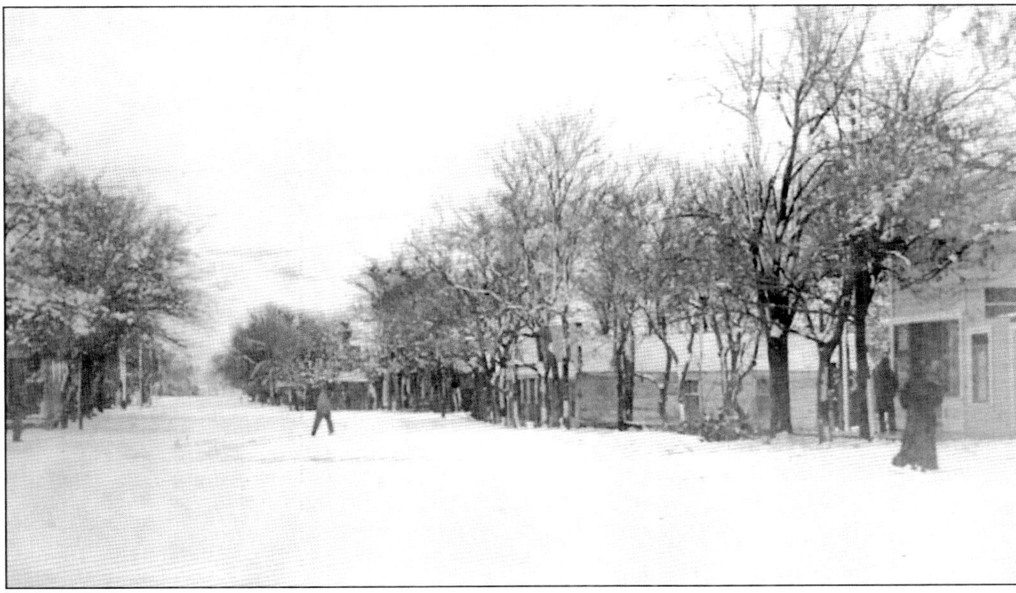

Many early climbers discovered that Whitney was subject to sudden storms. Here, Lone Pine endures a snowfall in a photograph from around 1910.

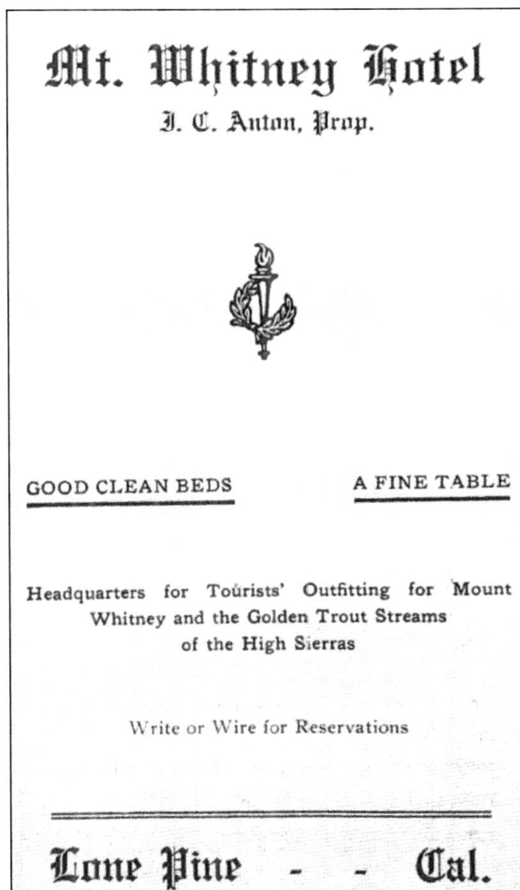

The Mount Whitney Hotel positioned itself in its advertising early on as "Headquarters for Tourists Outfitting for Mount Whitney and the Golden Trout Streams of the High Sierra."

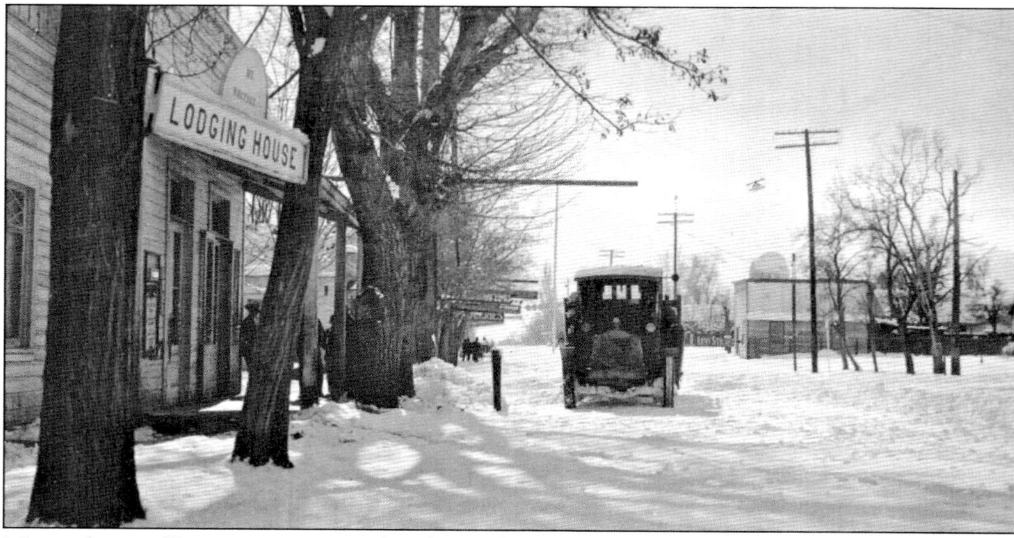

Many places of business recognized early on the marketability of Mount Whitney as a tourist destination. This photograph shows the Lone Pine Hotel, an early lodging for adventurers. Even today, many businesses have Mount Whitney in their names.

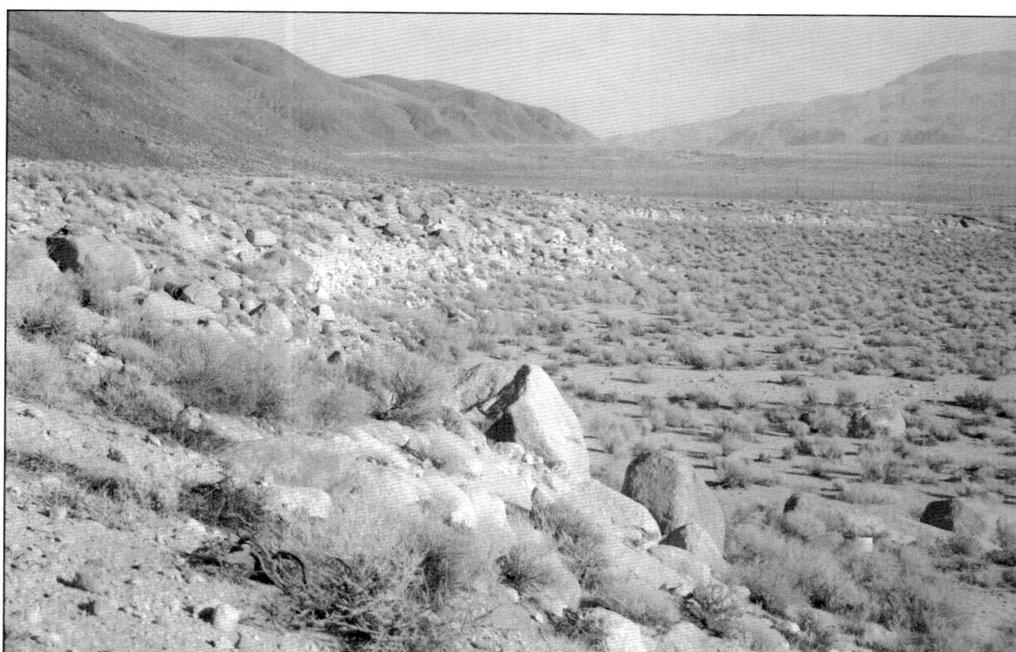

Early on the morning of March 26, 1872, the valley floor dropped 25 feet in some places, flattening the town of Lone Pine. J.D. Whitney and Clarence King rushed to the area to study the event. (Langley.)

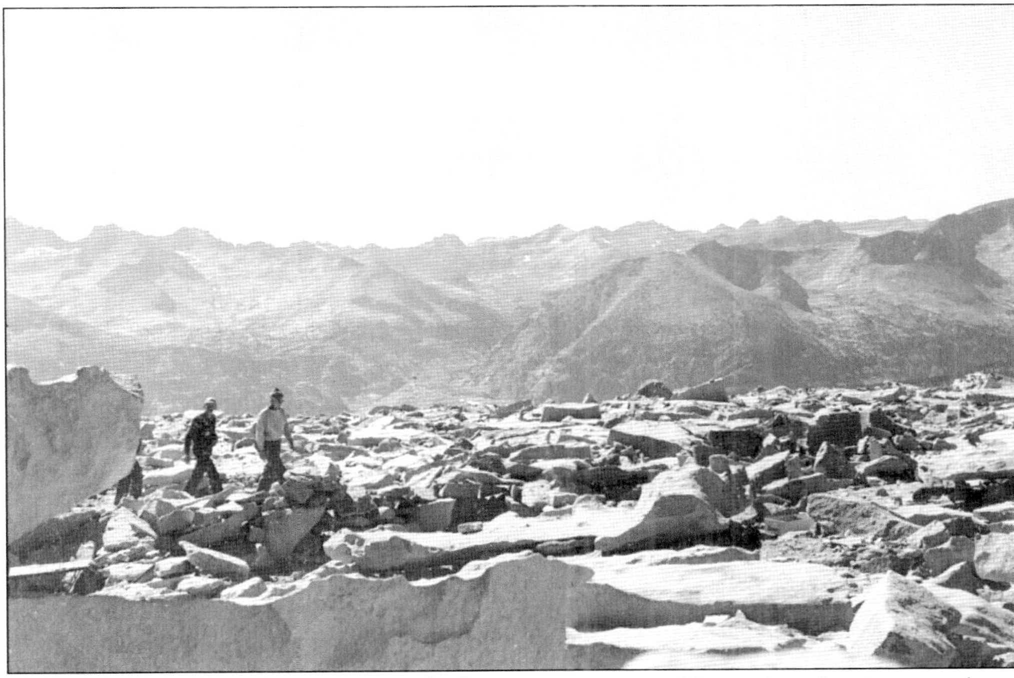

The summit of Mount Whitney, a goal of so many, is pictured here. A rock cairn, not shown in this photograph, is where many have their photograph taken to prove they actually achieved the summit.

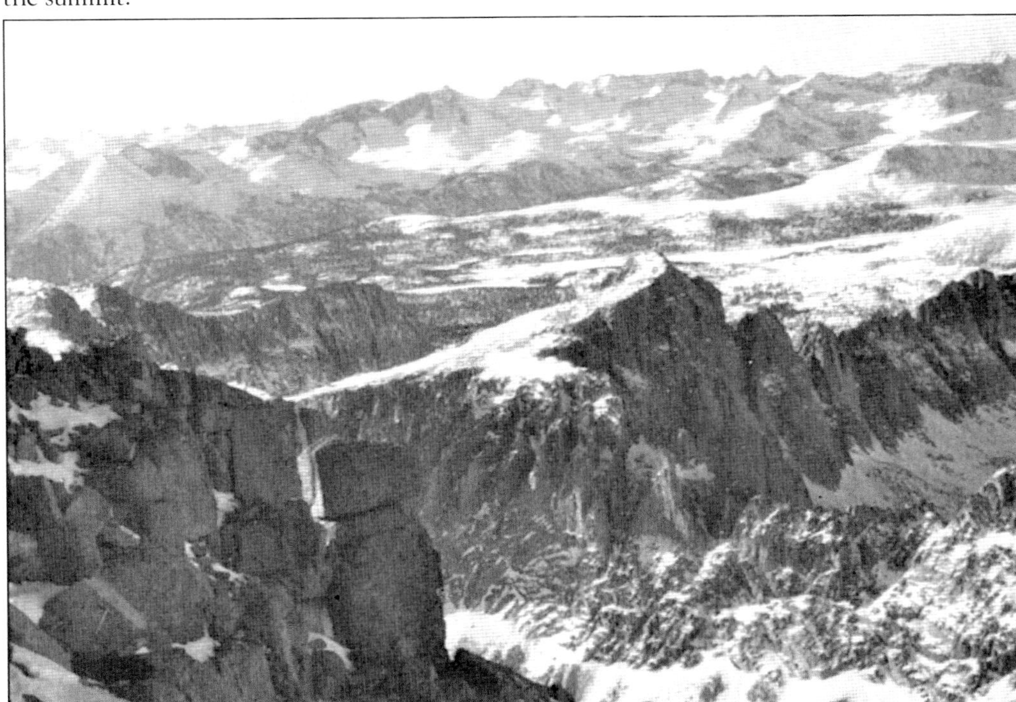

What might one see on the way up, near the top? Here is a view of surrounding peaks.

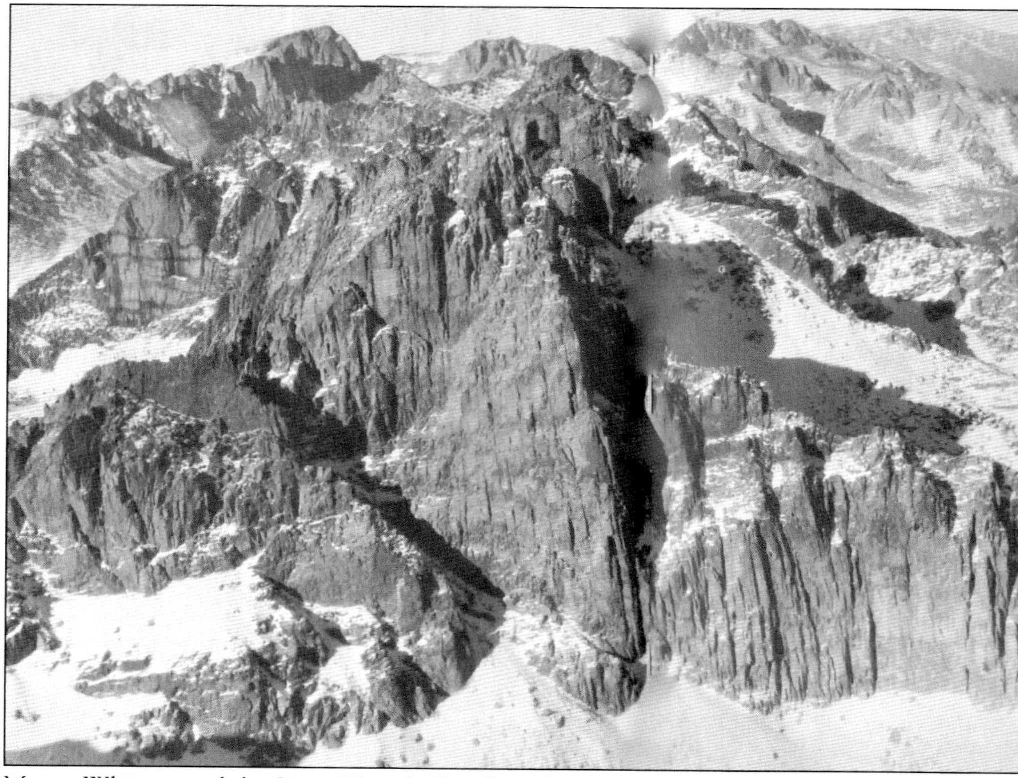

Mount Whitney and the Sierra Nevada East Face dominate Lone Pine and the southern Owens Valley. (Branson collection.)

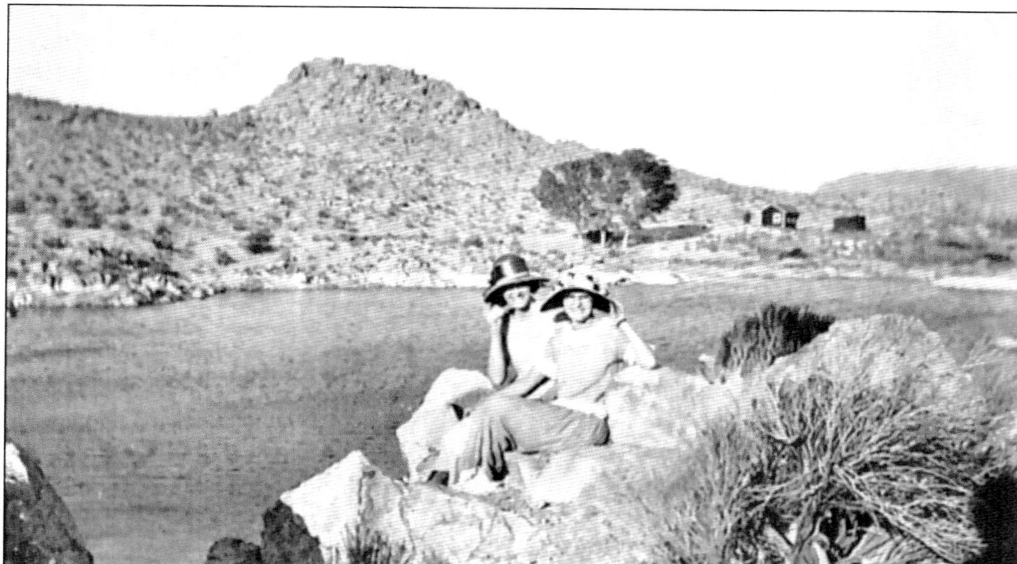

Although it would be a few decades before they succeeded, women were SOON challenging the mountain as well. This photograph shows Mary Ince (left) and Belle Andrew. At the time, Belle became the second woman to ever climb Mount Whitney. (Kathryne Wingfield.)

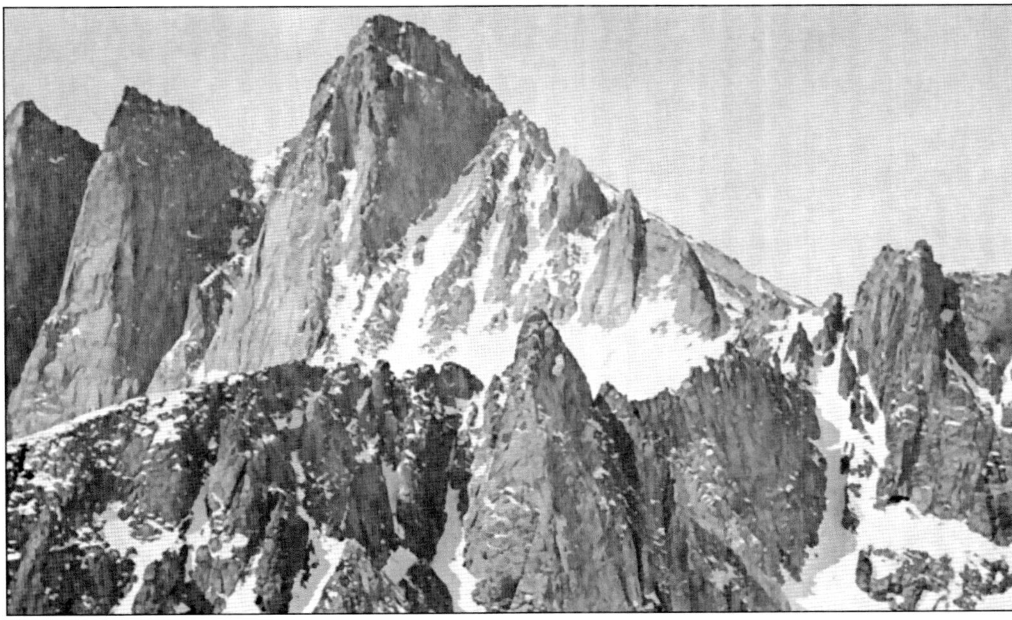

The East Face of Whitney, called the "mountaineers route" by Norman Clyde, is shown here. It remains one of the most challenging ways to approach Whitney.

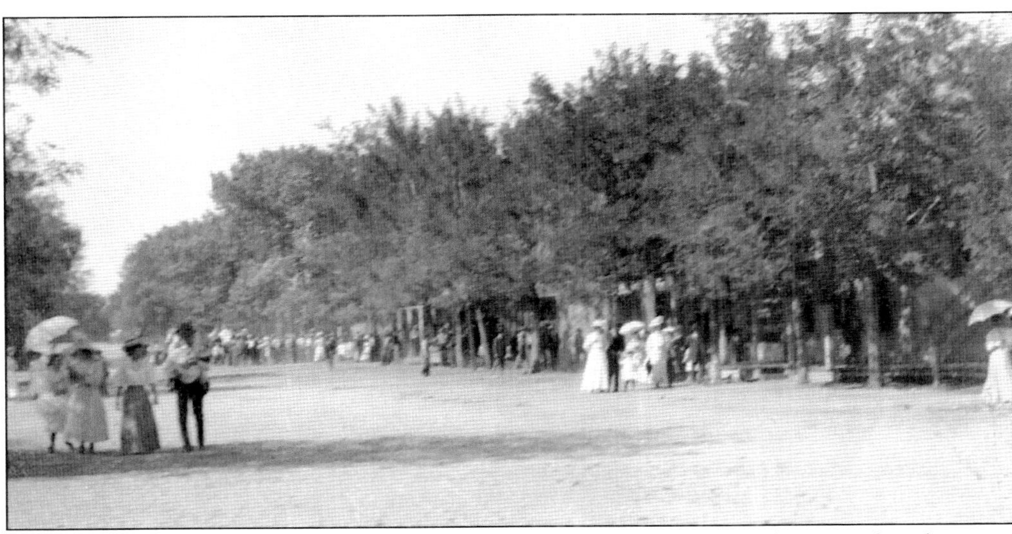

Lone Pine in the summer, perhaps this is A July Fourth, is a wonderful time. After the initial exploration of the mountain, Lone Pine residents realized a true permanent trail would be a great attraction and addition to local commerce.

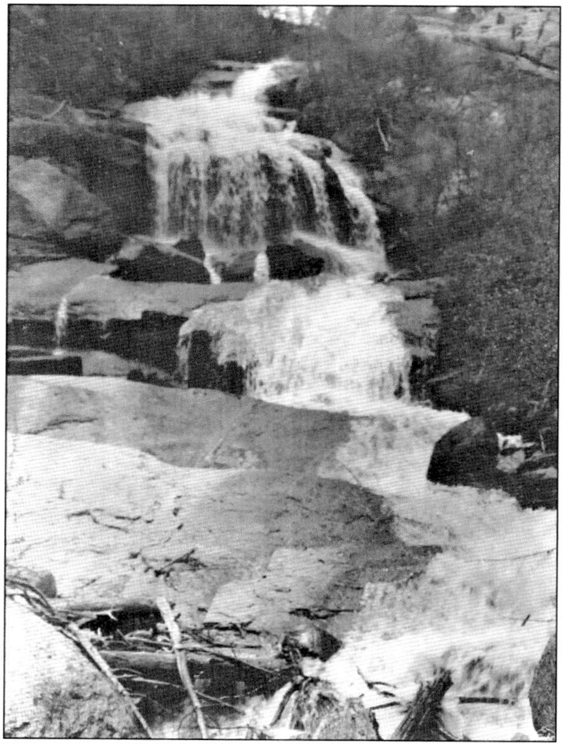

As the new century dawned, many in Lone Pine and the surrounding areas realized that the Whitney area presented many attractions good for the local economy. Here are the beautiful Whitney Falls at the Portals. (LPFHM.)

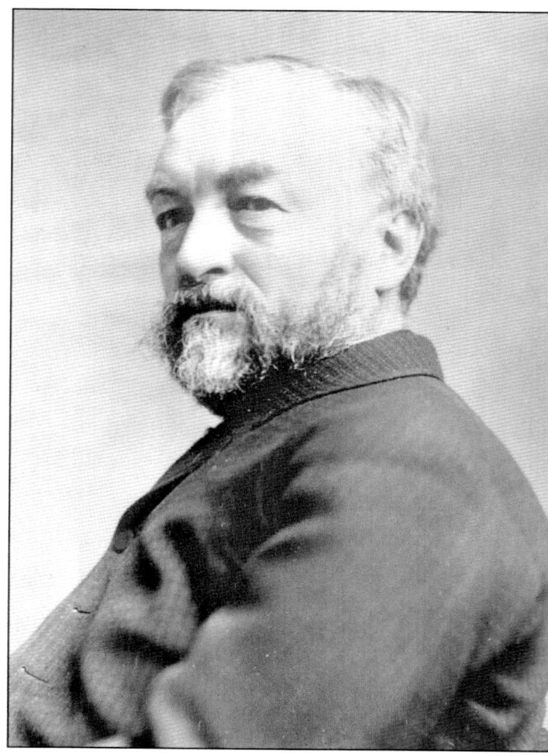

Samuel Pierpont Langley was an astronomer at the Allegheny Observatory and visited Whitney as part of an expedition in 1881. He studied solar radiation and absorption at higher altitudes and spent a famous night at the top of Whitney. He was one of the champions of a permanent observatory on the summit.

Three

GETTING THERE

If identifying and actually climbing the true Mount Whitney for the first time was a challenge, establishing its official name was a vexing problem as well. In *The Story of Inyo*, W.A. Chalfant writes, "'Old' Mount Whitney bore the name for three or four years, while there were attempts to give the high summit some other name. 'Fisherman's Peak,' 'Dome of the Continent,' and 'Dome of Inyo' all had supporters. Eventually, the name Whitney was finally established by law through the action of the California Legislature, but it took almost eight years.

In October 1873, John Muir, apparently lacking some important information that Clarence King had learned the hard way, decided to take on an ascent of Mount Whitney. He mistakenly climbed Mount Langley, from which point he could see the higher peak to the north. Muir actually returned to Independence, not Lone Pine. He summited from the "forbidding" east wall. In *The Mountains of California*, Muir says, "For climbers, there is a canyon which comes down from the north shoulder of the Whitney Peak. Well seasoned limbs will enjoy the climb of 9,000 feet required for this direct route, but soft, succulent people should go the mule way." Two years later, Muir again returned to the summit. He brought two companions and was now confident of the way. It seems generally to have been uneventful but taxing to his younger fellow travelers.

More and more parties began to climb Mount Whitney, not because it was any easier, but because more people thought they could meet the challenge since others had. In 1878, it appears that the first women summited. Anna Mills Johnson later wrote a reminiscence of the experience. Three other women had also been on the expedition and succeeded in getting to the top.

The visit of Prof. Samuel Pierpont Langley and his expedition in 1881 for scientific research had an impact that would eventually lead to the construction of a permanent trail up to the summit of Whitney. This led to the construction of the Smithsonian's permanent structure at the top, partially upon Langley's urging. Professor Langley, when he reached the summit of Whitney on August 22, 1881, was the director of the Allegheny Observatory and was soon to become the secretary of the Smithsonian Institution. He was there to study the amount of heat sent by the sun to the earth and variations in the levels of absorption based on elevation. He had studied the phenomenon at lower levels and wanted to increase his knowledge in high altitudes.

His writings are both scientific and rather poetic. In his paper "Report on the Mt. Whitney Expedition," Langley exclaims in writing upon reaching the summit, "The sky is the most deep violet blue, such as we never, under any circumstances, see near sea level. In an incomparably beautiful sky for the observer's purposes, such as I have not seen equaled elsewhere."

It took many more years of overcoming many daunting physical and financial challenges, but Gus Marsh announced on July 17, 1904, the completion of the pack trail to the summit. It was the people of Lone Pine who had the vision, the determination to find or raise the funds, and the perspicacity to see it through, thanks to Marsh's heroic leadership.

A crew was put to work at first with Reuben Spear in charge and $700 to build the trail. When determination and the money ran out, they were within three miles of the summit. At this point Marsh took over and found more funds. To accomplish the final leg of the venture, the Inyo Supervisors had contributed $200, then $300 more. Using the technique of basket social and dance, the women of Lone Pine raised $69, while the town of Independence contributed $85 and Keeler $67. Further funds were raised by individual contributions, often at some sacrifice by the locals.

In the *Papers of Gustave Marsh*, Marsh writes, "During the time putting up the building I stayed on top 43 days. I had 15 men to start with and only 5 at the finish. We had a terrible thunderstorm when we were almost done. Our cook was knocked down by a flash of lightning at 9 o'clock at night and one flash almost finished us all. St. Elmo's Fire, we did not know what it was. So you can guess how scared we was . . . I got everything completed 24 hours ahead of time and $250 below my estimate. So I was happy."

His grandson George F. Marsh gathered much of Gustave Marsh's story and history in 2000 to support the naming of Mount Marsh to commemorate the accomplishments of this hero. Those materials were used in the writing of this section.

Mount Marsh was approved on January 10, 2002, by the United States Board on Geographic Names (USBGN) and is in the National Geographic Names Database that is part of the Geographic Names Information System (GNIS).

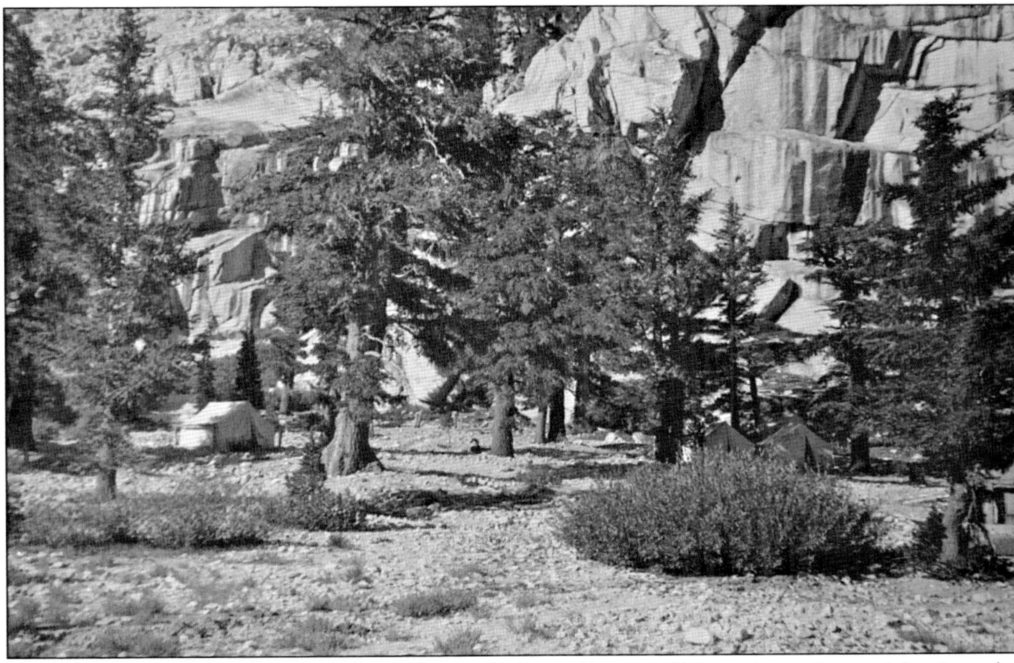

Langley set up a camp for scientific study not far from Outpost Camp, shown here. After Langley moved on to the Smithsonian, he became very active in promoting the building of the observatory for scientific study. The observatory, built by Gustave Marsh, is the same rock building found at the top of Whitney today.

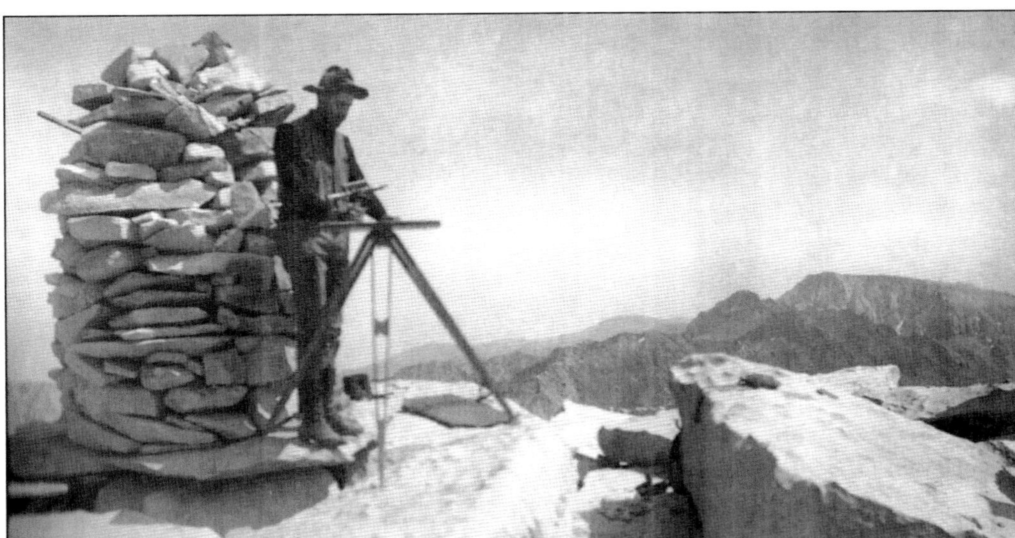

While this photograph is from a later date, the image shows scientific instruments on the summit of Whitney similar to those brought in by Professor Langley.

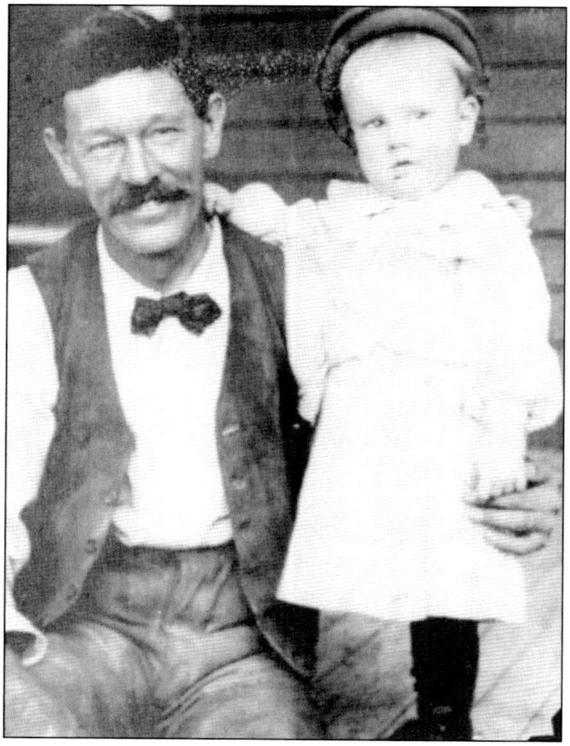

Gustave Francis Marsh lived from 1869 to 1946 and was born in England. He first climbed Whitney in 1901 and realized the value of the landscape to the local economy and to national pride.

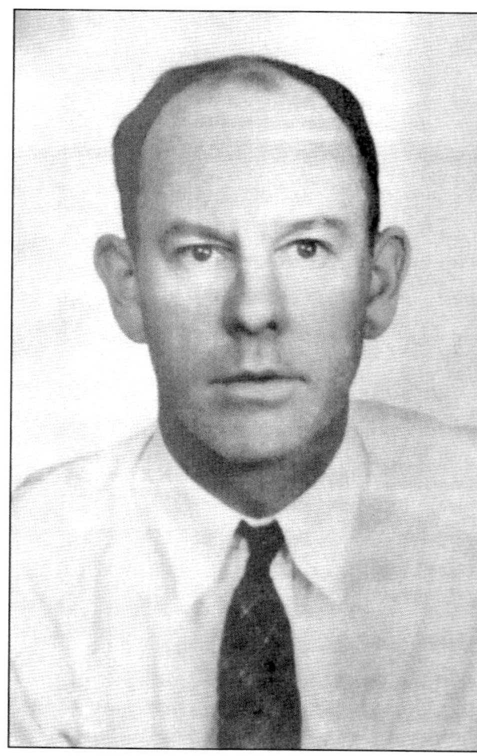

The Whitney Trail had already begun, but many obstacles suggested failure when Marsh took over managing the project in 1903.

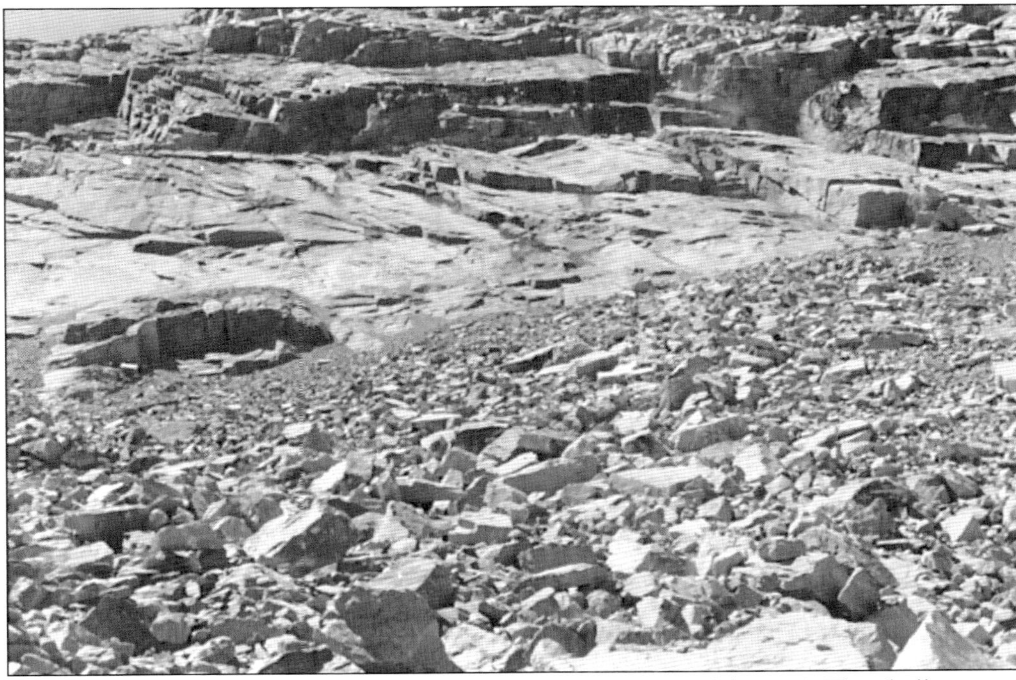

There appear to be few photographs of the actual construction of the trail. The challenge was not only physical but one of securing financing to complete the work. This photograph shows some of the terrain that had to be traversed by the trail. (Relles Amick.)

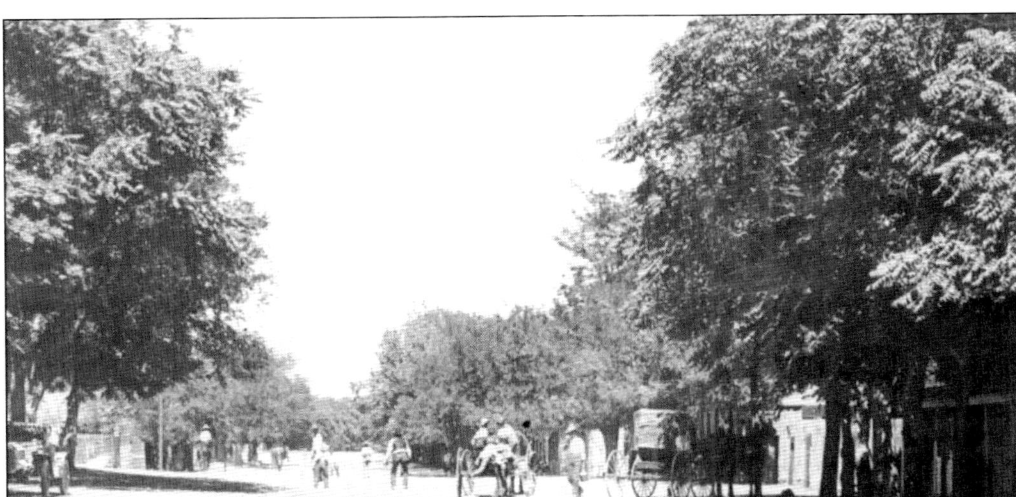

Inspired by Marsh and realizing the importance of having the permanent trail for attracting visitors to the area, Lone Pine, Independence, and Keeler residents all helped in raising funds for the project.

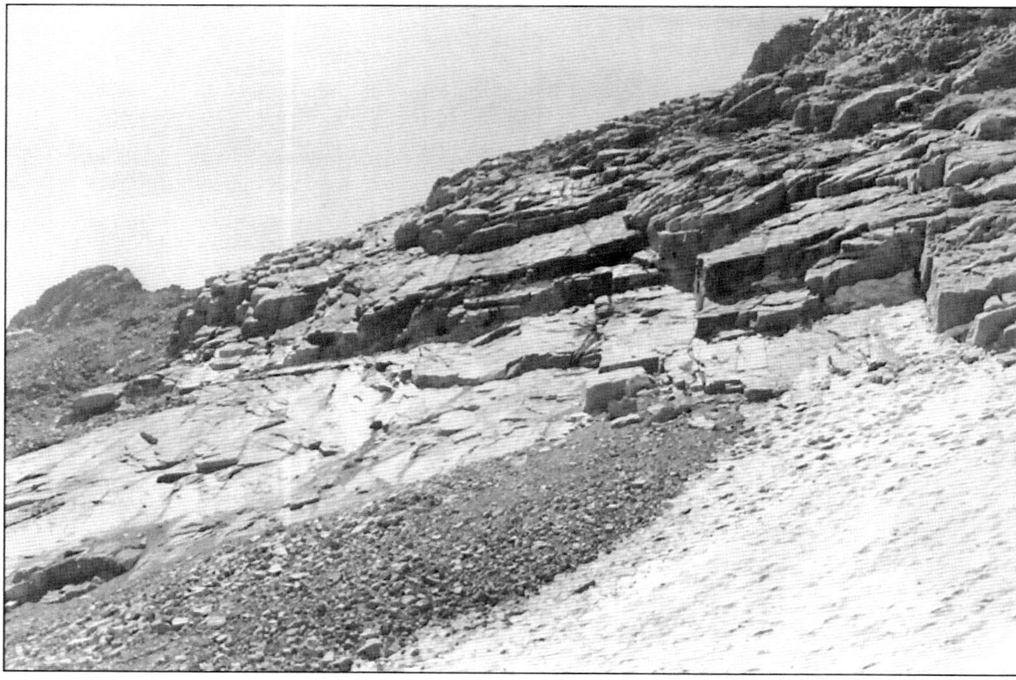

The first year of construction was interrupted by winter storms. This is a photograph of the terrain to be cut by the trail.

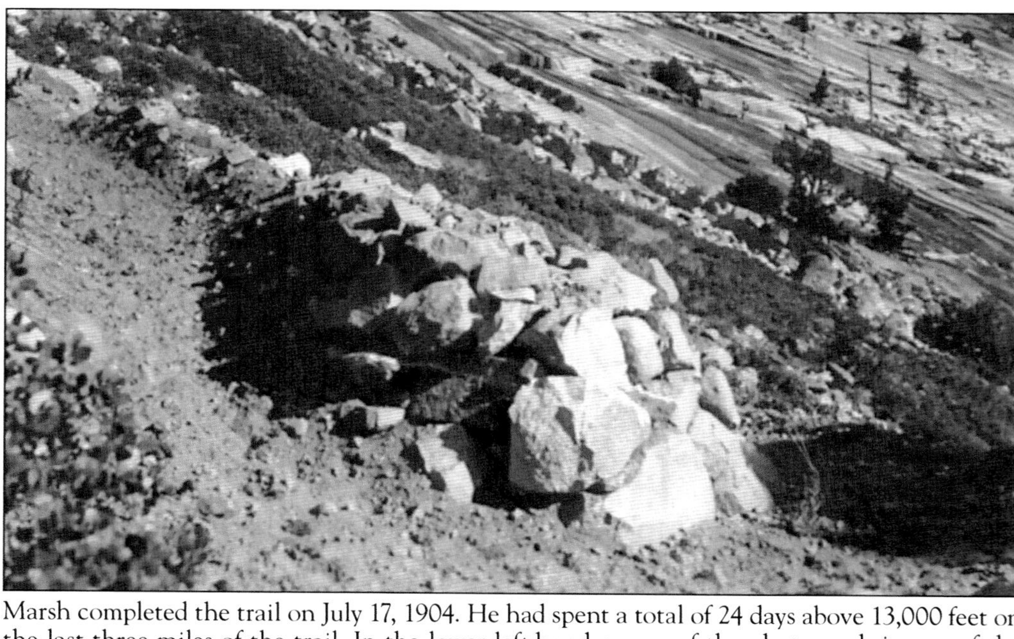

Marsh completed the trail on July 17, 1904. He had spent a total of 24 days above 13,000 feet on the last three miles of the trail. In the lower left-hand corner of the photograph is part of the newly established trail.

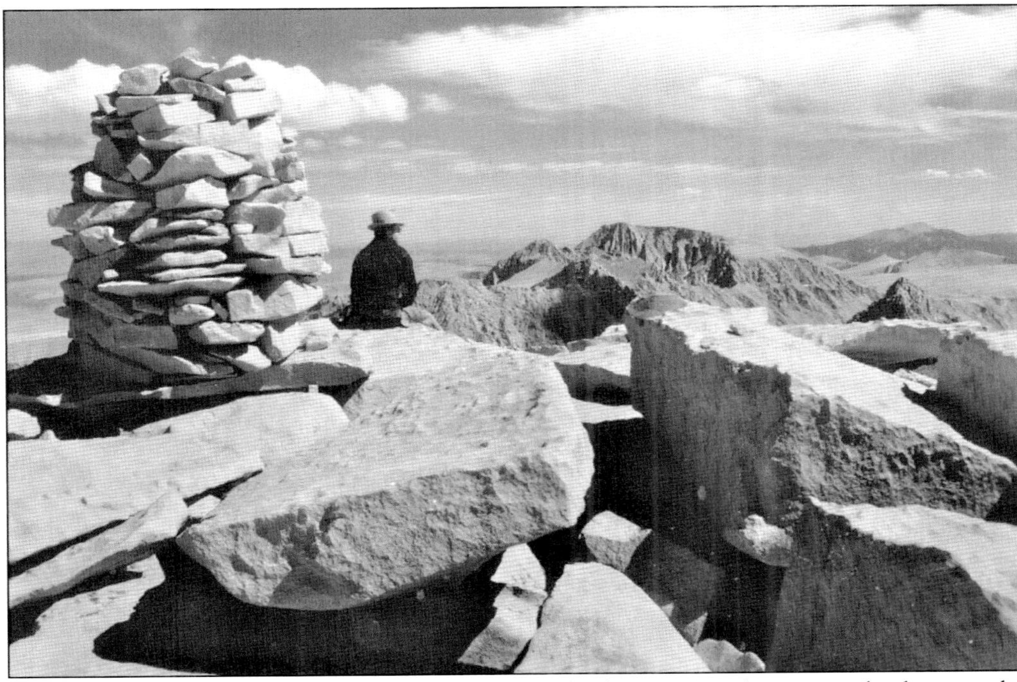

A "summiter" sits and enjoys the view from the top of Whitney. A rock cairn marks the spot, the goal of the newly established trail just after the start of the 20th century.

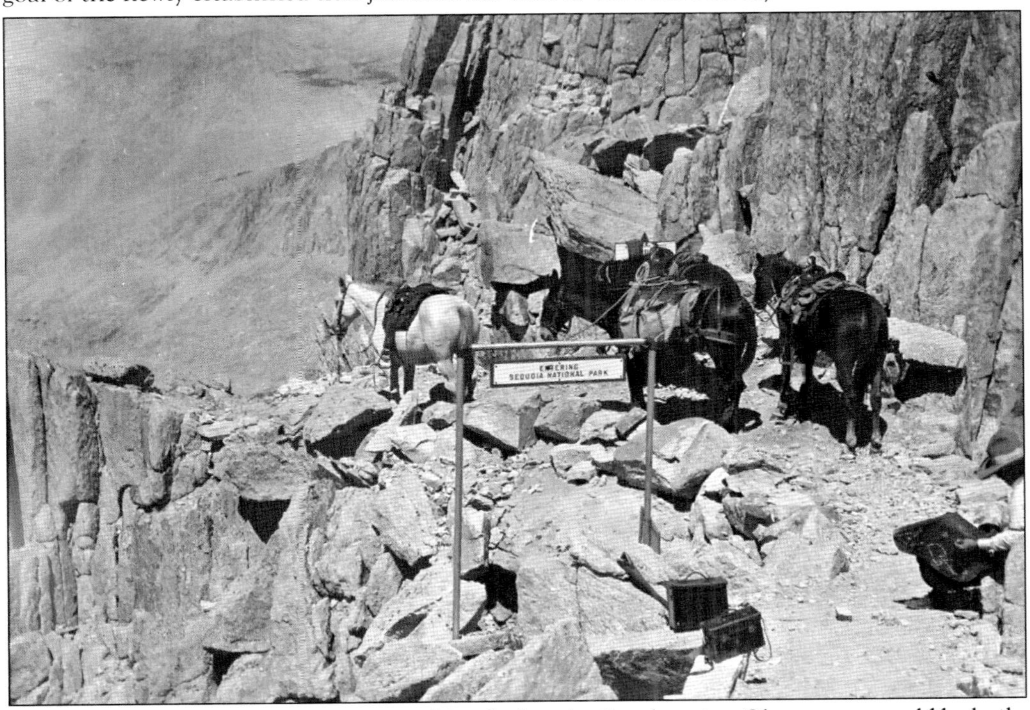

The Whitney Trail had to be maintained first before the Smithsonian Observatory could be built. Notice the trail is actually in Sequoia National Park as shown by this sign.

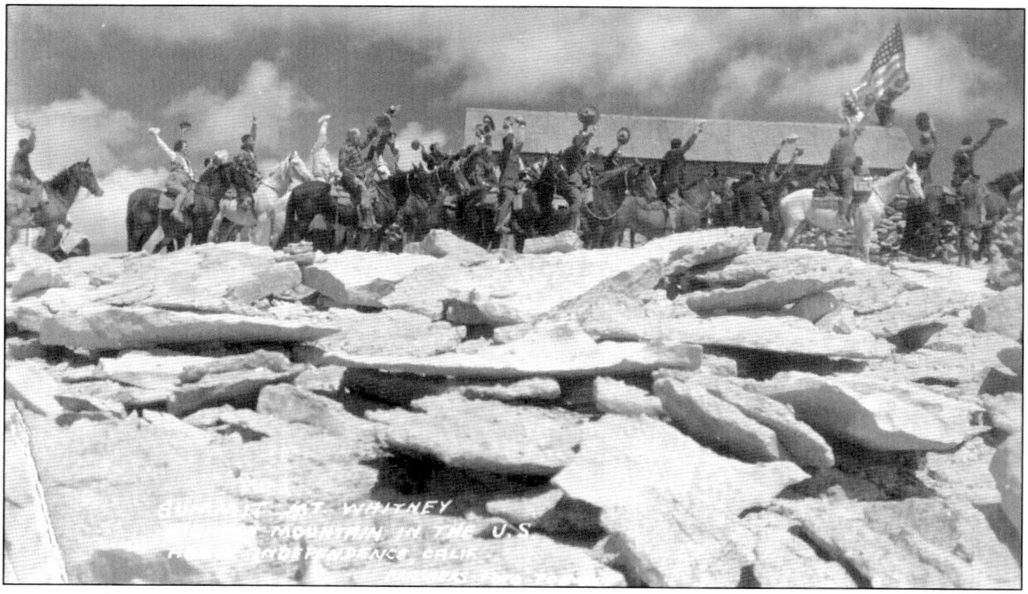

In 1909, the observatory was completed after Marsh spent 43 days on the summit of Whitney, 30 days continuously. Here, a group on horseback celebrates arriving at the top. The Summit Shelter, as the observatory is sometimes called, is seen in the background.

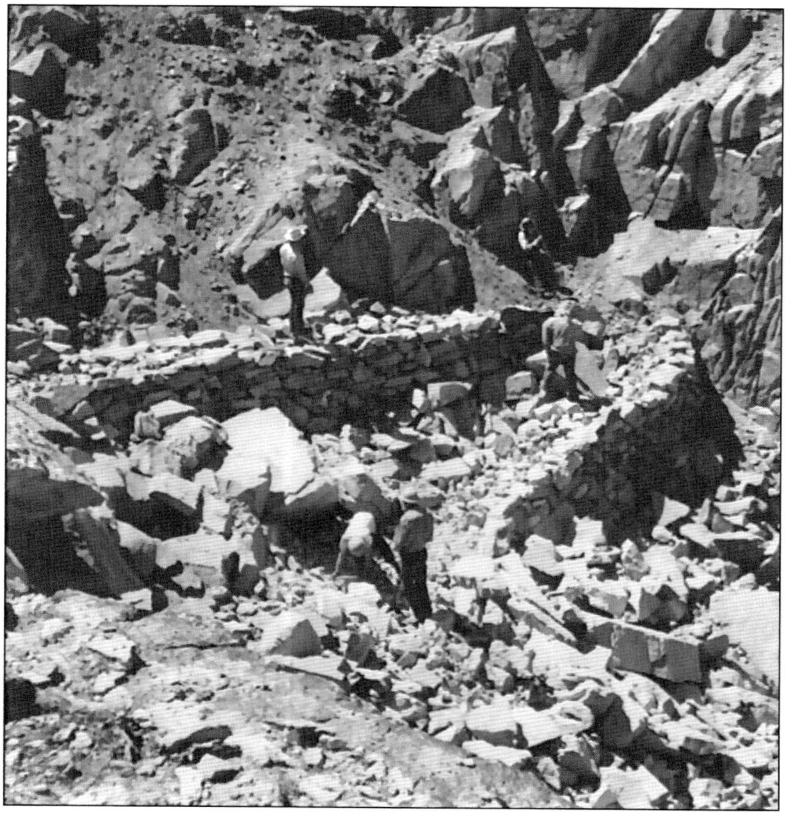

In the 1940s, more construction was done on the trail by local workers that resulted in creating the famous 99 switchbacks of the trail today. (Relles Amick.)

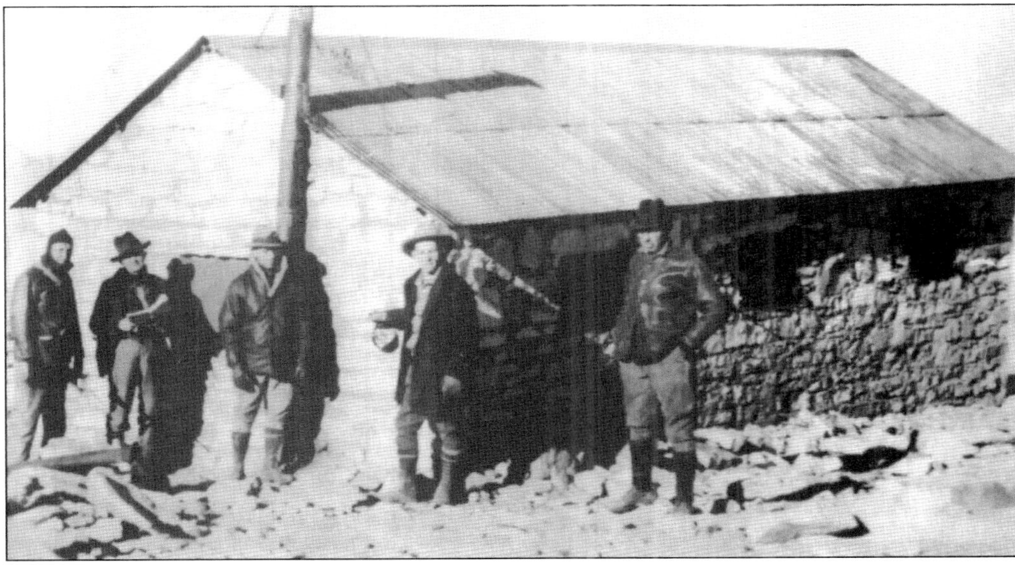

The Smithsonian Observatory was used for several scientific projects, including those done by Prof. Alexander George McAdie and Prof. Charles Greeley Abbot.

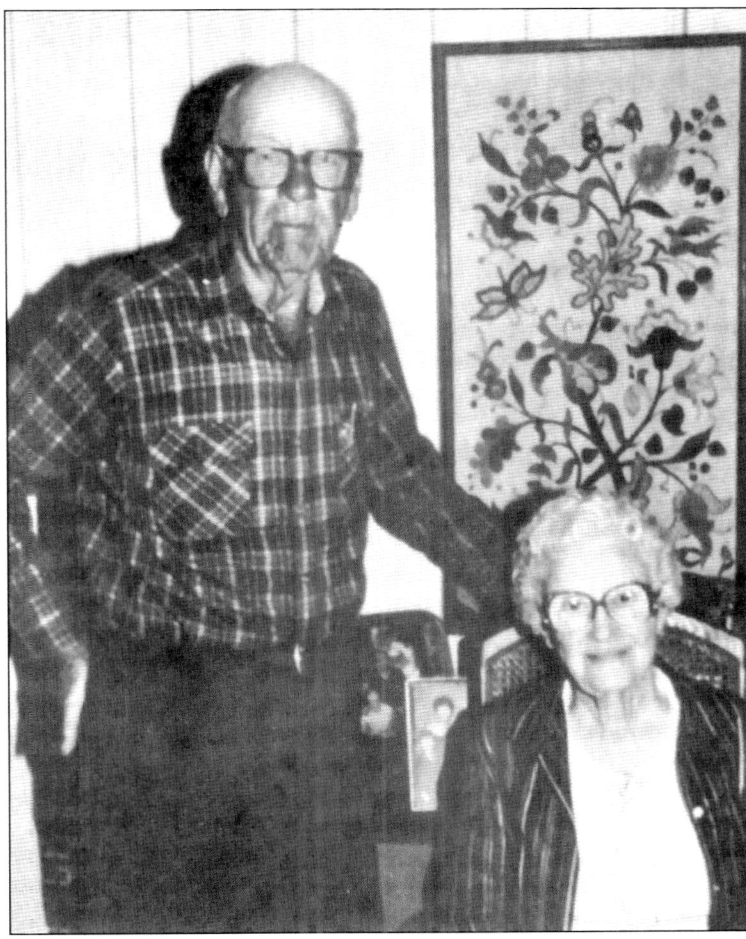

Because of all his hard work for the community and his adopted country, Gus Marsh had a peak finally named for him on January 10, 2002. His accomplishments live on, but Marsh—seen here with his wife, Zoe, at a late age,—never lived to see the mountain named for him.

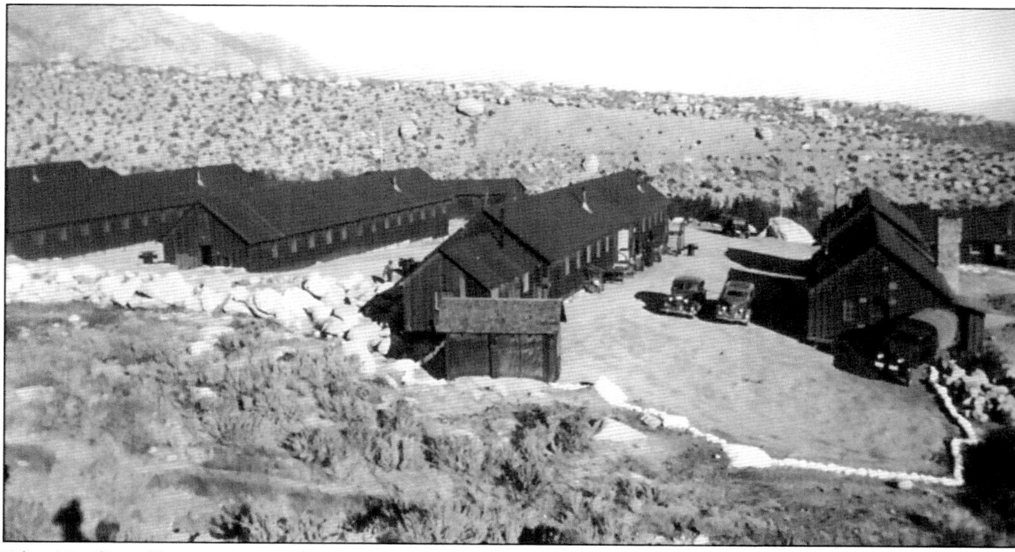

The Civilian Conservation Corps was involved in building the Whitney Portal Road in the 1930s. The buildings seen here were located in what is today known as Lone Pine Camp Ground area. (Mildred Langston collection.)

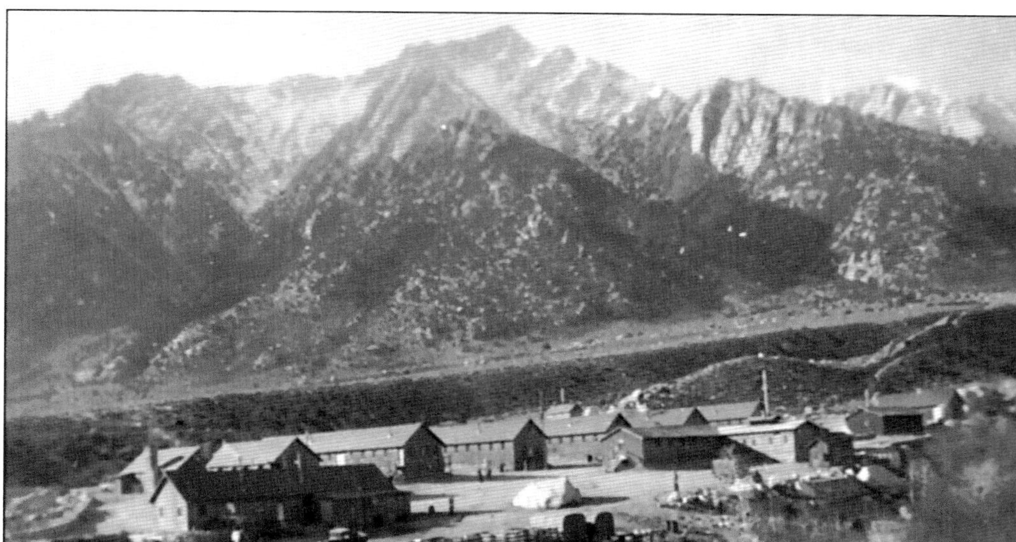

This is another view of the CCC camp located at the foot of Mount Whitney. (Mildred Langston collection.)

Icicles hang from the roofline at the CCC camp dorms. (Mildred Langston collection.)

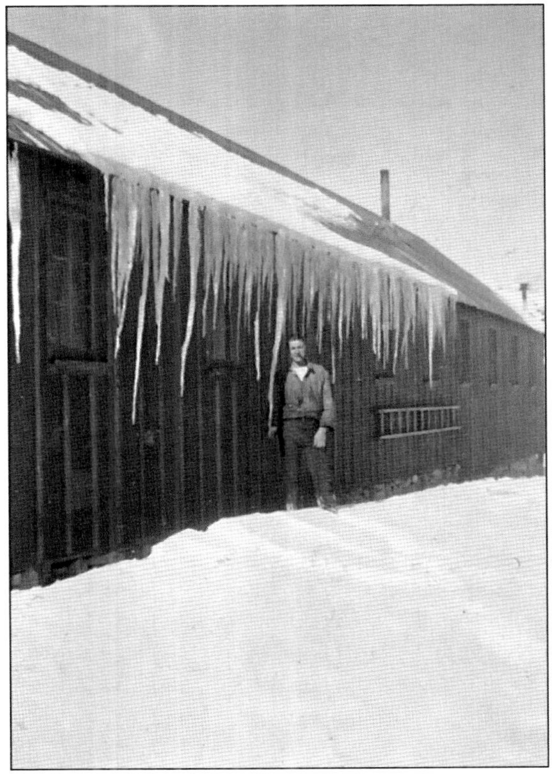

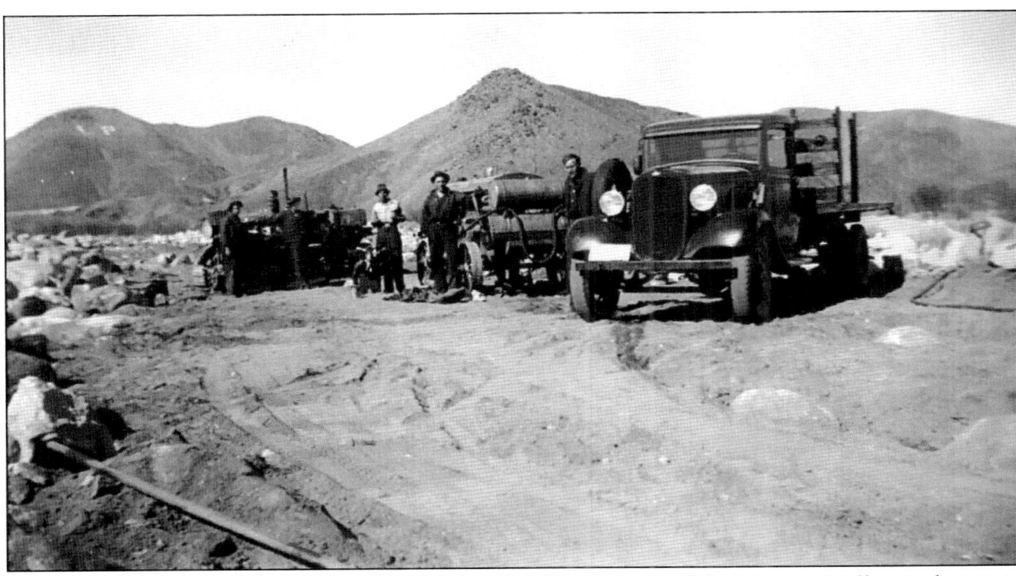

Building the Mount Whitney Portal Road in the lower areas of the Owens Valley is shown in this photograph. The road combined with the trail allowed visitors and adventurers much freer access to getting there. (Mildred Langston collection.)

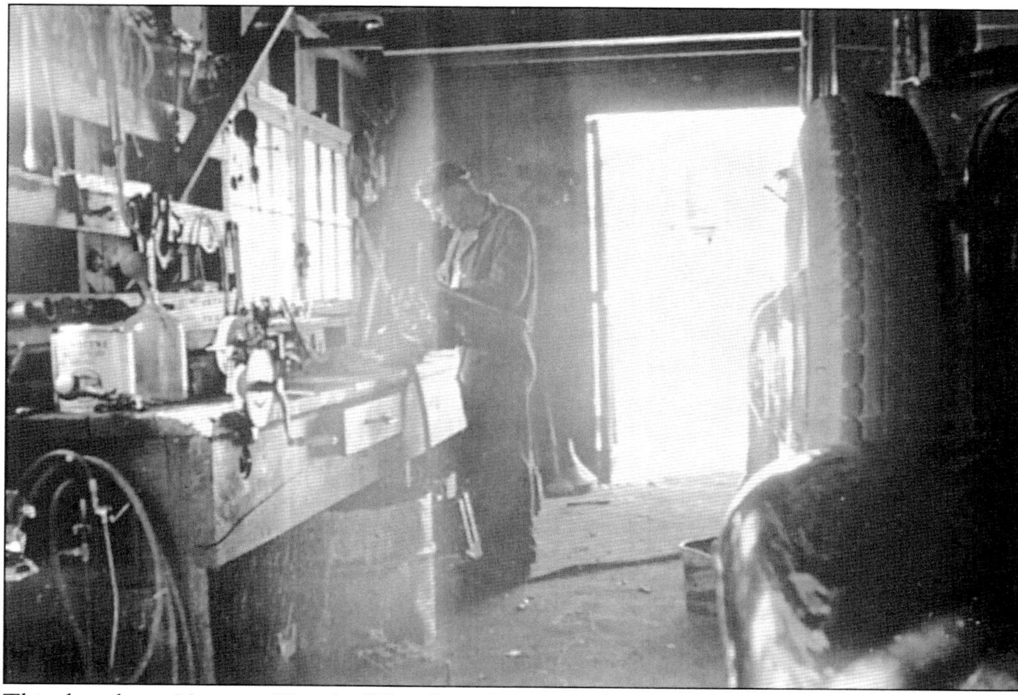

This shot shows Norman "Smithie" Smith in the garage that maintained the vehicles that helped build the road to the Portal and the heads of the Whitney Trail. (Mildred Langston collection.)

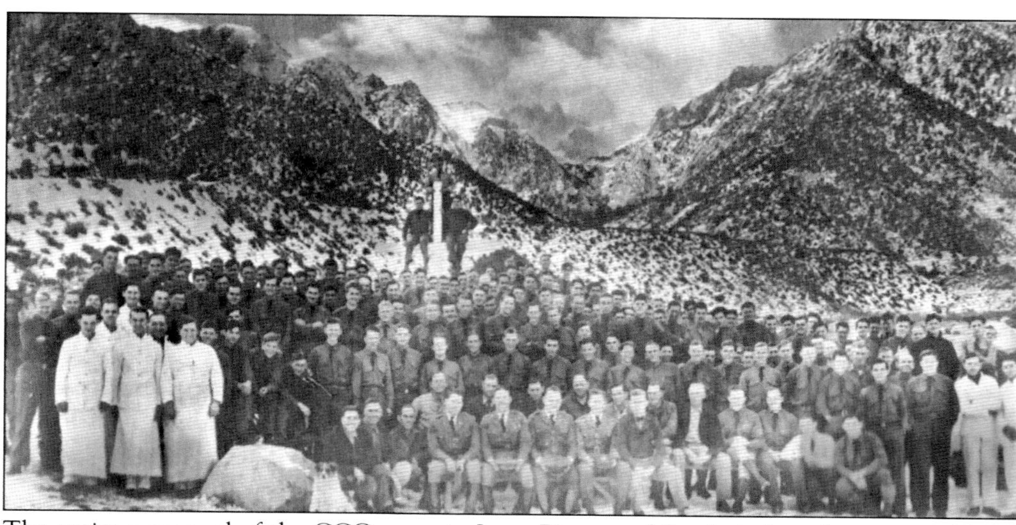

The entire personnel of the CCC camp in Lone Pine stand for their formal portrait at Easter time. (Inyo National Forest.)

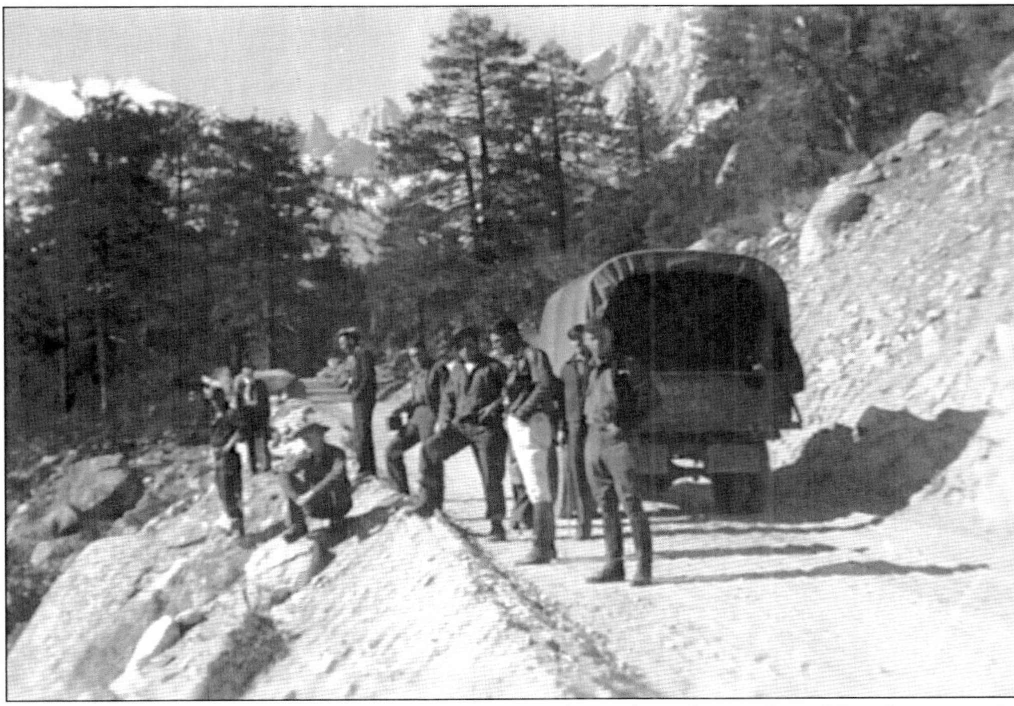

A group of engineers and construction workers stands on the Whitney Portal Road cut into the side of the cliffs below Whitney. (Mildred Langston collection.)

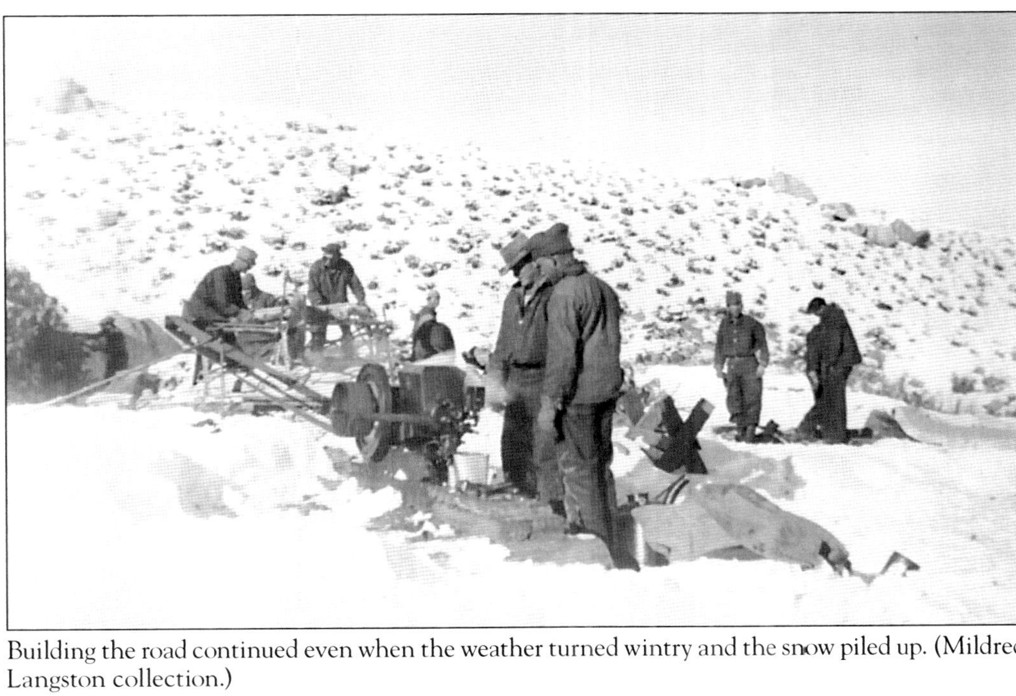

Building the road continued even when the weather turned wintry and the snow piled up. (Mildred Langston collection.)

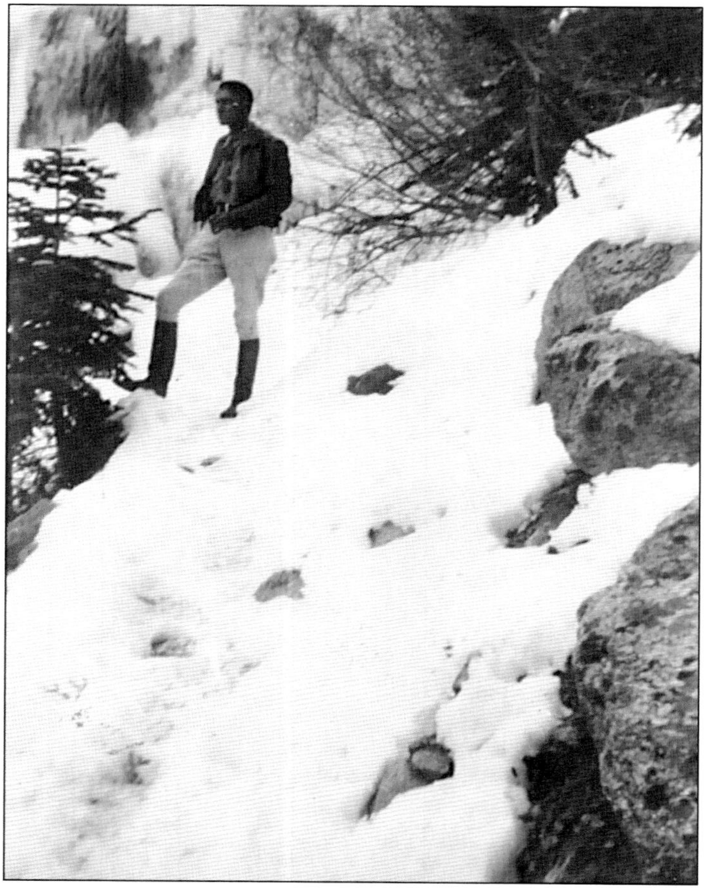

Construction of the road slowed to a crawl when the weather dropped snow measured in feet above the CCC Camp. Here, Norman "Smithie" Smith overlooks the terrain. (Mildred Langston collection.)

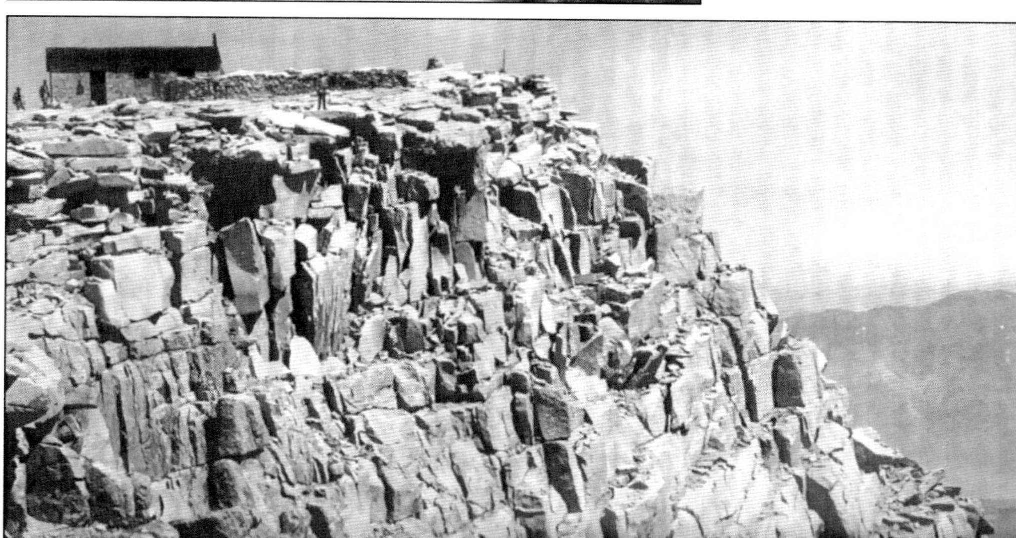

The Smithsonian Observatory is perched at the summit of Whitney, and the sharp cliffs near it show clearly in this photograph of the summit.

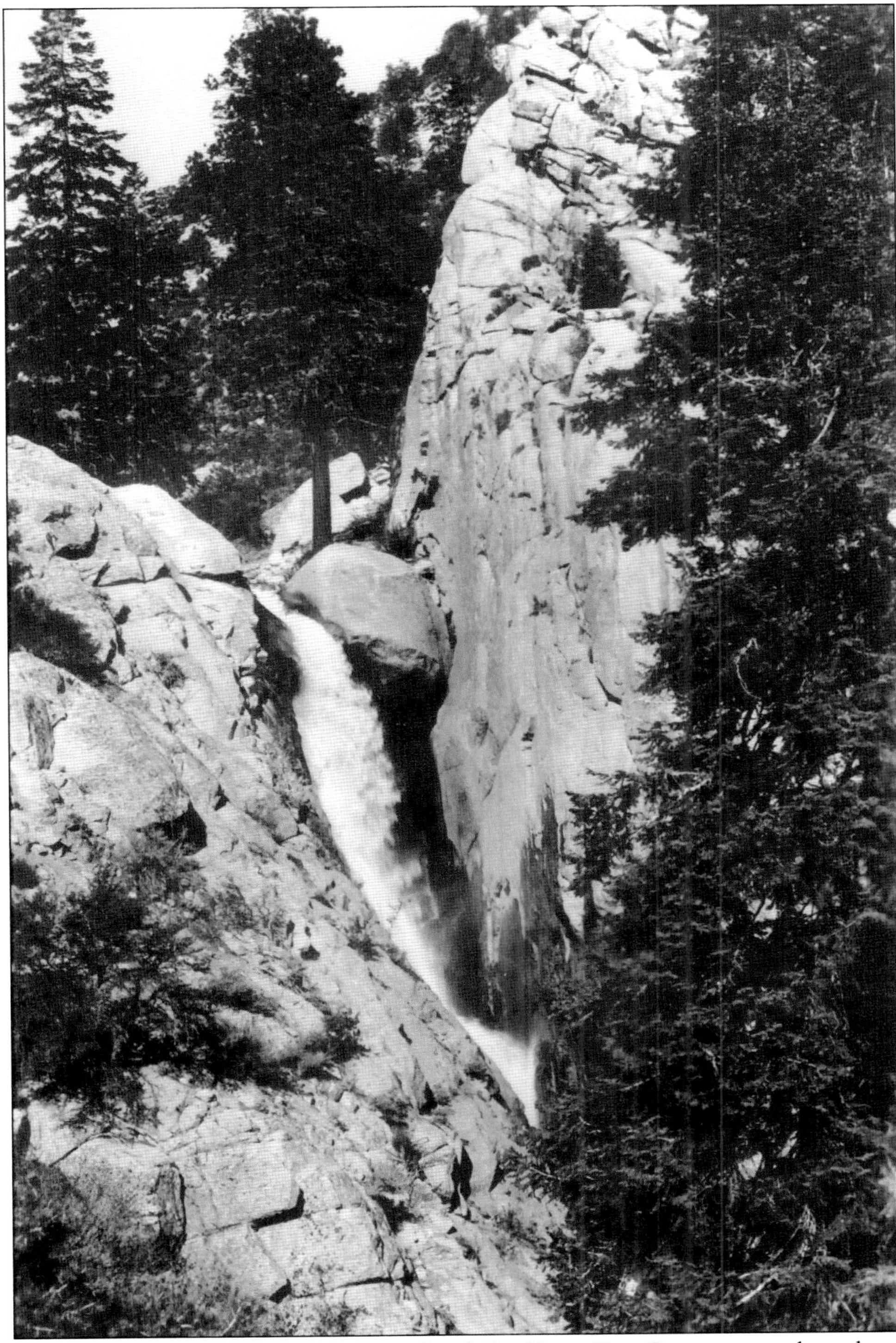

This waterfall tumbles spectacularly down the cliffs of Lone Pine Canyon near where the road turns north as it rises up the cliffs of Whitney. (LPFHM.)

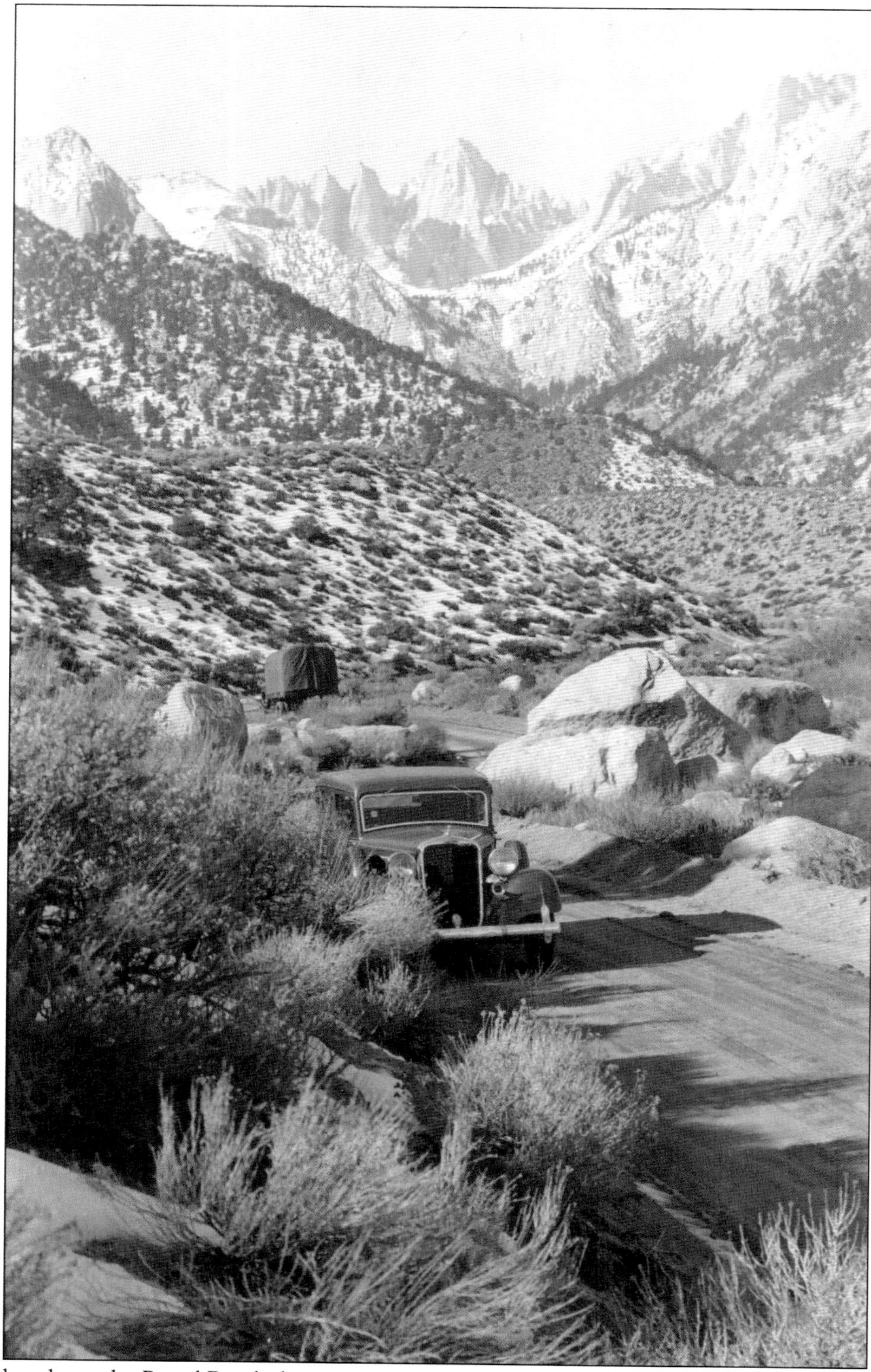

Further down the Portal Road, this car tries out the new road in the late 1930s.

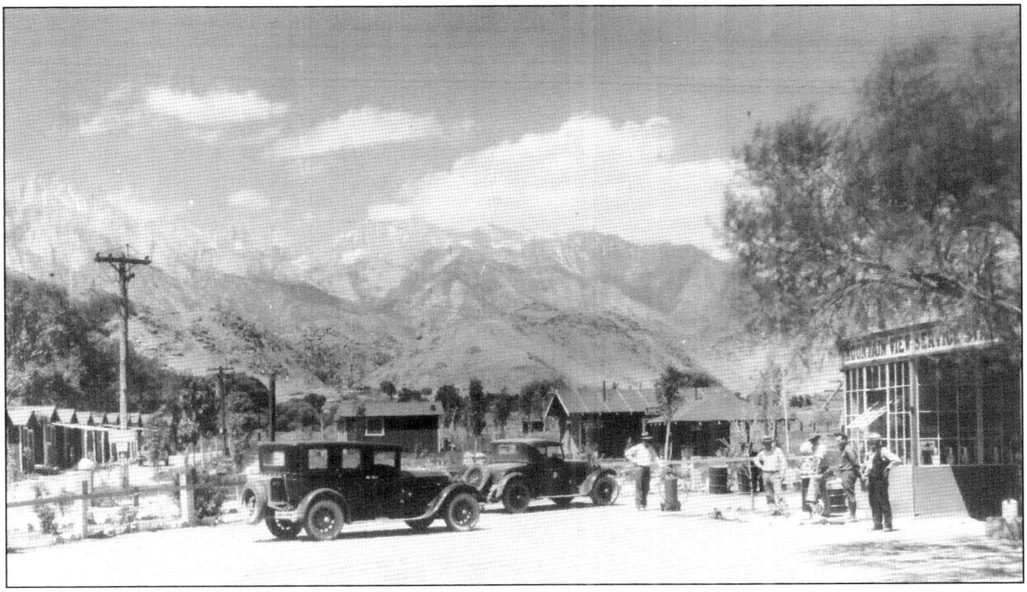

The new road encouraged more visitors to come to Lone Pine. The Mountain View Motor Court and Service Station sits with Mount Whitney in the background.

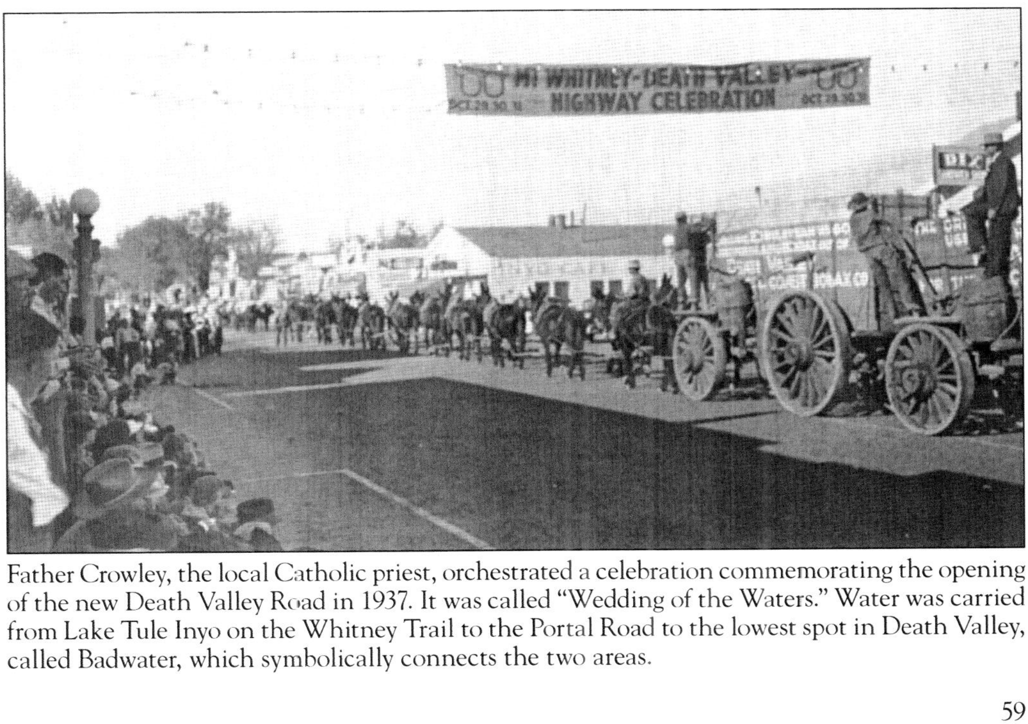

Father Crowley, the local Catholic priest, orchestrated a celebration commemorating the opening of the new Death Valley Road in 1937. It was called "Wedding of the Waters." Water was carried from Lake Tule Inyo on the Whitney Trail to the Portal Road to the lowest spot in Death Valley, called Badwater, which symbolically connects the two areas.

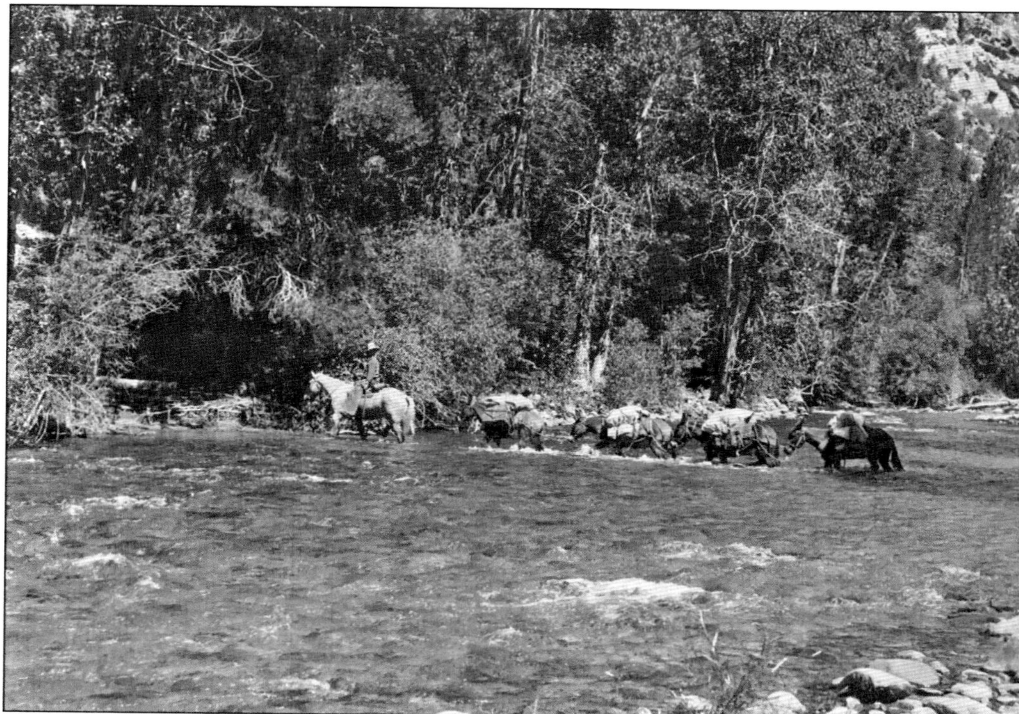

There are many ways of getting to Mount Whitney. Here, a guide leads a pack train across a swollen creek towards Whitney.

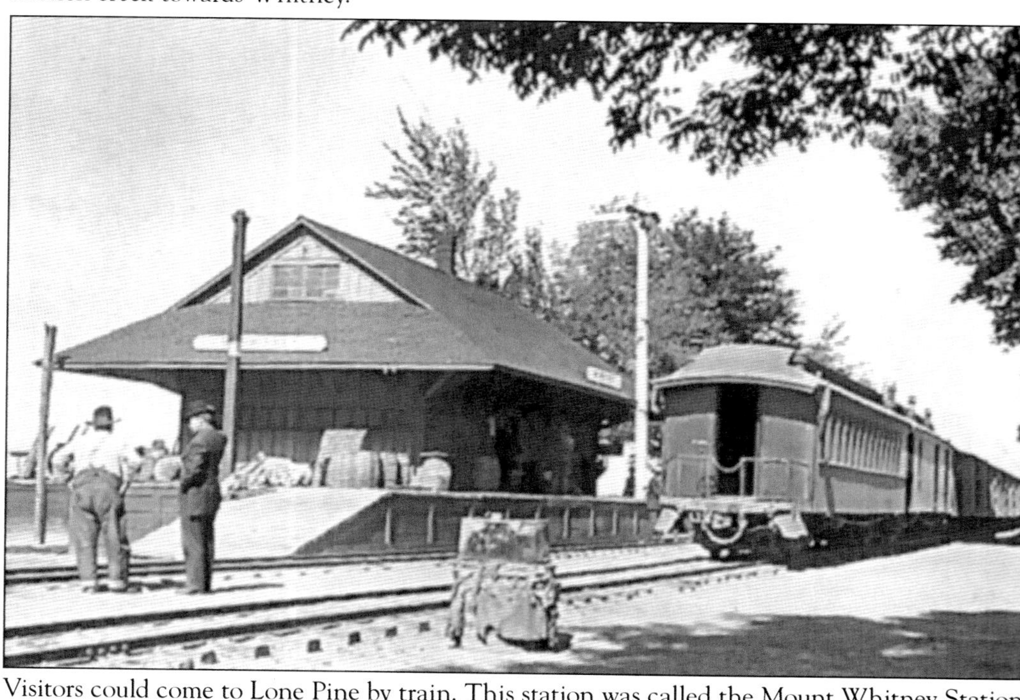

Visitors could come to Lone Pine by train. This station was called the Mount Whitney Station because of its strategic location for visitors to the mountain.

Four

PLAYGROUND

Evergreen forests, cool shady canyons, vibrant green meadows, and crystal flowing creeks have always been irresistible for locals and visitors to the Mount Whitney area—a lure to think about in the winter months at home. Deer, wildflowers, intensely blue skies, and trout-fishing have brought visitors each summer season to the scent of pine needles. The appreciation of natural quiet and beauty are firmly rooted in western heritage and the driving force that led to the creation of America's national park and national forest systems in the early 20th century. The Mount Whitney Trail, reached from Lone Pine, lies in the Inyo National Forest, which was established by proclamation in 1907 by Pres. Theodore Roosevelt. The trail winds through the John Muir Wilderness, created in 1964 by the passage of the original Wilderness Act.

The John Muir Trail from Yosemite to Mount Whitney was completed in 1938. As it is 219 miles long, backpackers must resupply along the way, often hitching rides into east-side towns for their general delivery food packages. The Pacific Crest Trail runs from Mexico to Canada and brings hikers by Mount Whitney on their way north each summer. Some are hiking the length of California, and others are heading north to Canada. A few complete the entire route before the snows begin. As the old proverb says, "Hunger is the best sauce," and it can be seen when these long-distance hikers arrive at the Whitney Portal Store and consume huge pancakes, juicy hamburgers, and French fries.

Sequoia National Park, created in 1926, extends up the west slope to the crest of the Sierra and the summit of Mount Whitney. This park's creation spelled the end of the cross-Sierra dream road to Visalia from Lone Pine, following the old Hockett Trail. Creation of the expanded Sequoia-Kings Canyon National Park in 1940 ended another cross-Sierra road dream over Kearsarge Pass to Grant Grove on the Kings River. Since then, in order to drive across the Sierra, travelers have had to go over Walker Pass from Ridgecrest or Tioga Pass in Yosemite National Park—an unbroken wilderness heritage that is roughly 200 miles long. As Aldo Leopold writes in *A Sand County Almanac* (1945), "Of what avail are forty freedoms without a blank spot on the map." That appeal of untrammeled natural landscape is the American West. It is the public's heritage.

Mountains anywhere are places for accidents. Whether involving hypothermia, heart attacks, falls, lightning, human error, or lack of preparedness, people die and are injured on Mount Whitney every year. The trail looks simple enough, though long. It is called a walk-up, where no technical skills are needed, but sudden changes in weather can soak hikers, and winds can seriously chill the body in minutes. Lack of proper rain protection and warm layers can quickly become life-threatening. In addition, hiking at high elevation lets a person feel the exertion of merely bending down and tying his or her shoes. Breathing becomes more labored the higher one goes. Less atmospheric pressure allows oxygen molecules to spread farther apart, so each breath contains less of this life-giving gas. The percentage of oxygen is the same at high or low elevation, but the air is thinner. This thin air also causes one to feel to warm in the sun and yet too cool in the shade. With the molecules spread farther apart, the air holds less heat.

Many people have the Whitney Portal Campground as their destination when visiting the Mount Whitney area. Enjoying the mountain air, doing some trout-fishing in the pond or creek, and taking short hikes are enough for these campers. This is a wild experience for these visitors who often travel from the cities and suburbs. Other visitors own one of the few dozen rustic summer cabins built on leased Forest Service land at the Portal. These cabins were constructed in the late 1930s, following the extension of the Whitney Portal Road from Lone Pine Campground to the Portal. Wildness is relative to visitors here. What is absolute is the awe that people feel when entering these mountains. It is the butterflies that can be felt in their stomachs as they in a meadow and the calmness that spreads through them when listening to natural stillness.

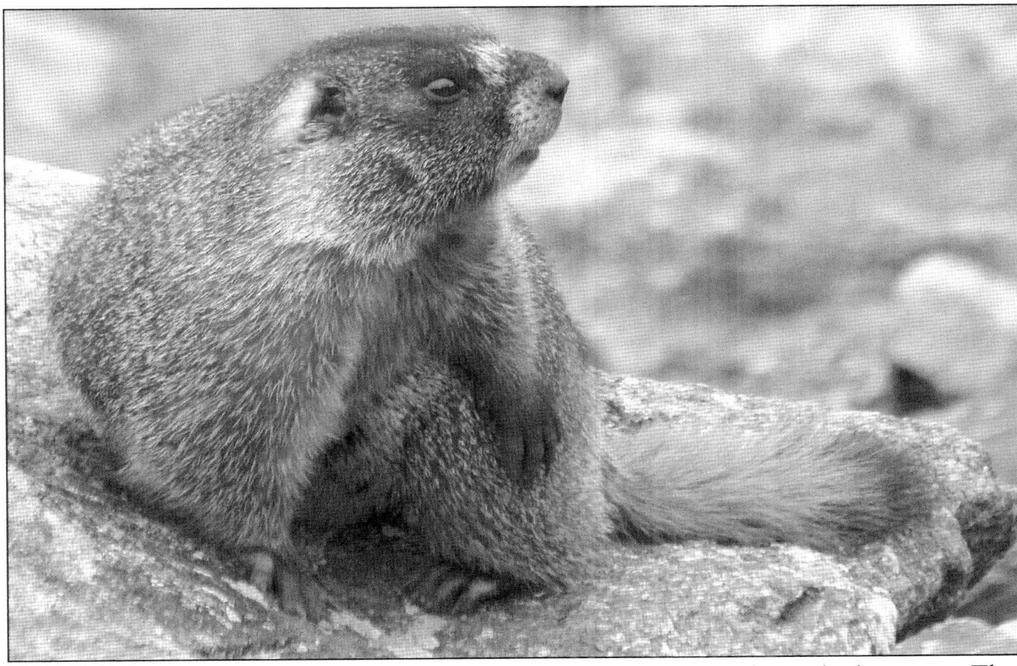

Yellow-bellied marmots lounge on the tops of boulders in meadows and open high country. They love the sun and also enjoy chewing into the packs of hikers when looking for goodies. (Ali Sheehey at Nature Ali.)

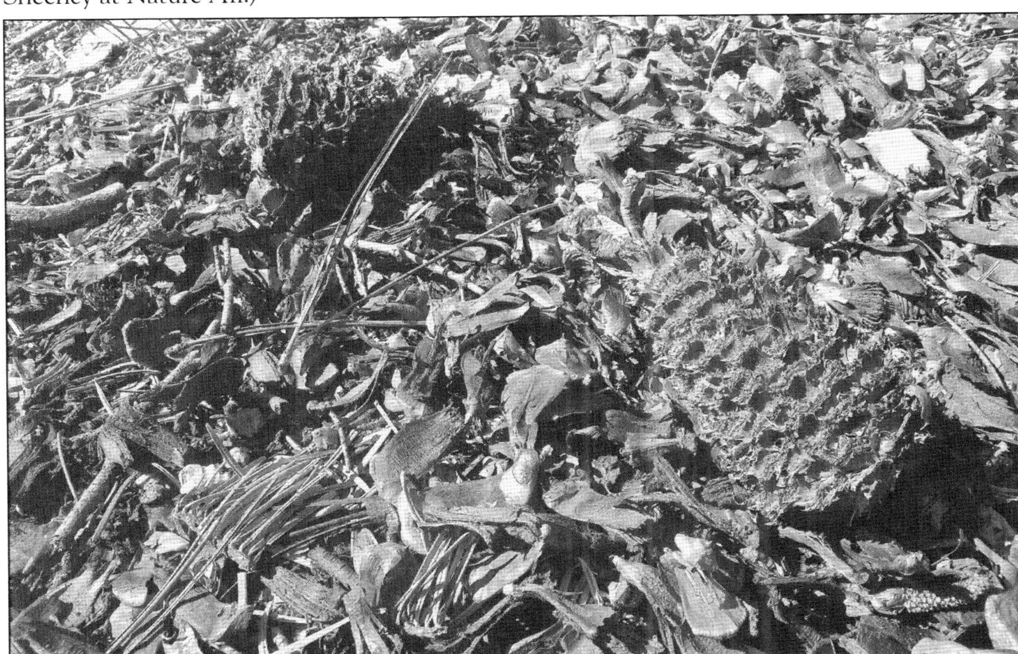

This is a chickaree feeding station. This tree squirrel takes apart pine cones for their seeds. Squirrels choose favorite sites on a rock or at the base of a tree where they leave piles of scales and cores. (Mike Prather.)

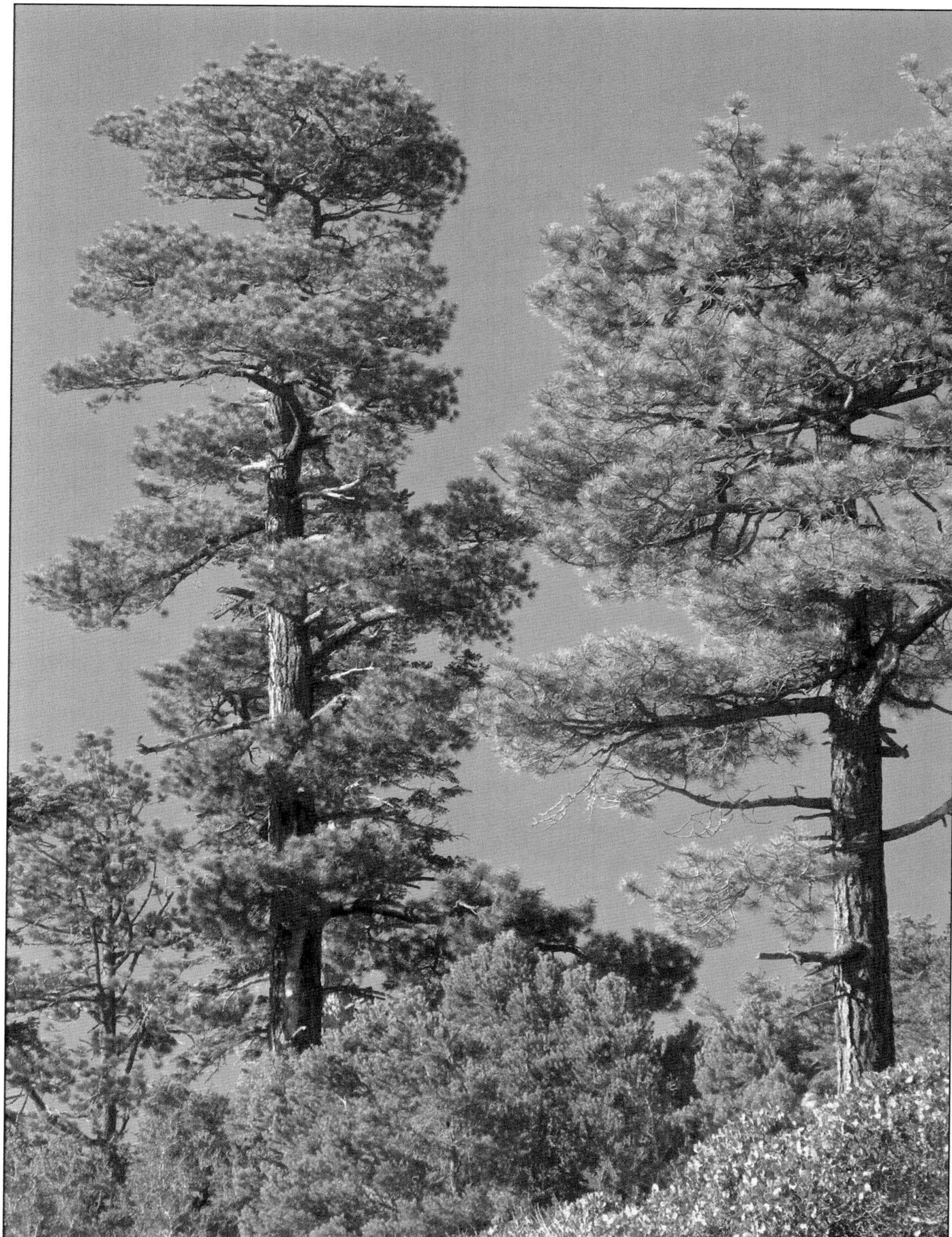

The Jeffrey pine is the largest eastern Sierra pine similar to the ponderosa pine of the west slope. The jigsaw puzzle–looking bark smells like vanilla in the warm sunshine. (Mike Prather.)

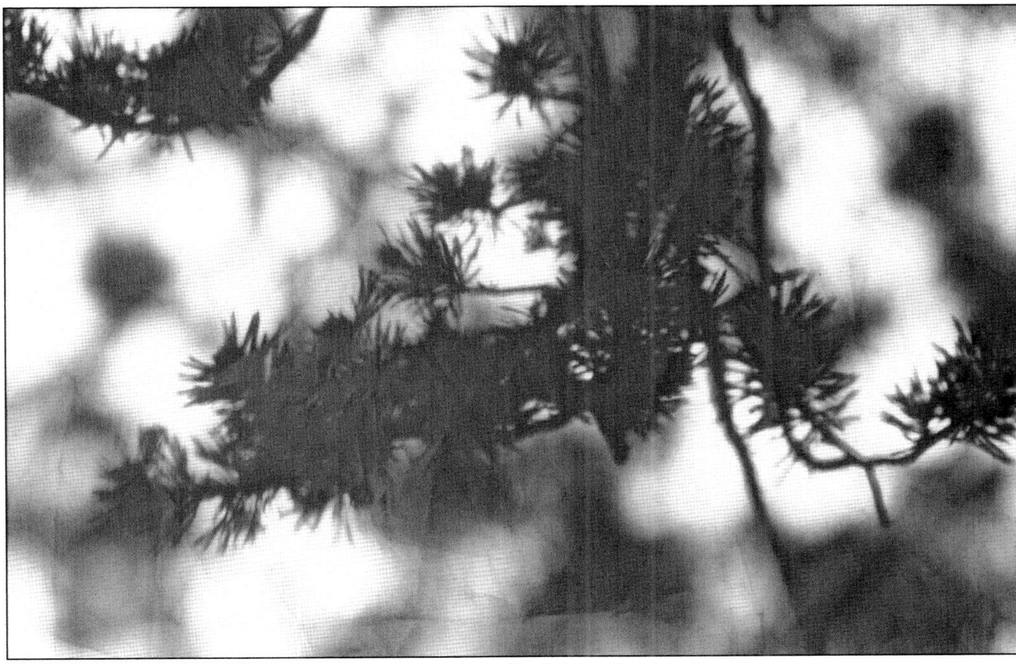

Pine needle shadows decorate a canvas tent wall. (Mike Prather.)

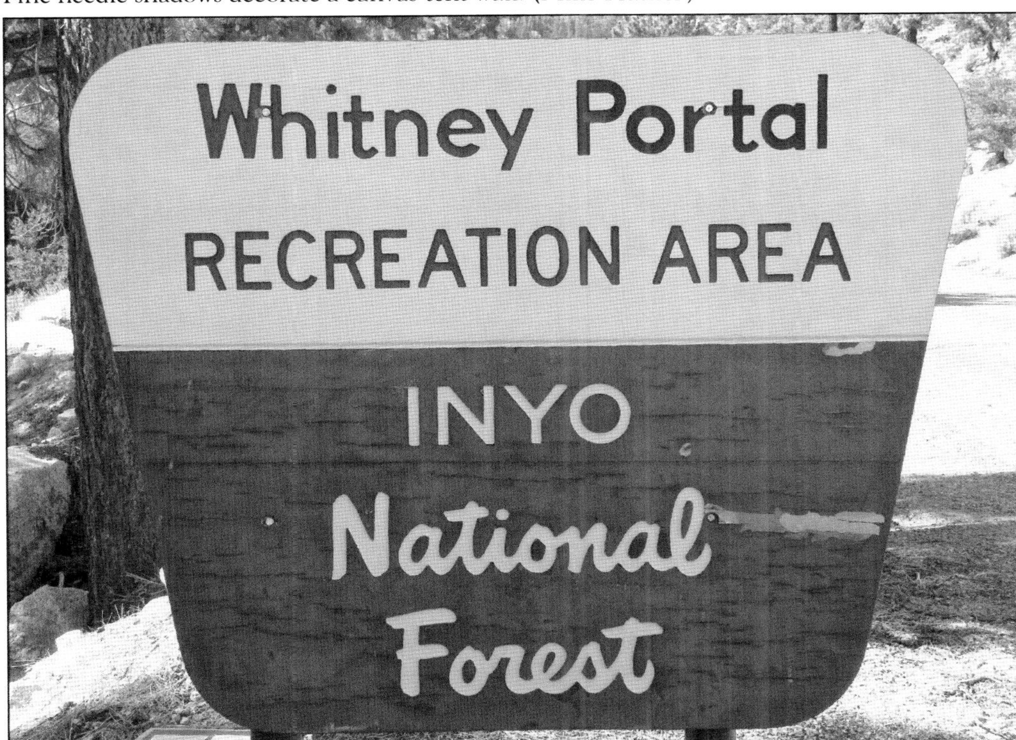

This sign welcomes visitors to the Whitney Portal Recreation Area in Inyo National Forest. Camping, hiking, climbing, and fishing take place here. (Mike Prather.)

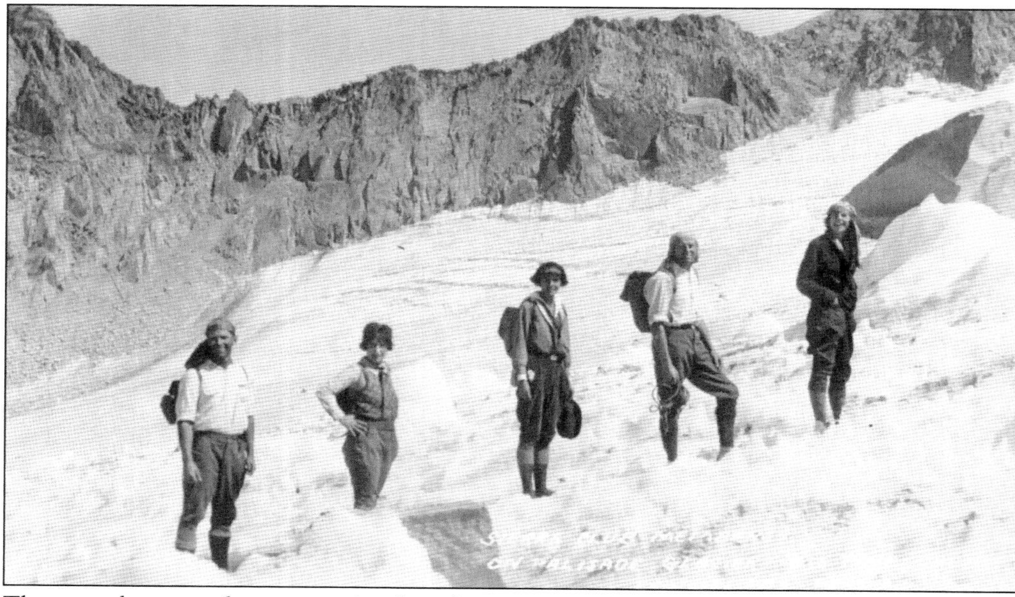

The term *pleasure-seekers* was used to describe mountain adventurers in the early days. The Mount Whitney region has attracted pleasure-seekers since Owens Valley was first settled in the late 1850s. *The Inyo Independent,* a local newspaper, reported on September 20, 1873, "Lone Pine folks at fishing a camp shot deer, caught trout, had raspberries and elderberries for pies and shortcakes and had two milk cows." In the era of no swamp coolers, residents of the Owens Valley who had the means would travel via pack stock (mules and horses) up into the Sierra for an escape from the summer heat. After the Whitney Portal Road was extended up to Hunter Flat (Whitney Portal) by the New Deal's Civilian Conservation Corps in the late 1930s, there were stories of Lone Pine families who would camp at Whitney Portal during the summer while dads would commute into town to work.

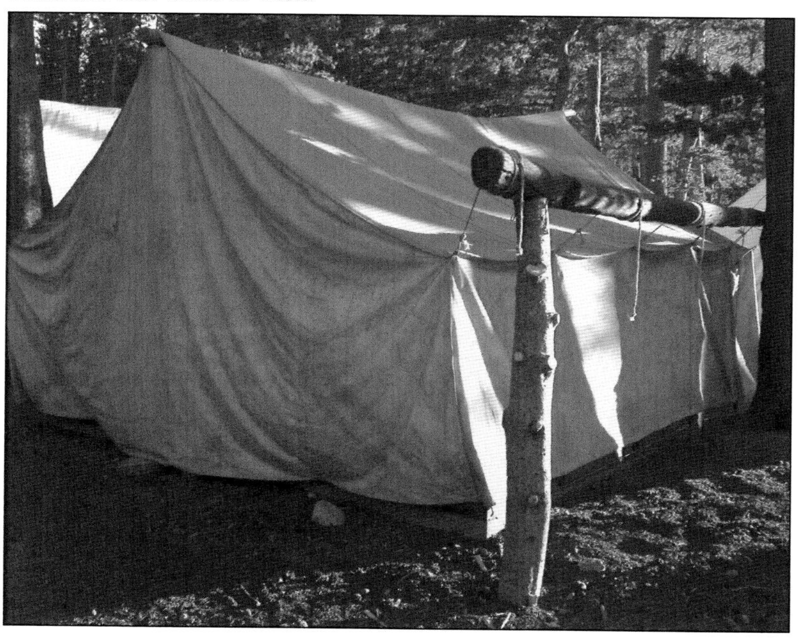

This photograph shows a classic canvas-walled tent that was used by pack trains. (Mike Prather.)

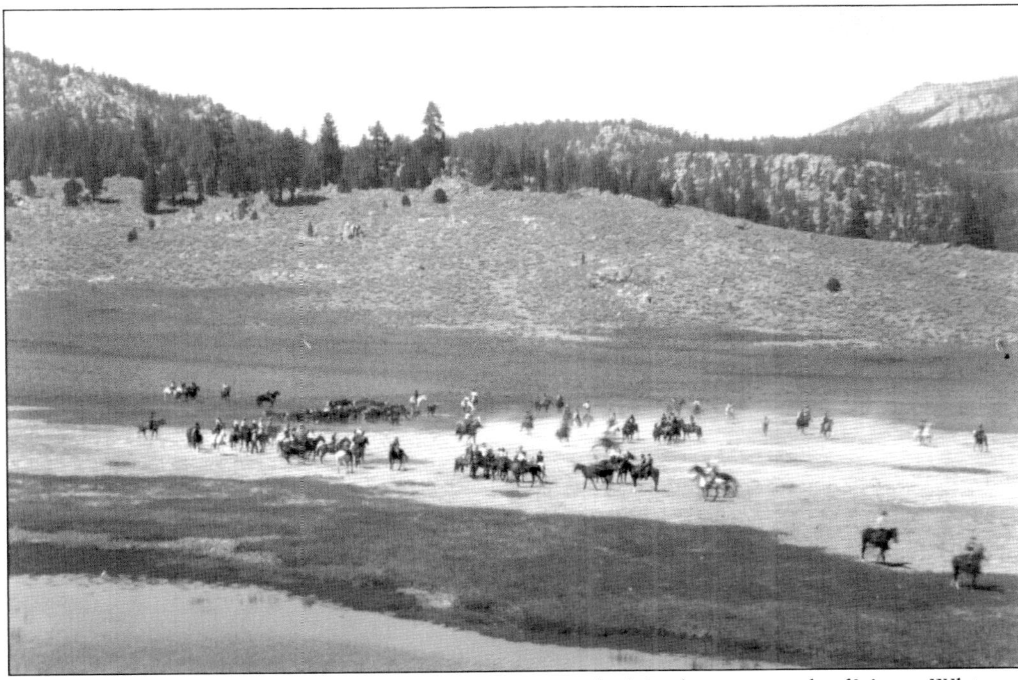

The Monache Rodeo was held by local cowboys in Monache Meadow, just south of Mount Whitney. No fences, gates, or chutes were needed for their displays of the skills of the cowboy.

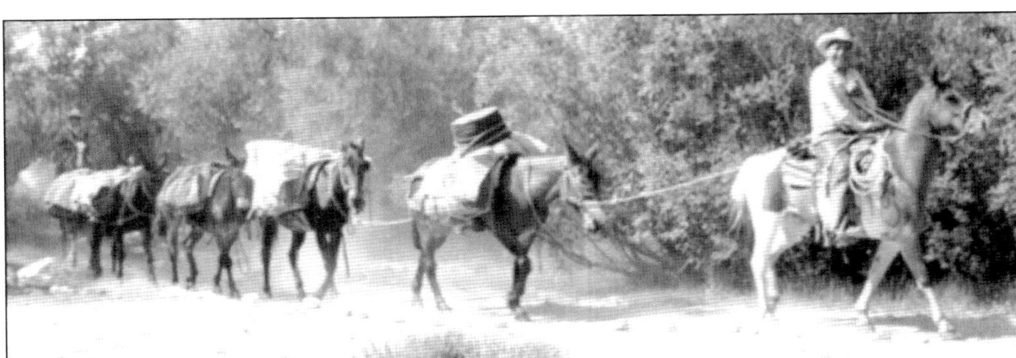

Mount Whitney Pack Train's Tommy Jefferson is leading a string. Local ranches had cow camps each summer that eventually provided ranch hands to take clients into the Sierra Nevada. This evolution of modern packing outfits repeated an often seen adaptation of locals finding additional ways of making a living here in the Eastern Sierra. Packer outfits have taken visitors into the Mount Whitney area since the early 1900s. From the 1930s to 1972, the Mount Whitney Pack Trains were in operation locally. One packer has said, "We are an old-style profession in a high-tech world."

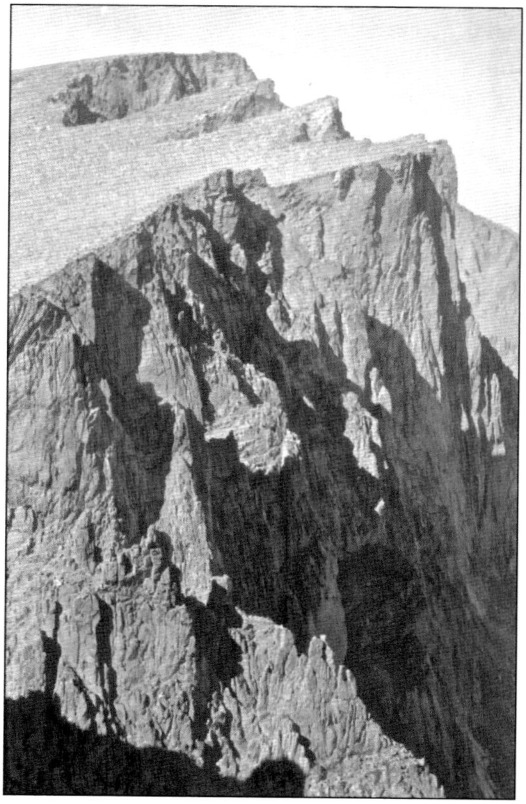

The tiny Summit House in this photograph gives a sense of the size of the mountain.

Shoeing is hard anywhere, but in the snow on the summit of Mount Whitney, it is extreme.

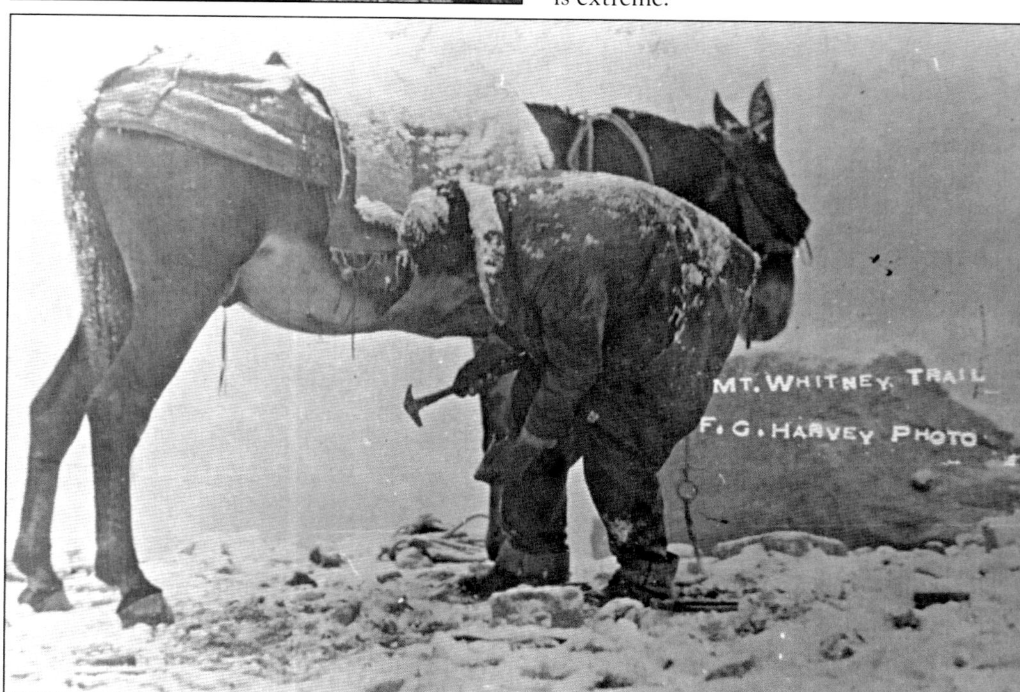

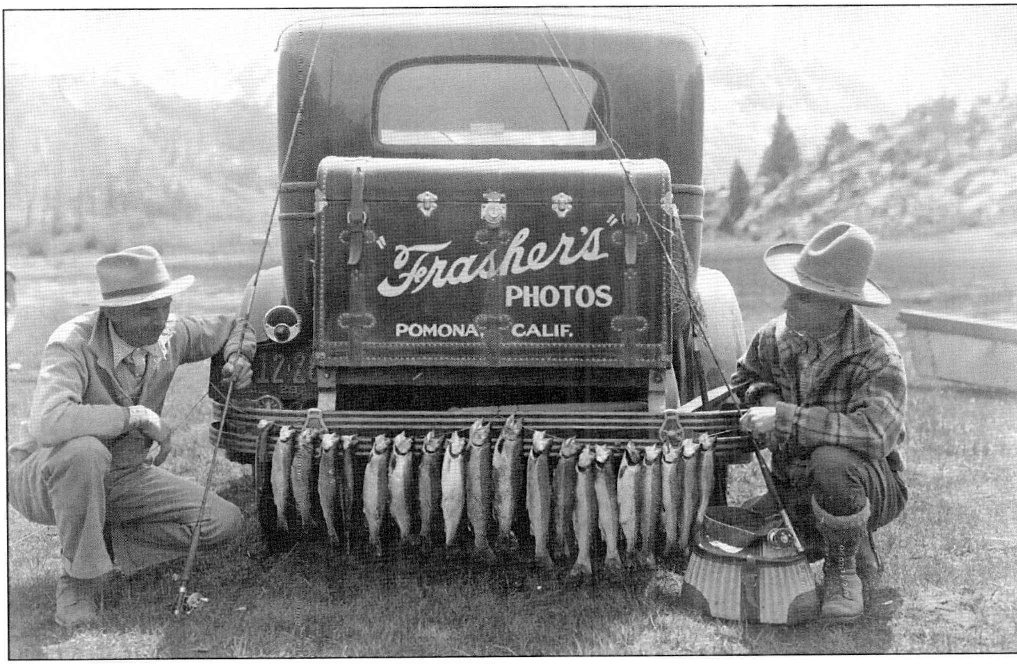

Burton Frasher, the famous photographer and postcard creator, is displaying a string of fish that was caught here in the Eastern Sierra.

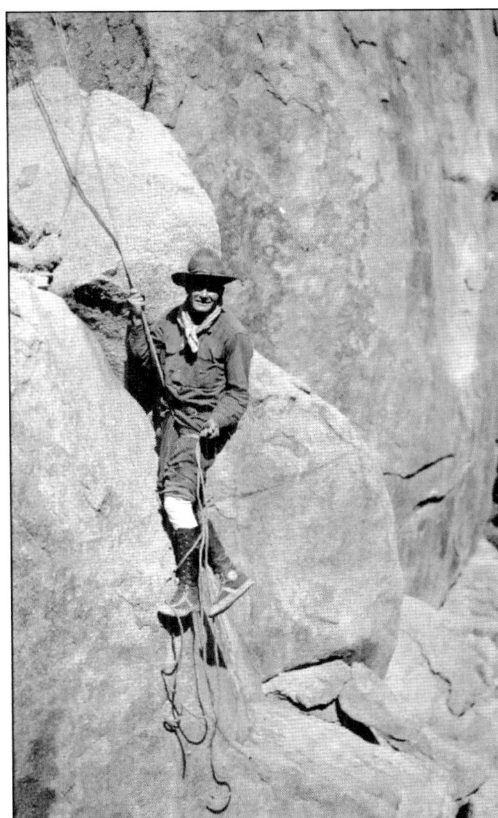

Norman Clyde is photographed climbing with rope. In the 1930s, Sierra Club mountaineers were schooled in European climbing methods by members of the Appalachian Club. This involved proper roping up and the use of pitons or anchors for protection. Norman Clyde and Sierra Club climbers in the early years made use of hemp rope, pitons, and hob-nailed boots. In later years, climbing clean, or the use of removable anchors, became more of the standard. This style of climbing did less damage to the rock from drilling and hardware placement. Routes up the East Face of Whitney in 1931 via the North Fork of Lone Pine Creek and the Mountaineers Route pioneered by Muir and named by Clyde were executed. In the 1940s, nylon rope and tents, tubular aluminum, and goose-down mummy bags allowed trekkers to reach the high country more easily and stay with more comfort. Winter camping and winter ascents became more common as the season for mountaineering became 12 months.

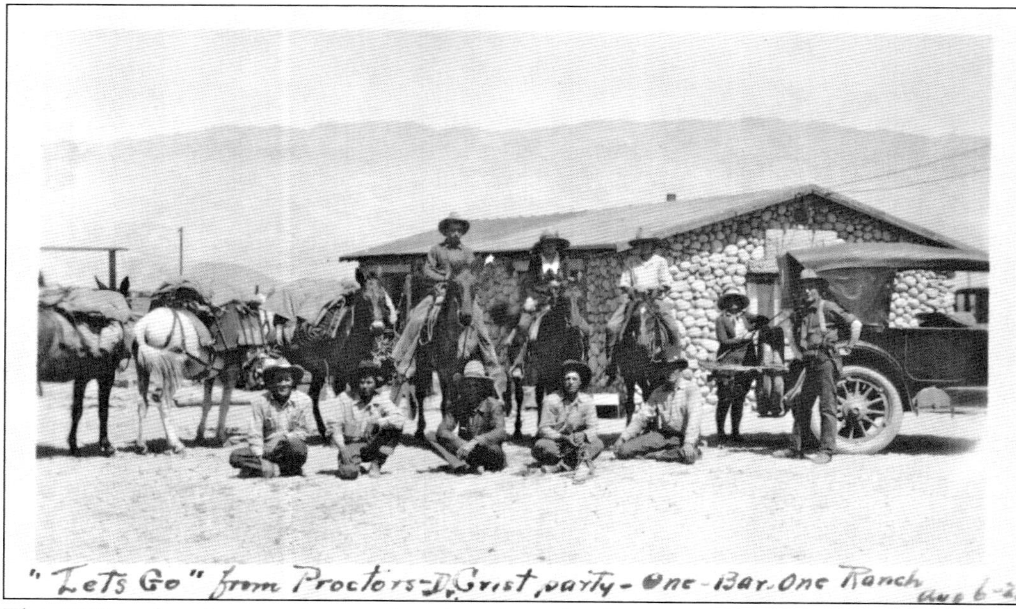

This 1923 pack train party is up and ready to leave for the mountains. Most trips to the top of Mount Whitney in the early years were up its gentler western slope. But in 1904, Lone Piners led by Gus Marsh constructed a trail up Lone Pine Creek from the Owens Valley. Pack trains could now climb to Trail Crest and on to the summit or down the backside to Crabtree Meadows. This trail made possible the later construction of the Summit House in 1909, also overseen by Marsh. Work crews in the 1940s improved the 99-switchback section of the route.

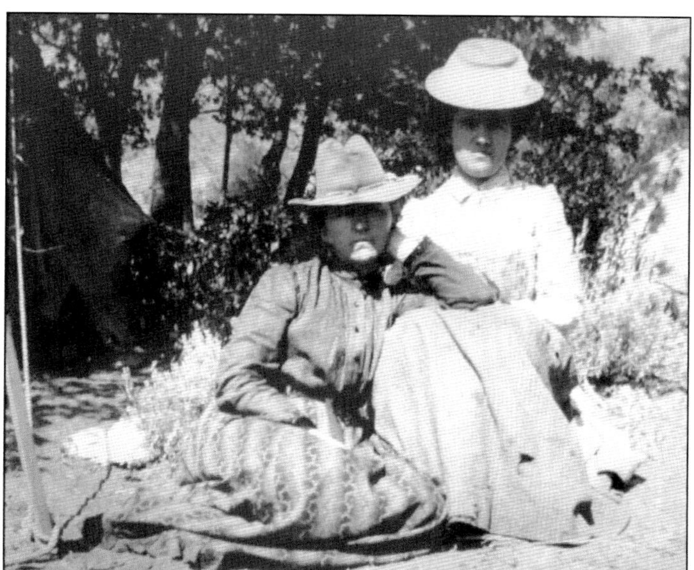

Tourist adventurers would come to the Mount Whitney area via horse teams and wagons or on the Southern Pacific Railroad. In 1898, four intrepid men left Pasadena in a horse-and-wagon team for a two-month trip to climb Mount Whitney from Lone Pine. The Sierra Club held annual High Trips from 1901 until the 1940s. In 1903, two parties totaling 169 hikers climbed Mount Whitney. Packers were said to be amused by these "foot burners" who would hike rather than ride.

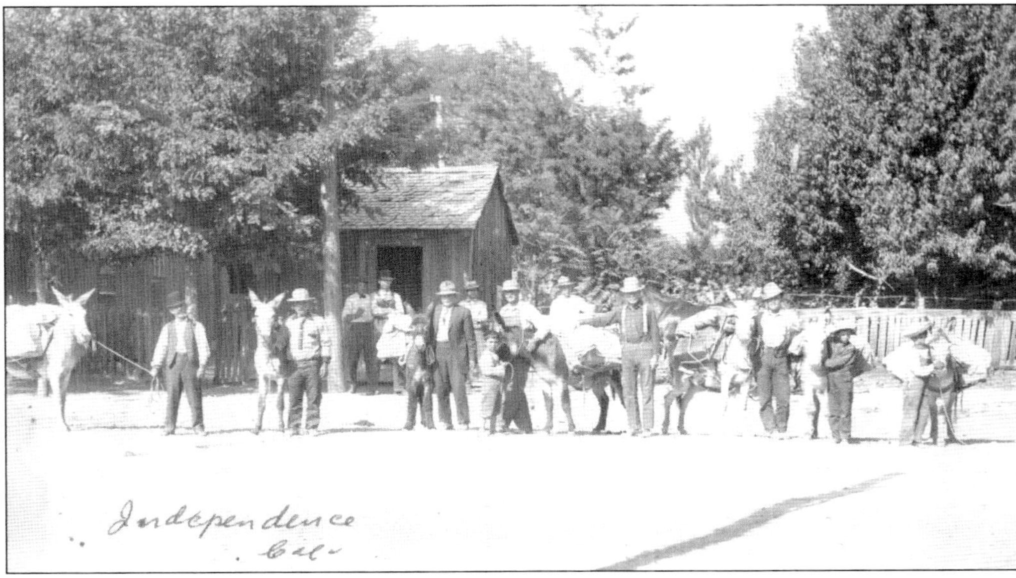

Burro strings have carried visitors' gear into the Sierra for many years.

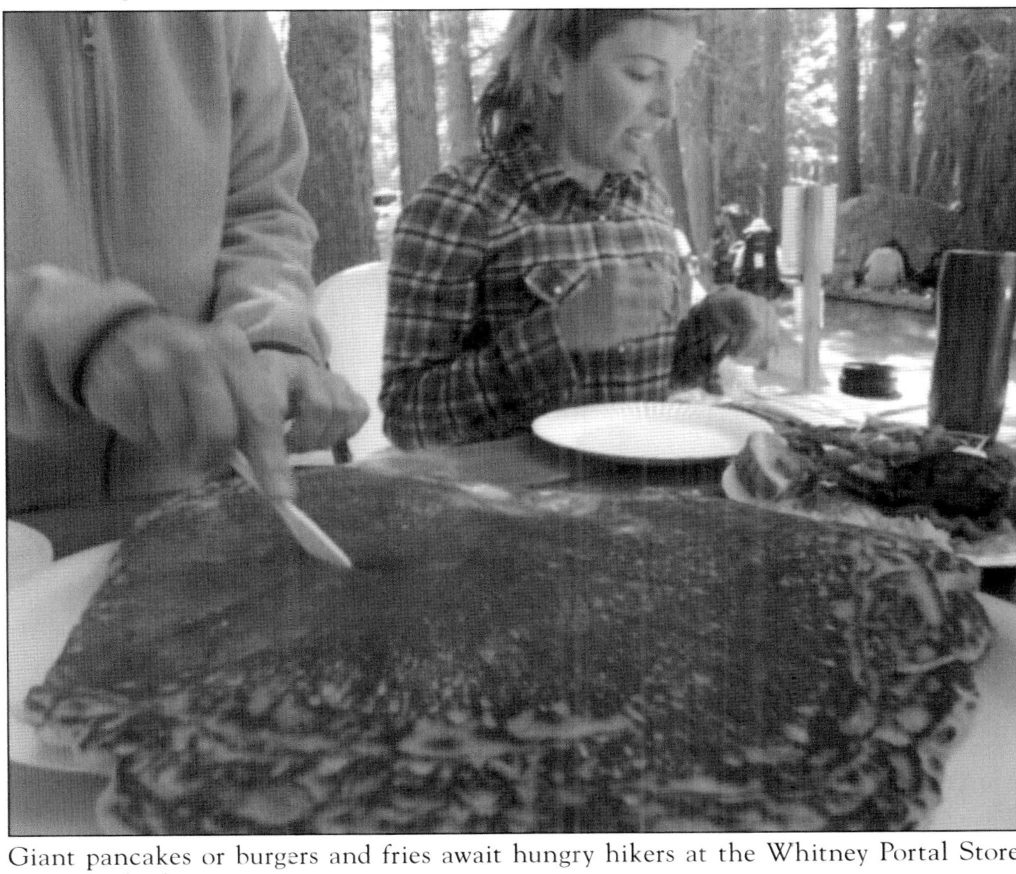

Giant pancakes or burgers and fries await hungry hikers at the Whitney Portal Store. (Mike Prather.)

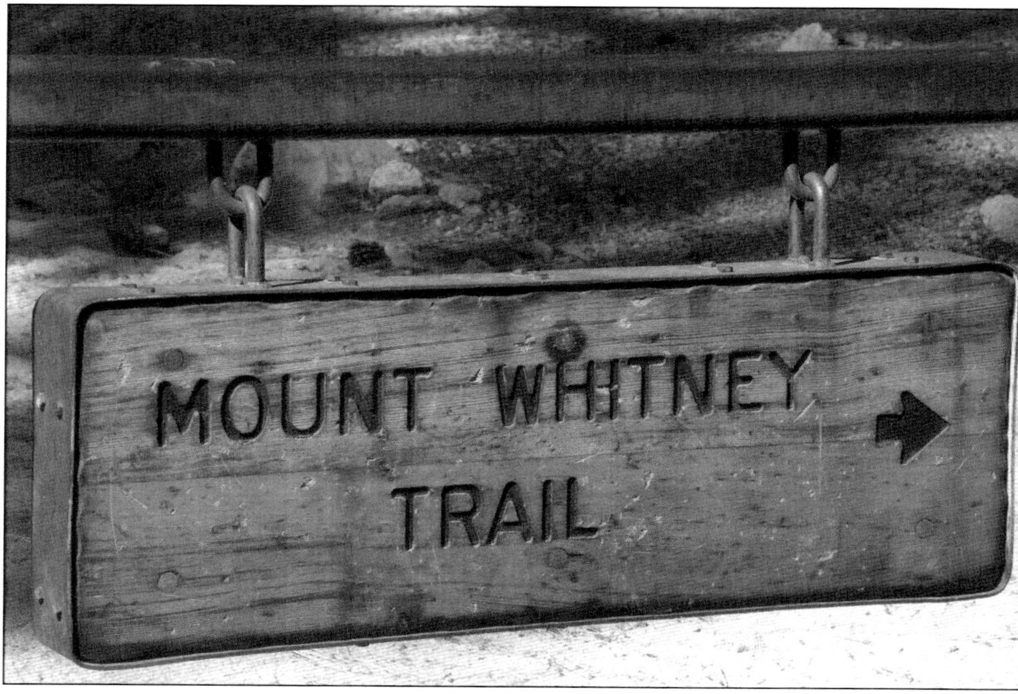

Only 11.3 miles and 6,000 feet of elevation gain gets one to the summit. Be prepared for the 99-switchback section when leaving Trail Camp heading for Trail Crest. Thin air is hot in the sun, cool in the shade. "Out of breath just tying your shoes," whispered one hiker. (Mike Prather.)

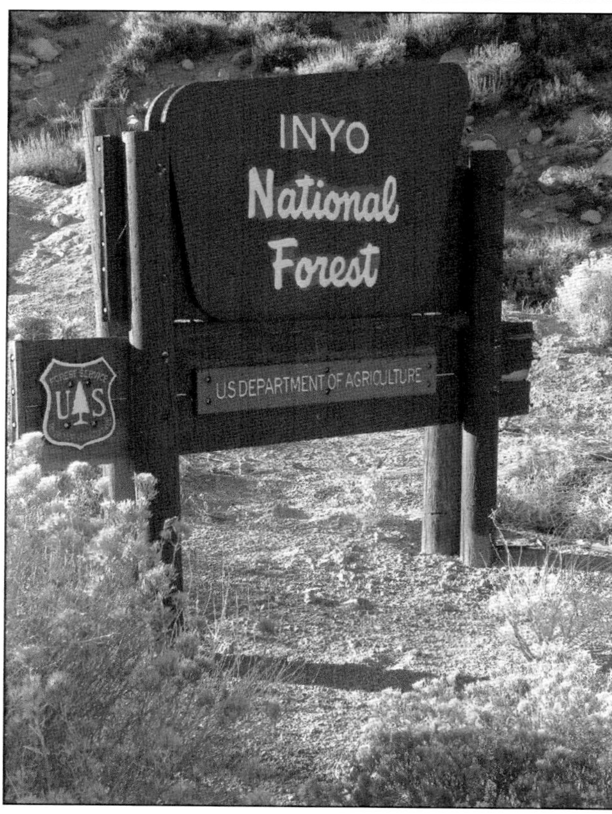

Inyo National Forest is primarily a recreational forest, stretching along the east slope of the Sierra in Inyo and Mono Counties. (Mike Prather.)

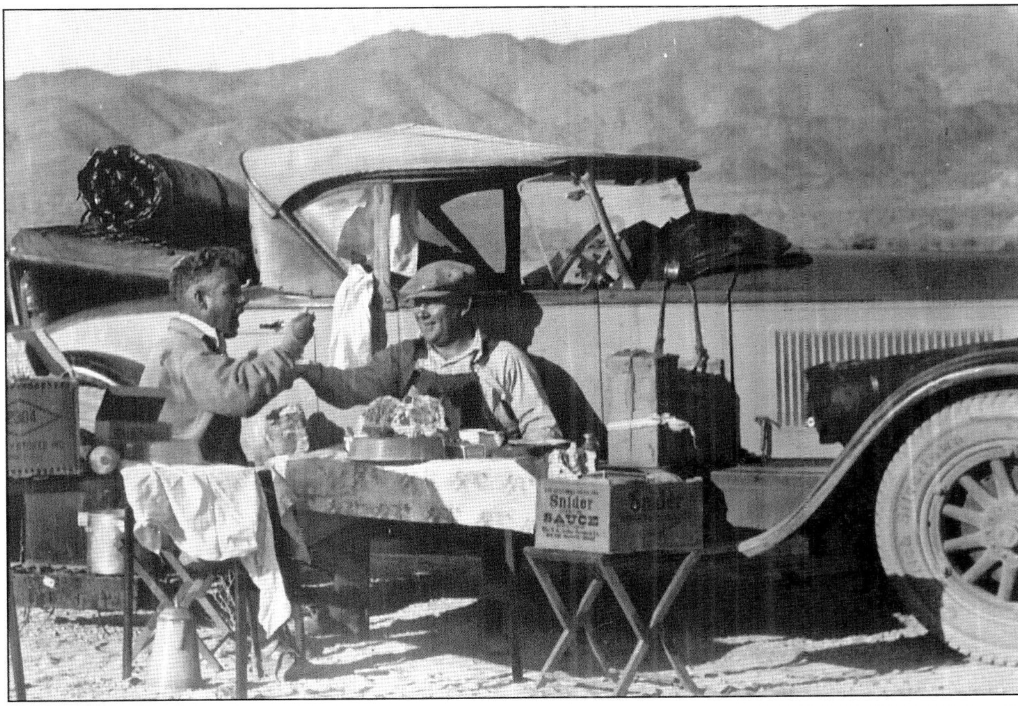

Highway 6 (later Highway 395) was paved in the 1920s, following the success of Henry Ford and the Ford Motor Car Company putting a car in nearly every garage. Americans were on the move, and they were now able to reach the Sierra from Southern California and elsewhere with an ease never before experienced.

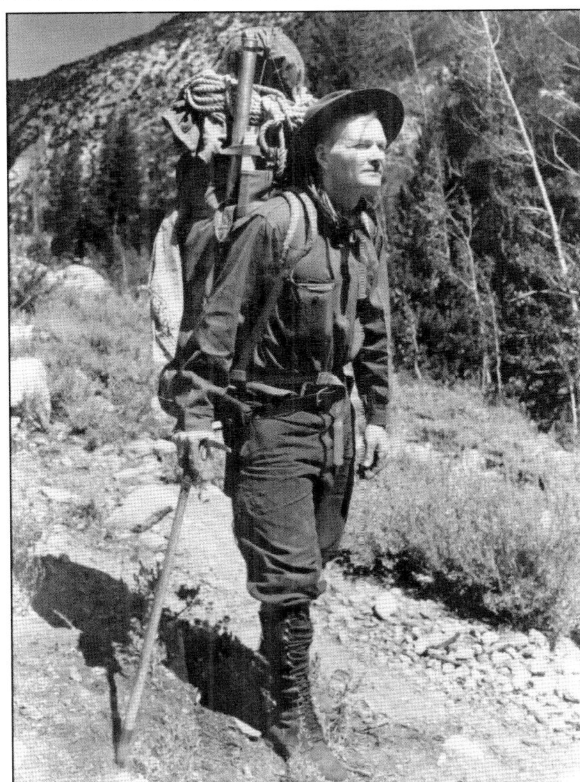

With his 80-pound pack, Norman Clyde was described as "a pack walking like a man."

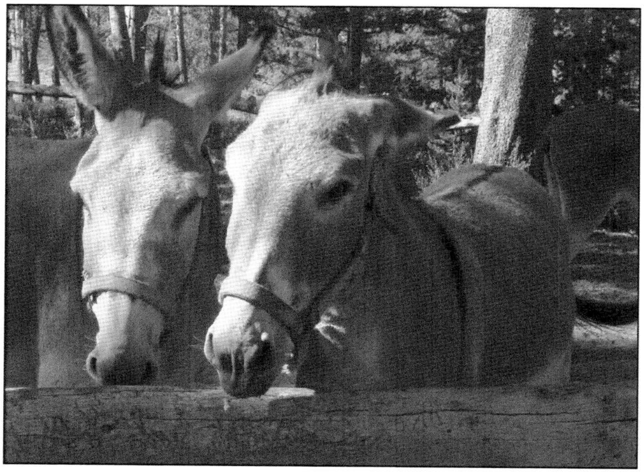

Burros have always been a part of packing. These burros help supply the Golden Trout Camp on Cottonwood Creek. (Mike Prather.)

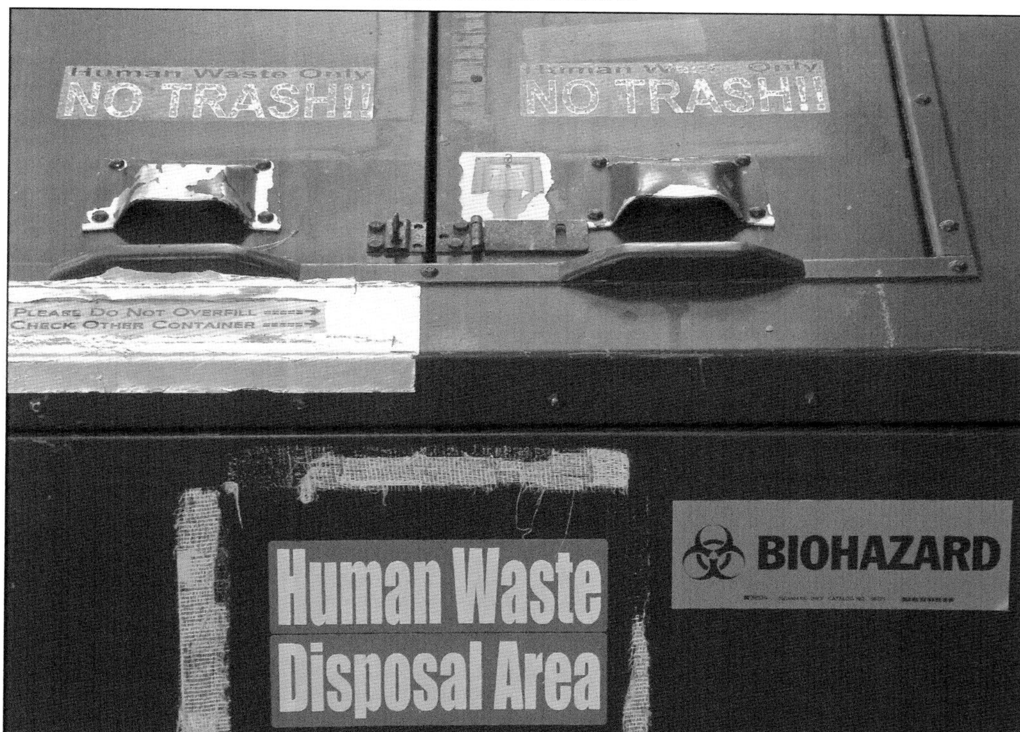

Pictured are human waste bins for Mount Whitney hikers. Crowds of backpackers eventually led to end of pack trains using the Whitney Trail. Nearby pack stations at Cottonwood Creek and Onion Valley continue to offer access into the backcountry on horses and mules. Backpacking rose in popularity starting in the 1960s; by 1974, a quota system for required permits was initiated. Today, nearly 20,000 people with 6,000 overnight permits set off up the trail to the top. Most hikers begin from Whitney Portal, while others hike in from the west slope. Inyo National Forest issues 100 day-hike permits per day and 60 overnight permits. Backcountry rangers patrol the trail, checking permits and providing assistance. This heavy use of the Whitney Trail by hikers has led to the requirement that all human waste be packed out by hikers. Bins for waste greet returning hikers to drop off their "wag bags." (Mike Prather.)

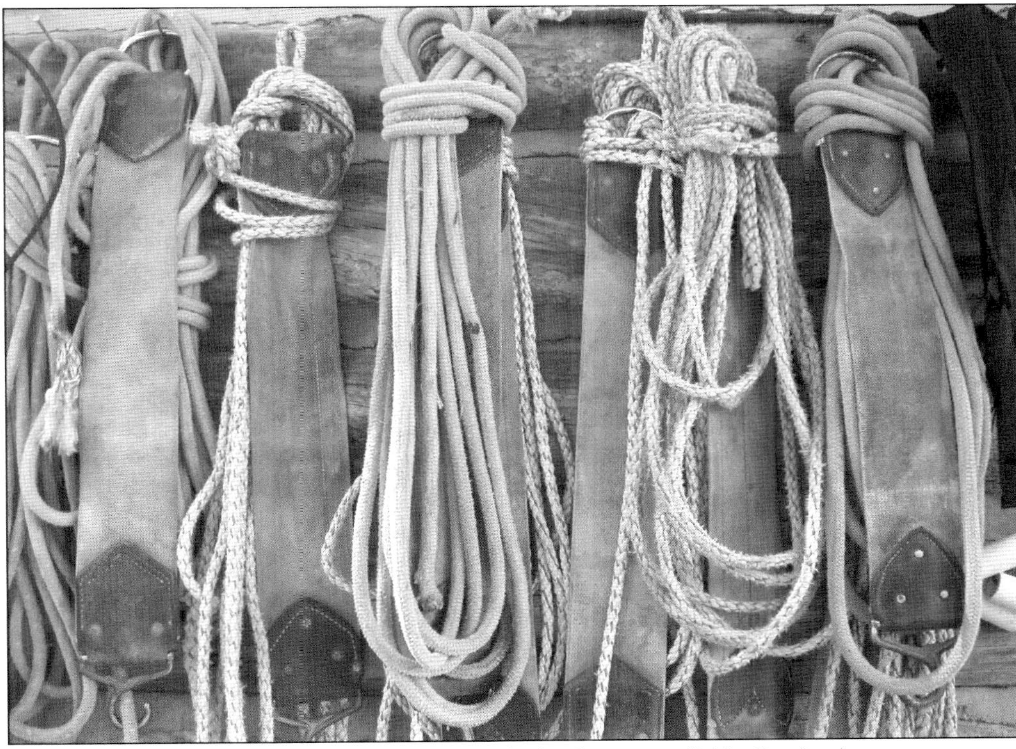
Packing rigging is ready for the next trip into the backcountry. (Mike Prather.)

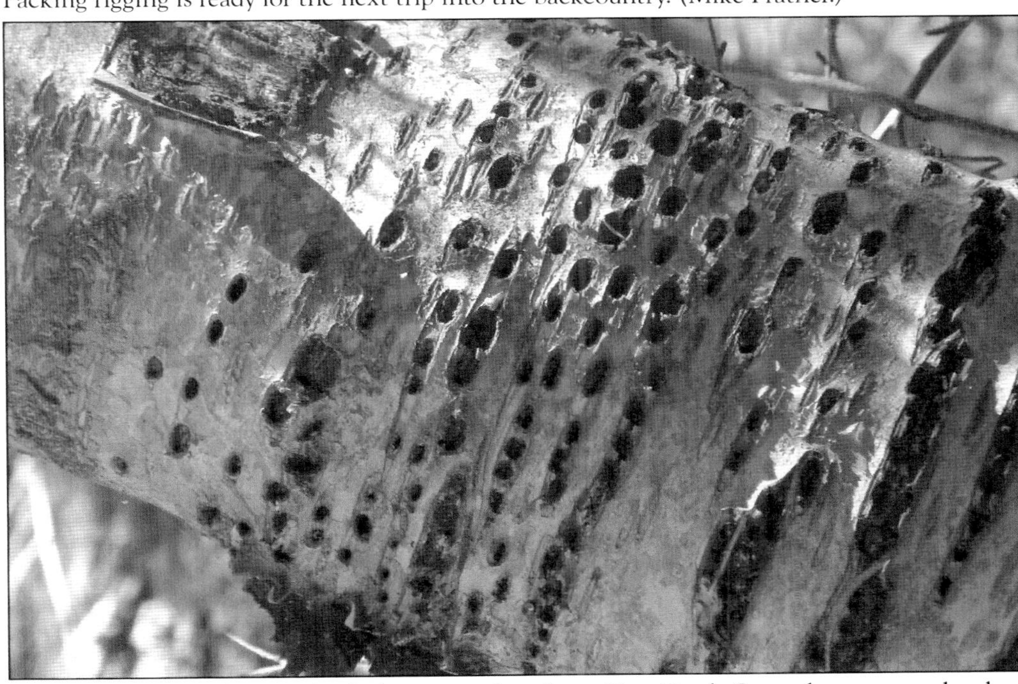
This water birch, with sapsucker holes, grows along Lone Pine Creek. Sapsuckers are woodpeckers that always drill their holes in a row. (Mike Prather.)

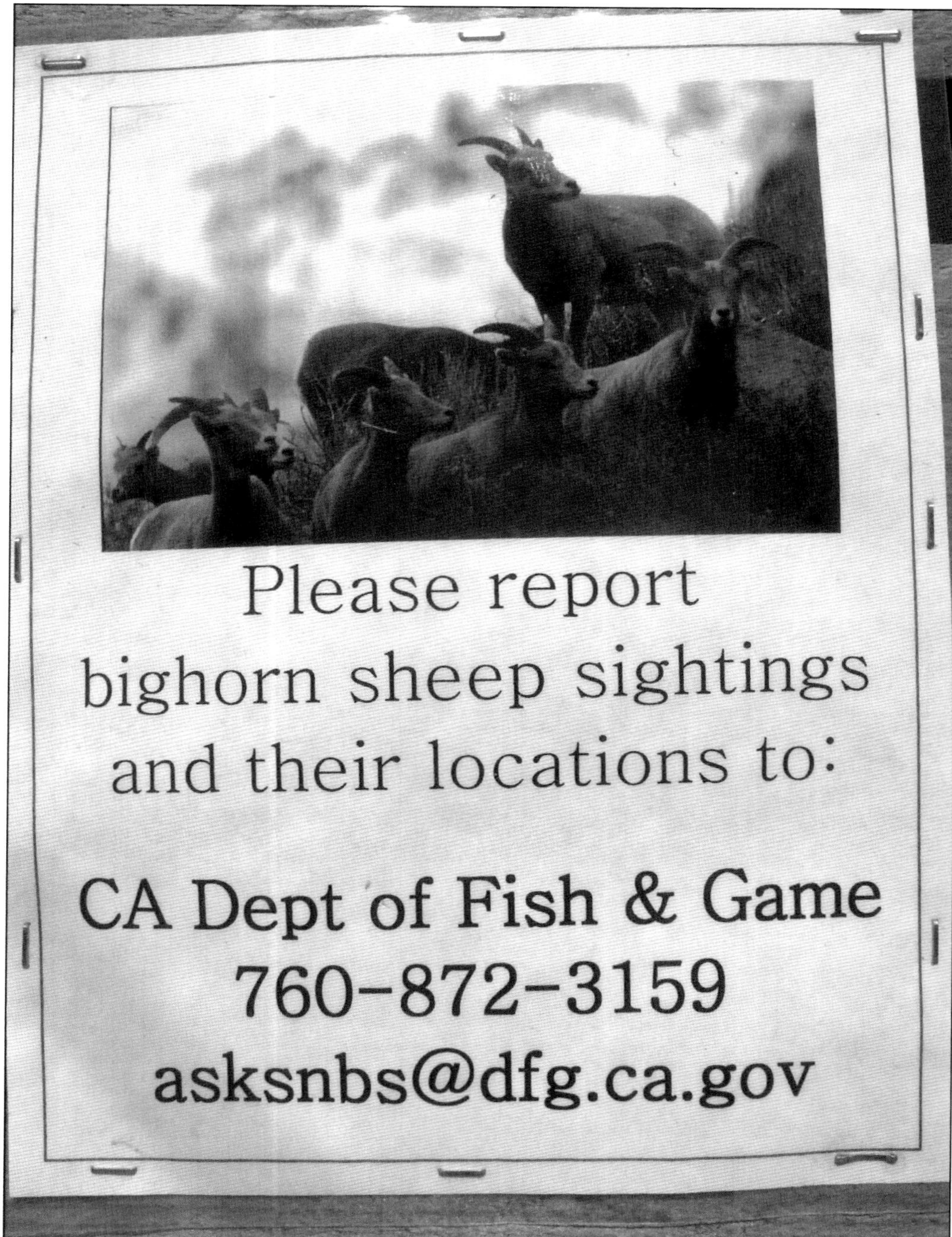

The California Department of Fish and Game closely follows the reintroduced bighorn sheep herd in the Mount Langley area. (Mike Prather.)

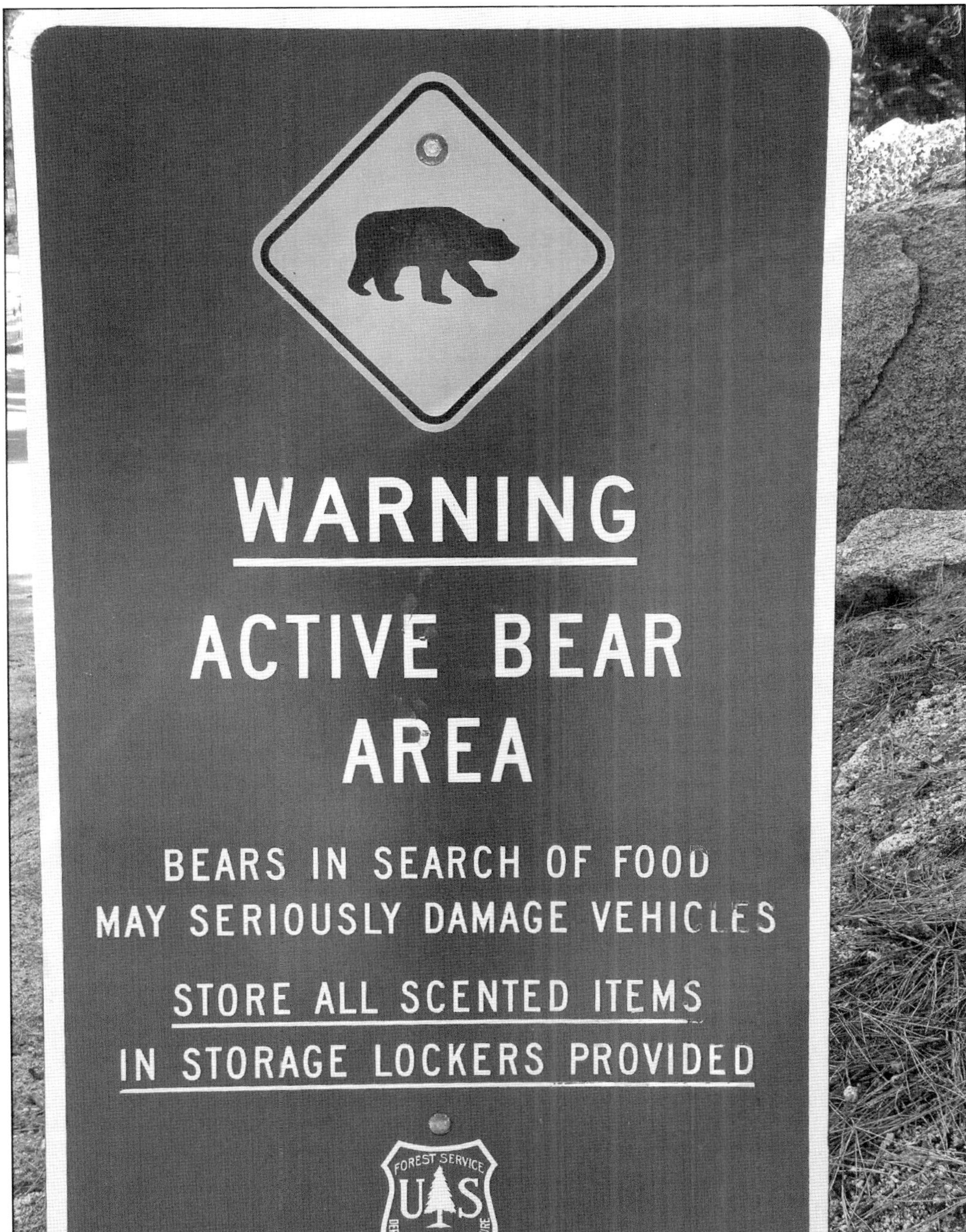

Campers and hikers are warned to follow the rules in bear country or risk a citation.

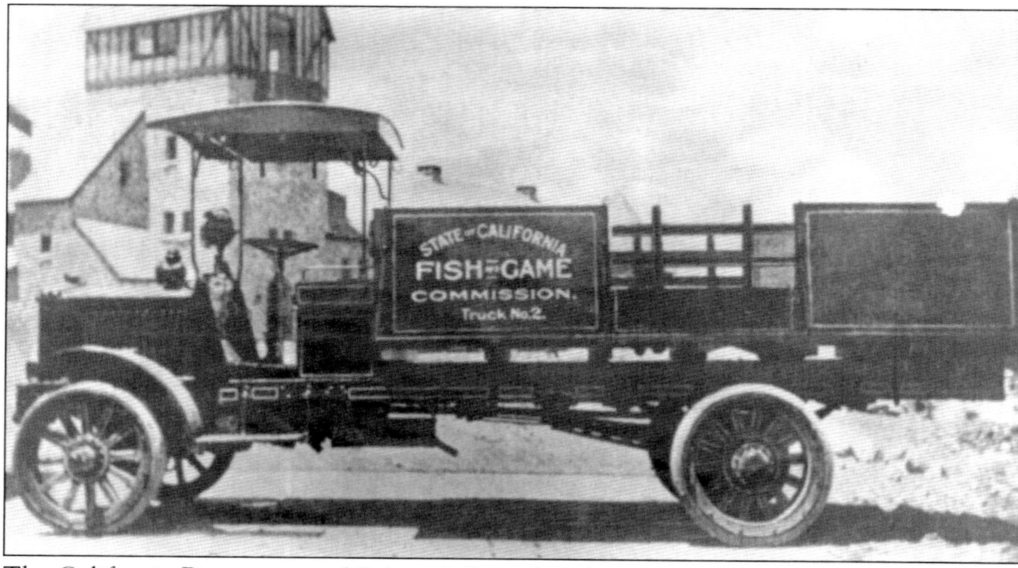

The California Department of Fish and Game hatchery truck at the Mount Whitney Fish Hatchery hauled eggs, fingerlings, and grown trout. No trout lived east of the crest in the Sierra; they have all been planted.

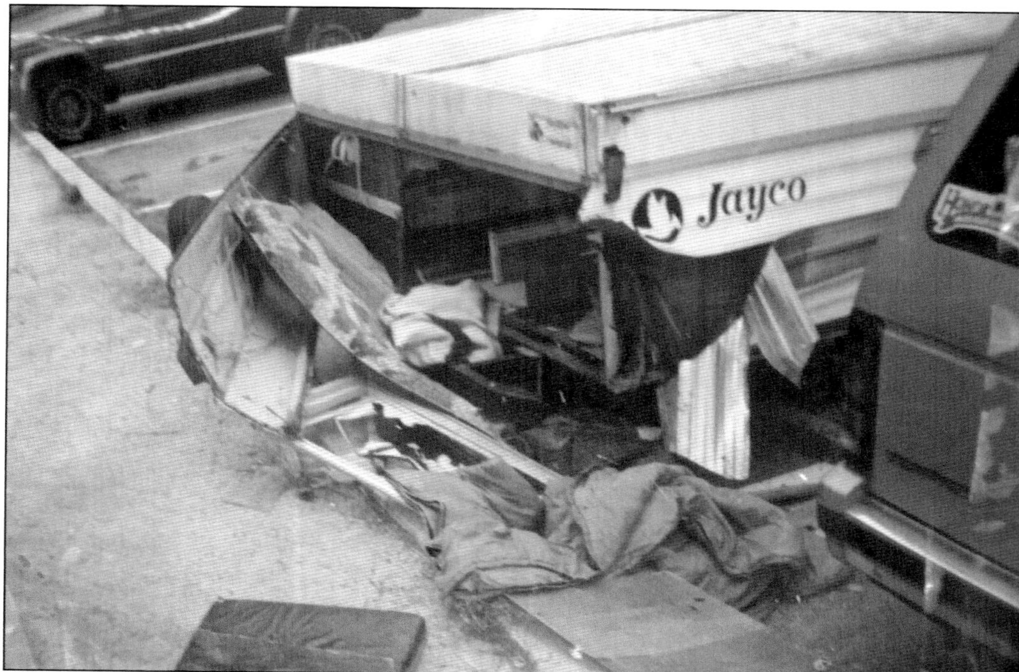

Never underestimate the power of a hungry black bear. Strong and with long claws, the bears can rip open cars, trailers, and even cabin windows. Humans are rarely harmed, but these so-called problem bears are often killed by authorities who have no other recourse. Out of kindness, the advice for visitors is, "A fed bear is a dead bear." So, do not feed bears or leave food in trailers, vehicles, or tents. Violators are given citations. Backpackers are required to carry bear canisters for food—extra weight, but thoughtful of bears. (Mike Prather.)

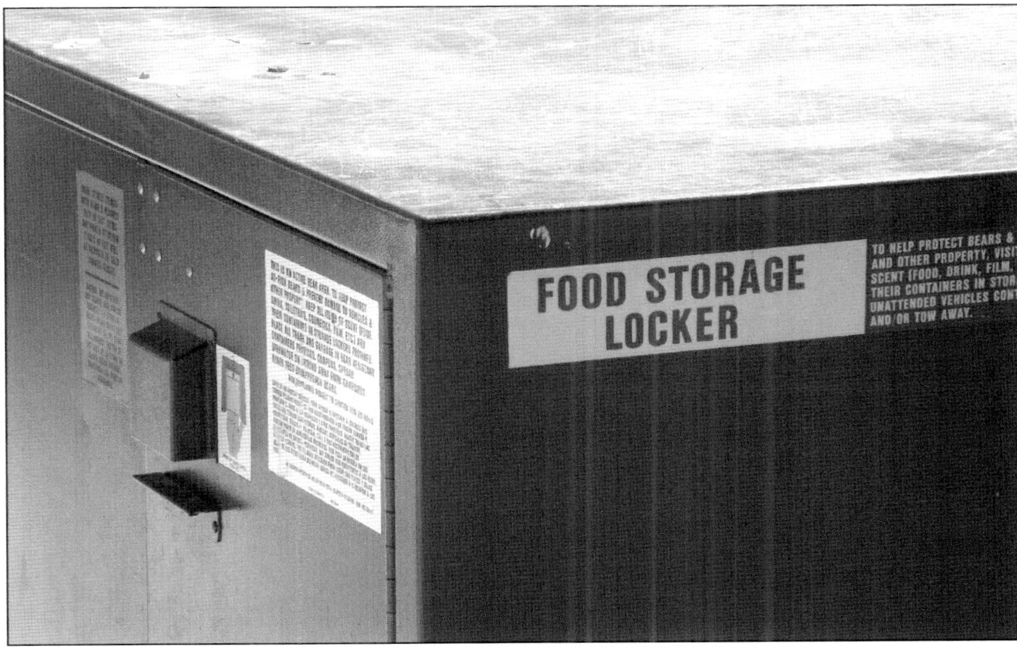

Bear boxes protect food and also protect bears. These secure metal boxes are provided by the Forest Service in all camping areas and trail heads to assist people in complying with this regulation. (Mike Prather.)

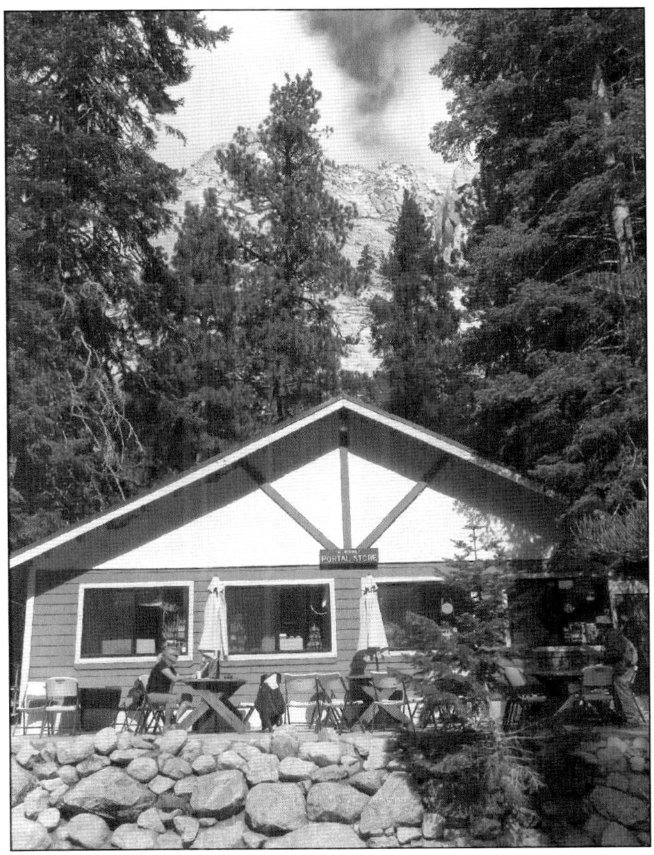

The Whitney Portal Store not only has supplies and food, but lots of information on trail conditions and preparations for hikers and campers. (Mike Prather.)

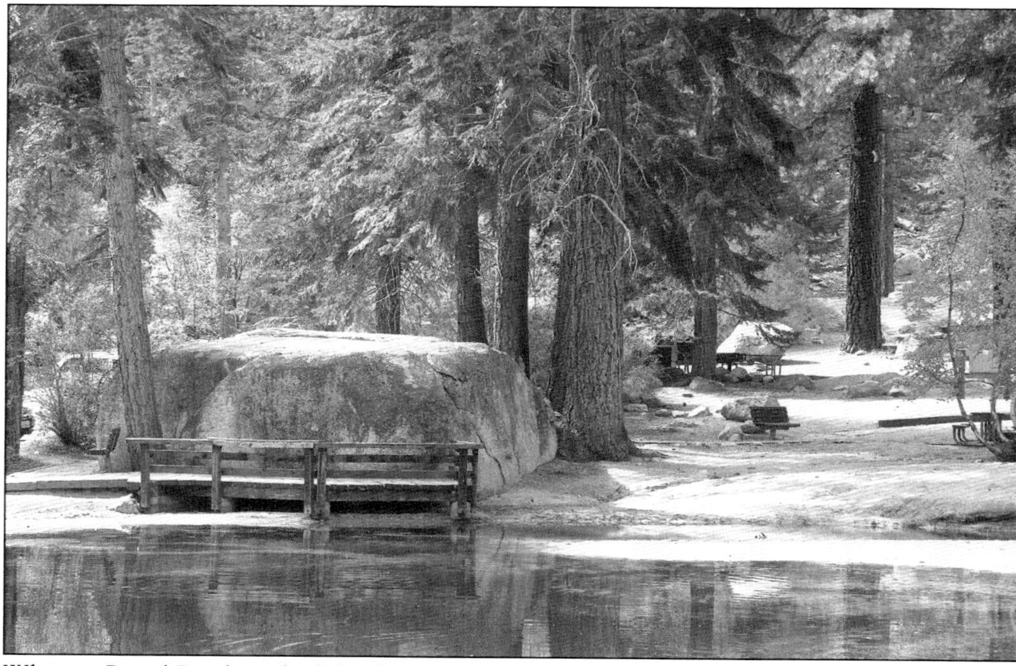

Whitney Portal Pond was built by the New Deal's CCC boys in the 1930s. It is planted with fish for those stalking the elusive trout. (Mike Prather.)

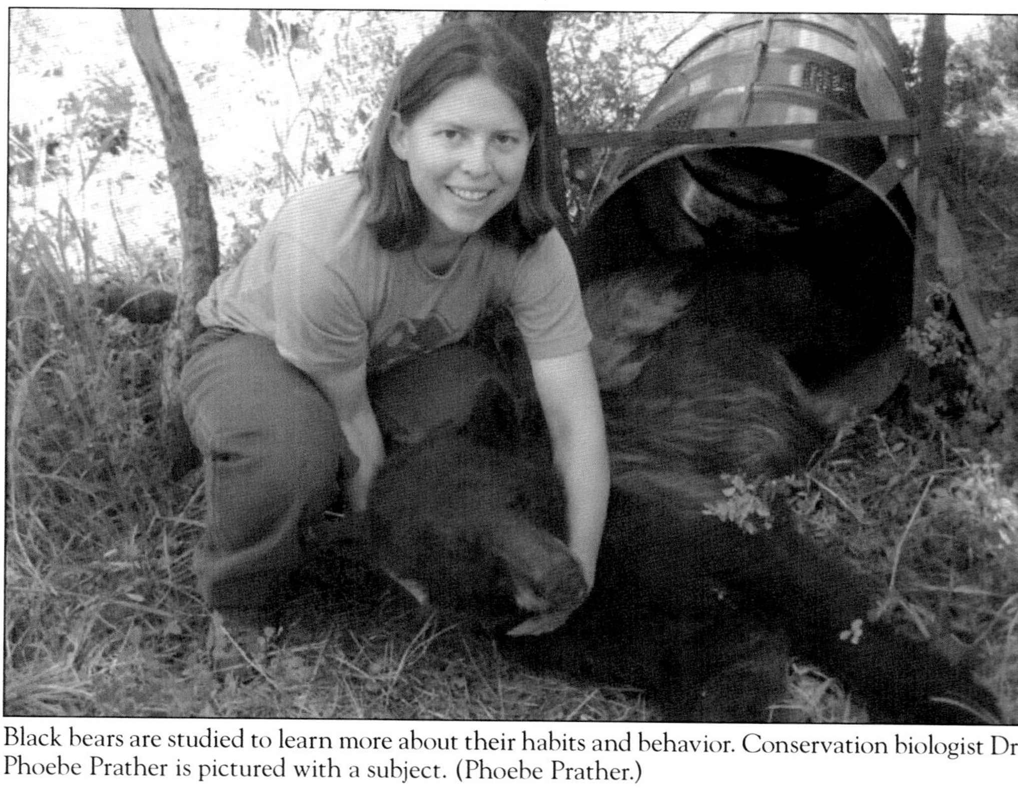

Black bears are studied to learn more about their habits and behavior. Conservation biologist Dr. Phoebe Prather is pictured with a subject. (Phoebe Prather.)

Five

The Written Word

In his book *Mountains of the Mind*, Robert Macfarlane writes of the possession that mountains can take of one's mind. He begins, "Three centuries ago, risking one's life to climb a mountain would have been considered tantamount to lunacy. The notion barely existed, indeed that the wild landscape might hold any sort of appeal."

Macfarlane notes the sheer physical "stoniness" of mountains as a fact. He speaks of the pursuit of fear, perceptions of the stream of time limned by glaciers and ice on the granite, and altitude and the summit and view it shapes in the human mind.

In *The Mountains of California*, John Muir writes: "Along the top and extending a good way down, was a rich pearl-gray belt of snow; below it a belt of blue and dark purple, a marking of the extension of the forests; and stretching along the base of the range a broad belt of rose-purple; all these colors, from the blue sky to the yellow valley smoothly blending as they do in a rainbow, making a wall of light ineffably fine." He then calls the range "the Range of Light."

Clarence King walked a path as an writer with one foot in scientific description and the other in the world of an accomplished literary author. This may stem from the fact that John Ruskin was King's aesthetic mentor. Rushkin's passion and writings on Alpine landscapes shaped King's response to the western mountains.

For a period of time, Mary Austin, one of the greatest western regionalists and feminist writers of the early 20th century, lived in Lone Pine at the base of Whitney. In *Land of Little Rain*, she writes, "Whatever goes up or comes down the streets of the mountains, water has the right of way; it takes the lowest ground and shortest passage."

Invited to spend the night by Langley in 1881, William B. Wallace wrote of his experience on Mount Whitney, which was published in *A Treasury of the Sierra Nevada*. "'The moon and her starry court' shone with increased brilliancy. Apparently more than double the number of stars were observable than can be seen from the valley, and while we know that every star is but a point of light without visible dimensions, yet in that clear, rarified atmosphere the stars we see from below appeared not only brighter but larger."

Paul Churchill recounted his attempt to conquer Whitney in March 1905 (also in *A Treasury of the Sierra Nevada*), with the redoubtable Gus Marsh, whom he described as "English and gritty; he is also a droll fellow and enlivened the day." Later he further states, "Marsh is a desert man by inclination. He made a bed for himself on some needles under the lee of a boulder despite my suggestion that he try the snow. Marsh is going to bed and has wormed his way into the sleeping bag as laboriously as a snake works his way out of his winter skin."

Both the novel *High Sierra* by W.R. Burnett and its movie version are wonderfully evocative of place. In this story, after an earthquake and a failed caper, Roy "Mad Dog" Earle has gone to Lone Mountain (read Lone Pine) and gone into the mountains. Earle senses his doom as he has dispatched Marie and Pard to safety, and he is traveling the Ballard Road. He stops in Lone Mountain (Lone Pine) and writes a note: "I'm sitting here under a tree in Lone Mountain writing this. I can see Mount Whitney and it sure is some mountain." His feelings of provincial safety and peace are illusionary. He knows it, and the reader knows it. Earle's fate awaits him on the broken face of the mountains.

Orland Bartholomew knew the Sierra and the dangers waiting there during the winter. Still, in 1928–1929, he took on the challenge of a winter assault on Mount Whitney. He wanted to record the scene from Lone Pine to Yosemite Valley. Fresno journalist Eugene Rose published Bartholomew's (Bart's) story, using firsthand accounts and the backcountry master's extensive journals to tell the story.

Norman Clyde is the most famous of the legendary mountaineers who have known Whitney. He is credited with more first ascents than Muir, King, and Brewer combined.

Poetry is a popular literary form for responding to or reacting against the challenge of Mount Whitney. Many poems celebrate a climber's exaltation at reaching the summit. Others recite exclamations of awe at the beauty and raw wildness of the terrain. Gary Snyder is a poet and prose writer who responds deeply to the alpine landscape, tempered by Zen Buddhist realization. Snyder has climbed Whitney multiple times. He lived with Jack Kerouac in a cabin in Mill Valley in 1955. He climbed with Kerouac up to the 12,000-foot elevation, and Kerouac captures the experience fictionally in his novel *The Dharma Bums*.

The human experiences centered on or around Mount Whitney have created and captured many diverse word images and visions.

The mystery of why people are drawn to mountains is one that authors have taken up many times. The writers of Whitney are no different. The air is thinner, and one's senses respond to all the physical cues of lightness. Here, many feel closer to heaven, the gods, or God. There is an ineffable quality of spirit in the height of mountains. (United States Department of the Navy.)

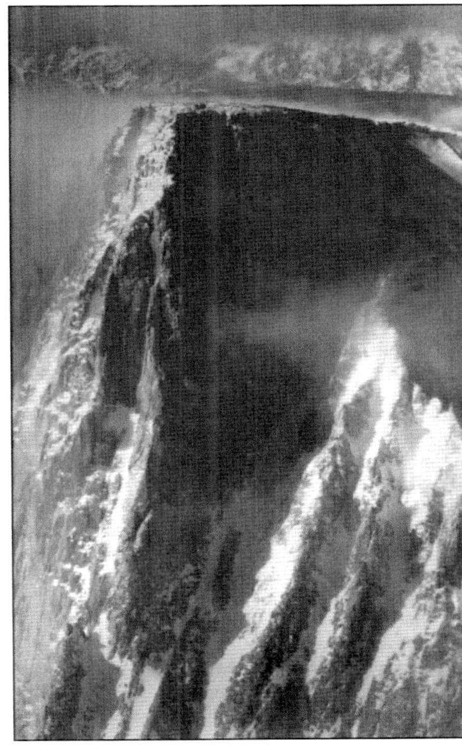

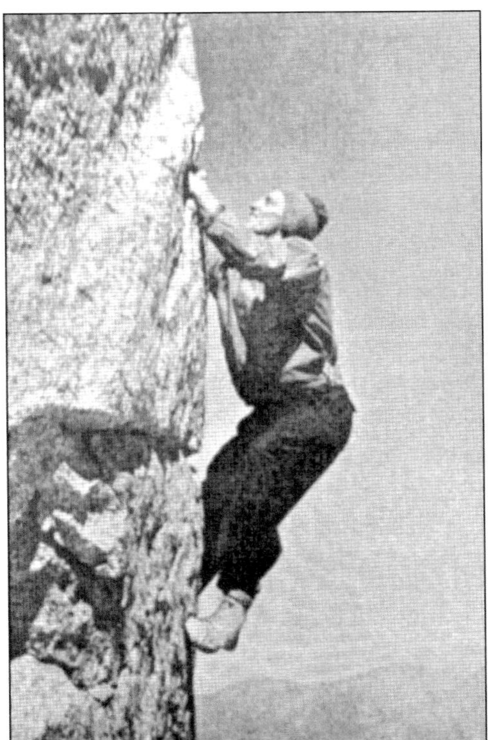

Mountaineers go to the mountains to experience the freeing emotion of fear. It is even possible to become addicted to the danger of climbing, of risking. The climber is unidentified.

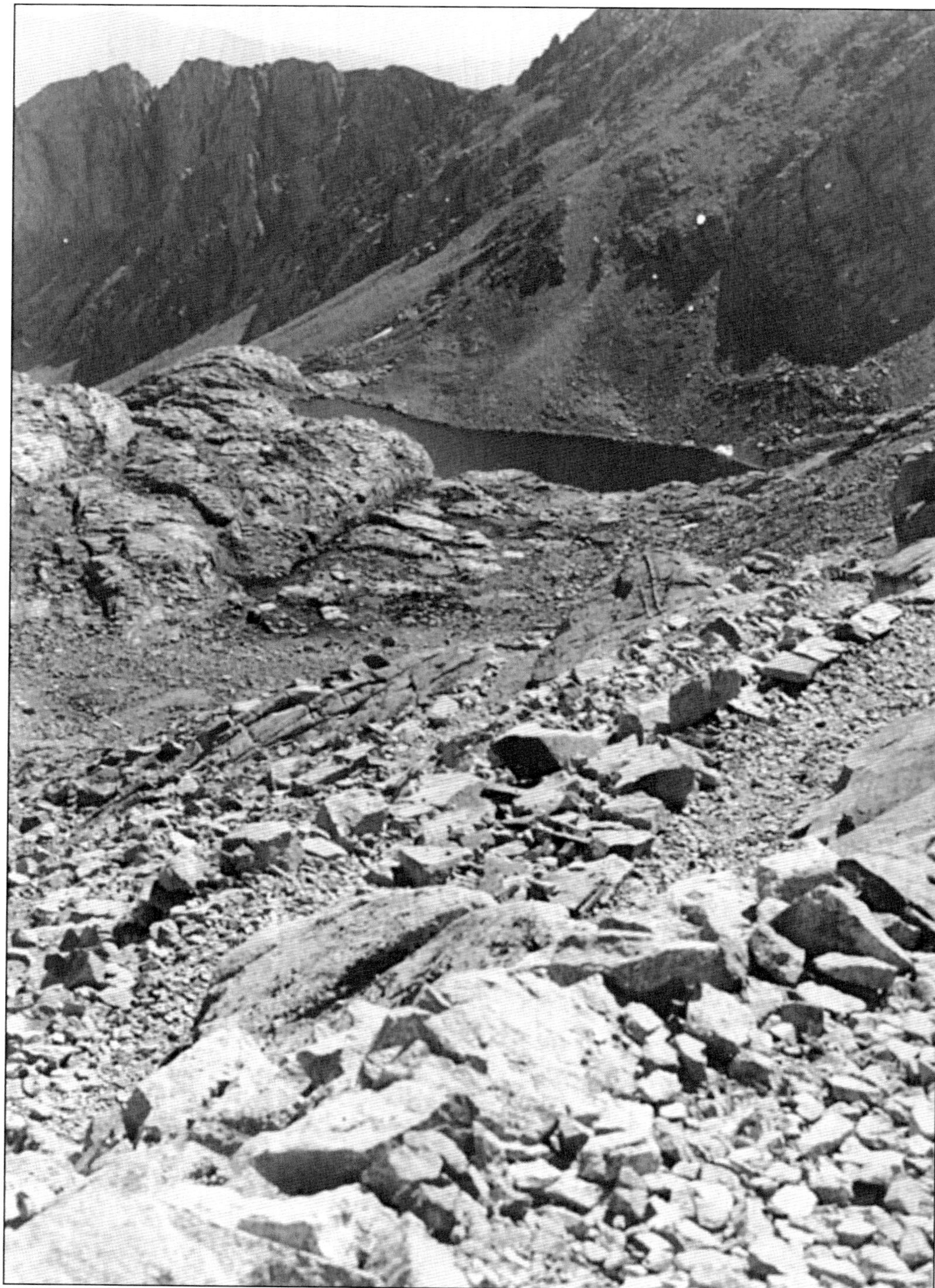

The stoniness of mountains is described many times by authors and nature writers. The mountain experience is one of hardness.

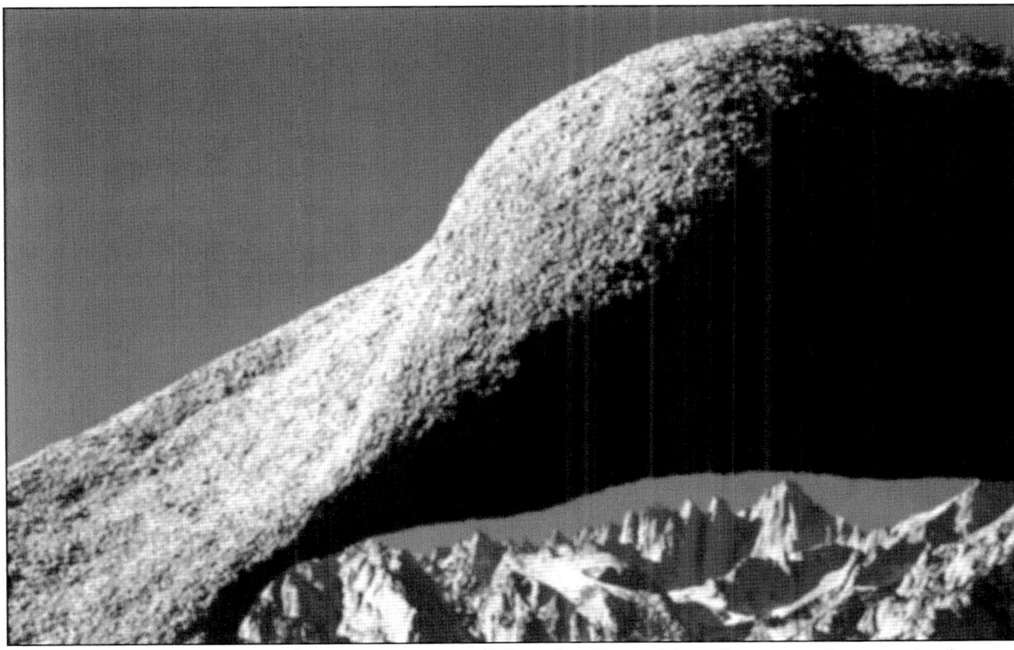

Mountains are almost timeless. It is estimated that the Sierra Nevada grows about an inch every century in some places. This photograph shows the mountain through the Mobius Arch, a favorite location for amateur and professional photographers. (LPFHM.)

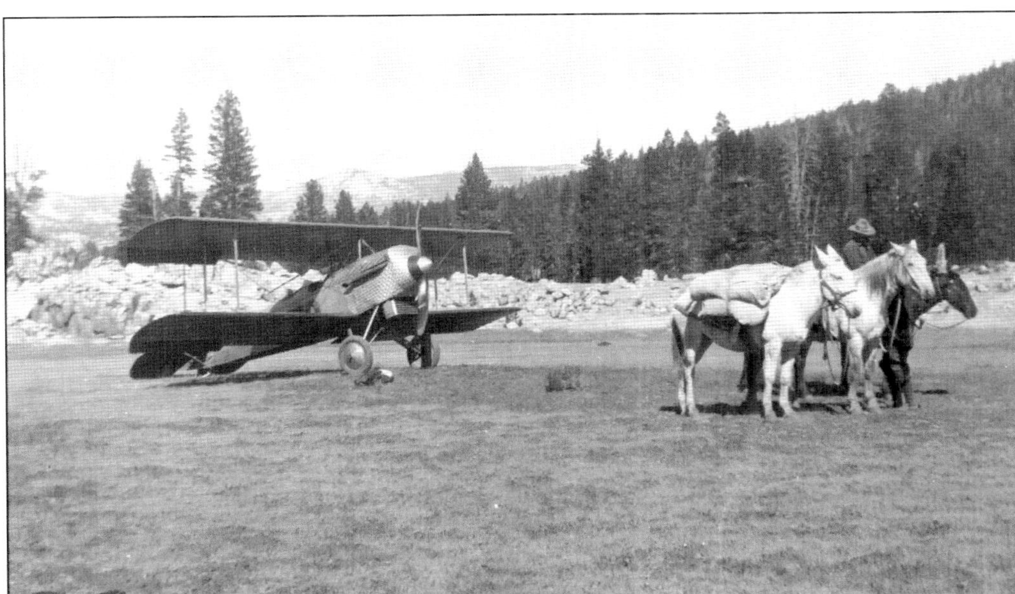

Some visitors to the high country and Mount Whitney would start with an air flight into Tunnel Airfield. It is now closed.

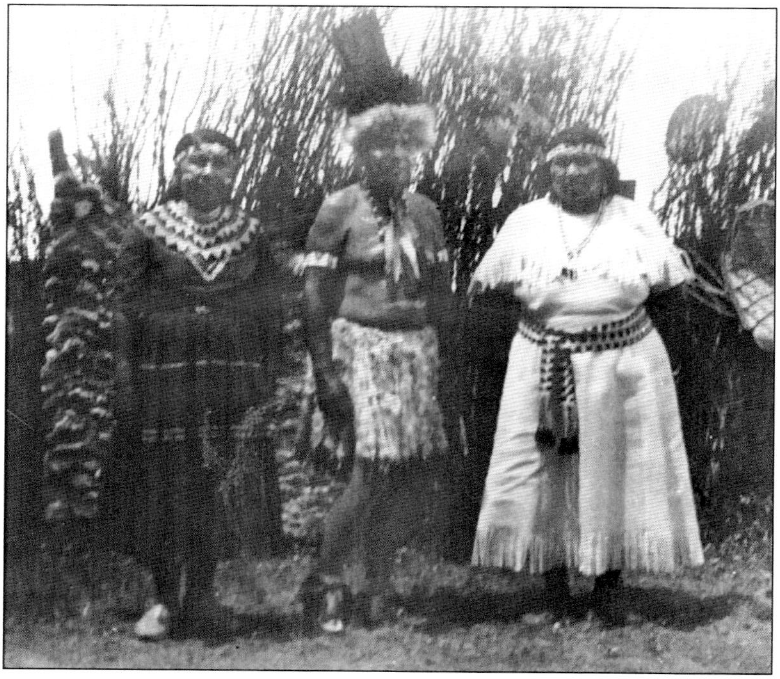

The original storytellers of Whitney, while not writers in the pen and paper sense, were the Paiute. The Paiute people in this photograph are Helen Archuleta (left), Herb Bellas (center), and Annie Jefferson.

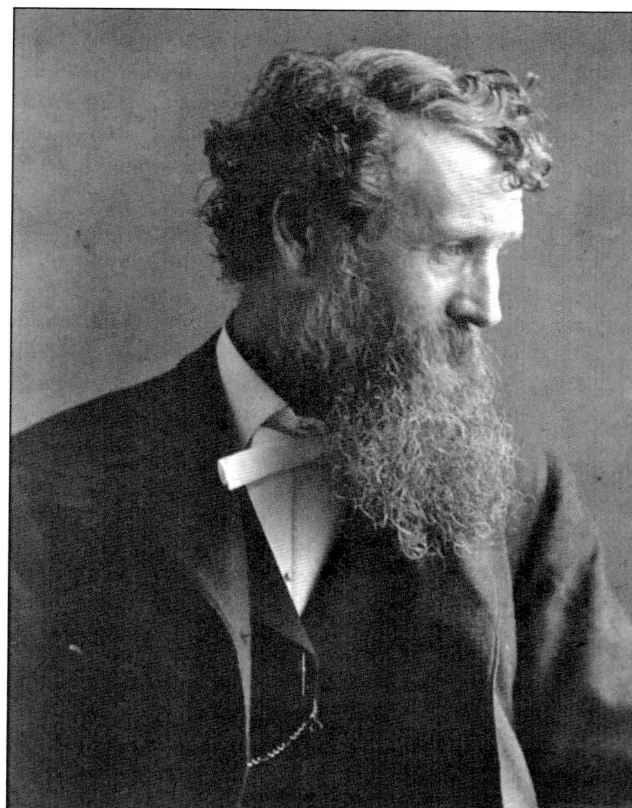

Among many other indelible descriptions, prolific writer John Muir called the Sierra Nevada "the Range of Light."

Clarence King created a classic book when he wrote *Mountaineering in the Sierra Nevada*. This photograph is not in the Sierra but captures the romantic image of the author as interpreter of nature.

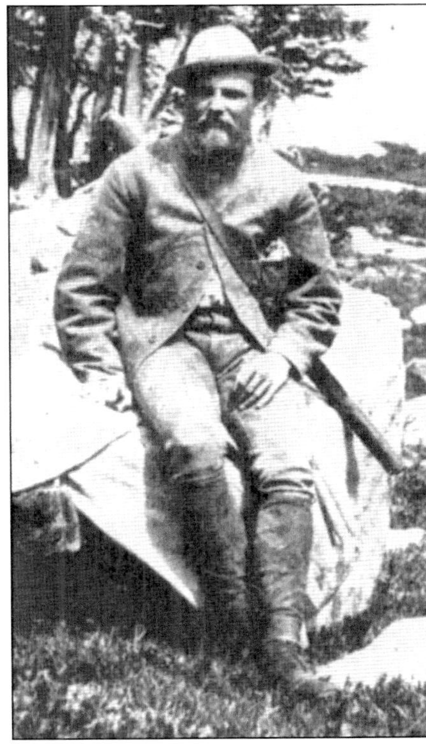

Many writers recount experiences in storms on Whitney. Clouds start to gather on the peak. Is it a storm in the making? (LPFHM.)

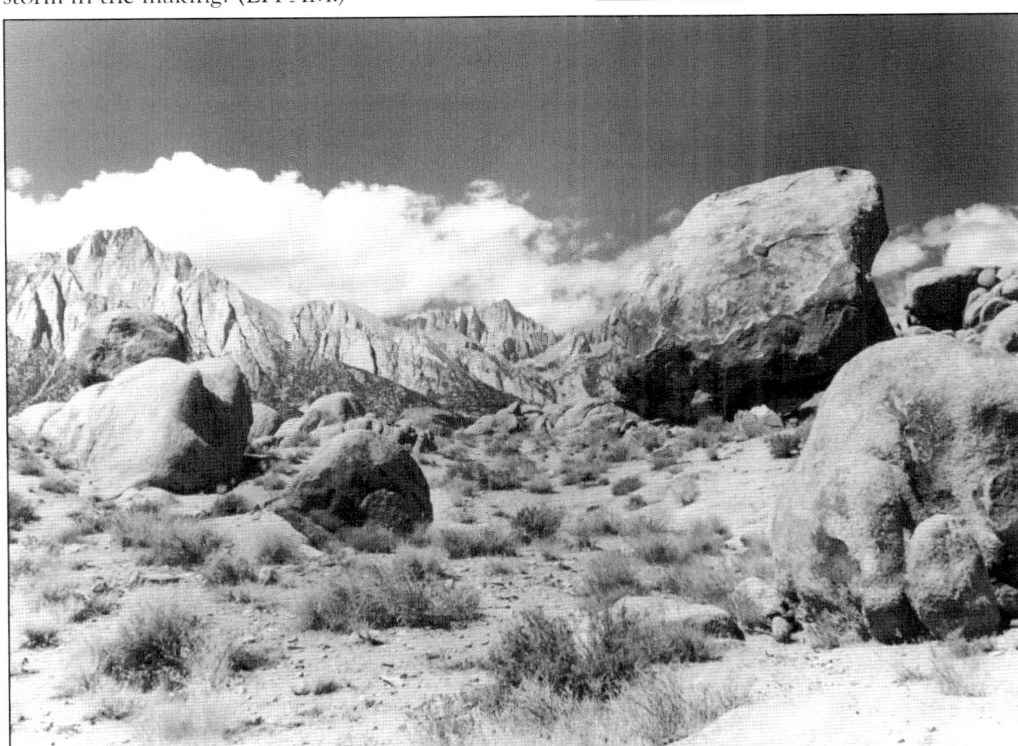

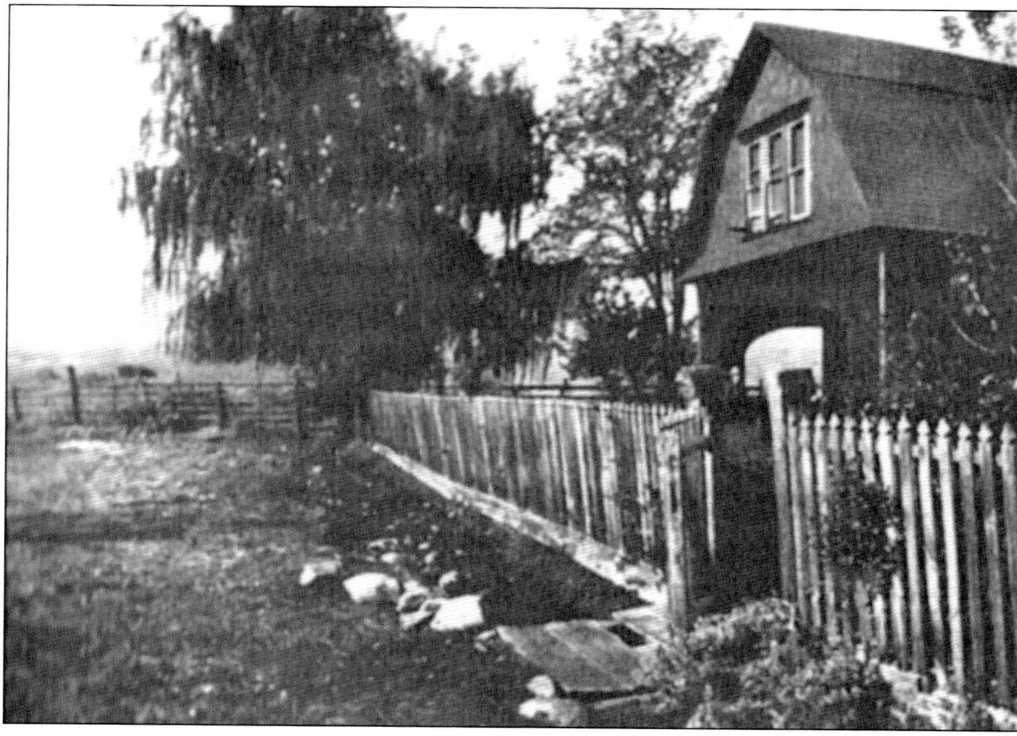

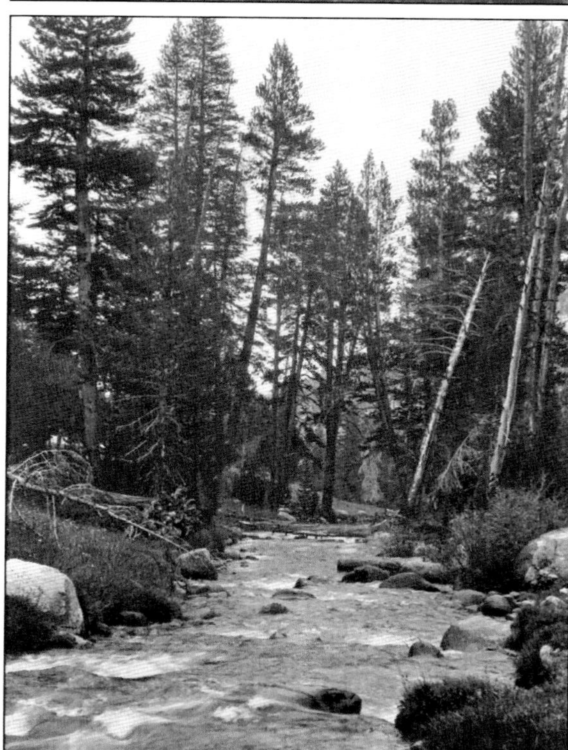

Mary Austin lived in Lone Pine, Independence, and Bishop in the Owens Valley. A naturalist, she also recognized the beauty and wisdom of the native residents when few others around her did. Here is the house in Independence where she wrote most of the classic *Land of Little Rain*.

Mary Austin wrote an essay about the "streets" of the mountains that reads like a prose poem. (LPFHM.)

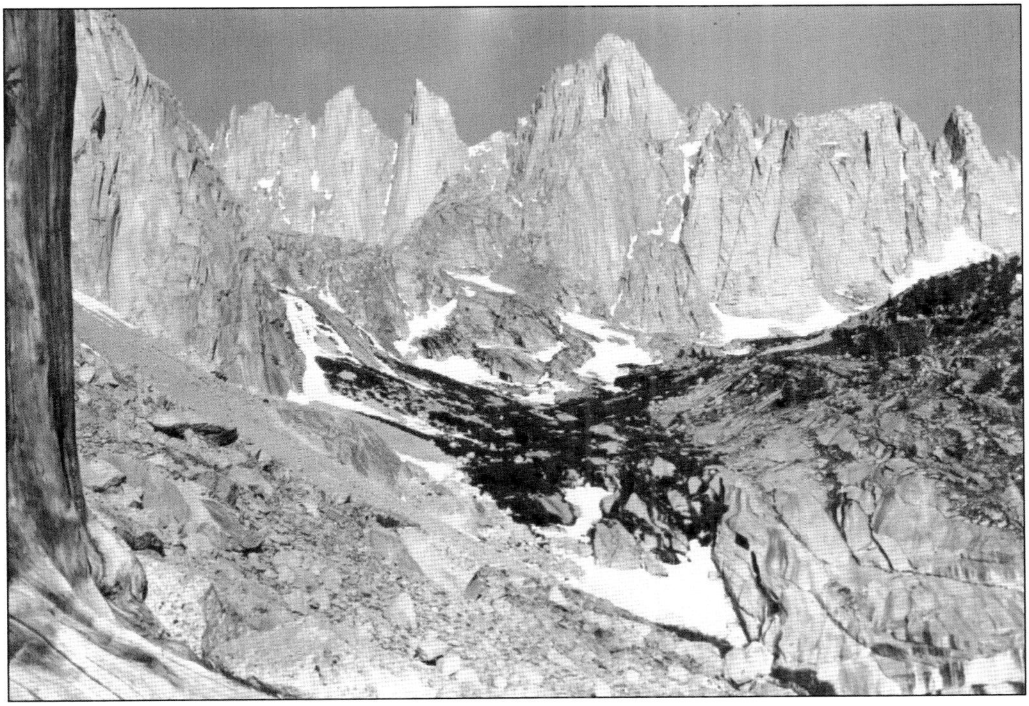

Writers often record their struggle to get to the top. The challenges are obvious in this close-up of Whitney. After getting there, many amateur poets write lyrically of getting to the summit. The exhilaration of success is obvious.

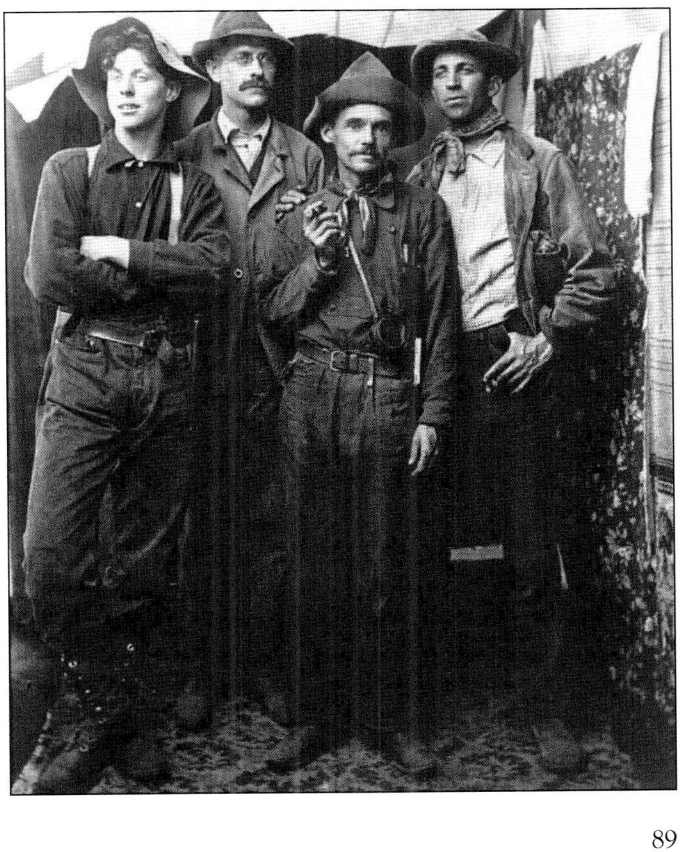

Joseph LeConte wrote of his experiences on Whitney. In this photograph are, from left to right, John Pike, Ed Hutchinson, LeConte, and Jim Hutchinson.

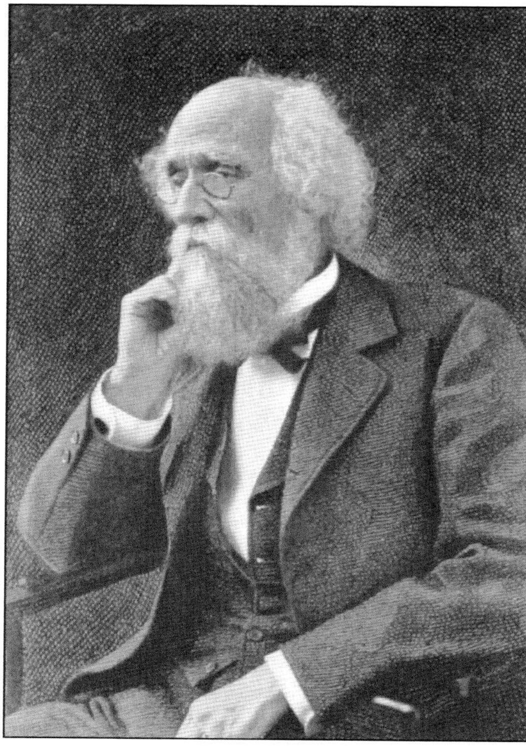

Joseph LeConte, who wrote of Kings Canyon and the Whitney Trail, is seen here in old age. He had more than 50 years of experiences in the Sierra Nevada to remember.

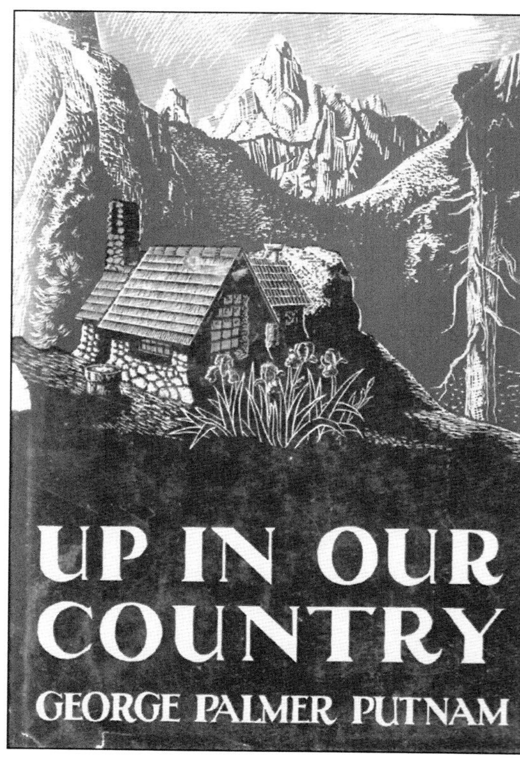

A publisher and husband to Amelia Earhart, George Putnam came to live at the Whitney Portal after her disappearance and wrote lovingly of his experiences in the area in *Up In Our Country.* (Duell, Sloan, Pierce.)

Francis Farquhar practiced what he wrote about in his book *History of the Sierra Nevada*, the classic text of human endeavors in the mountains.

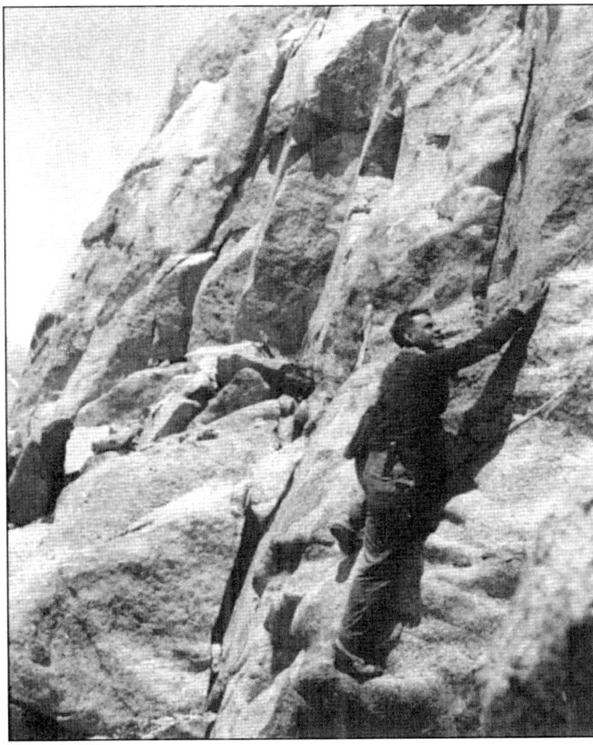

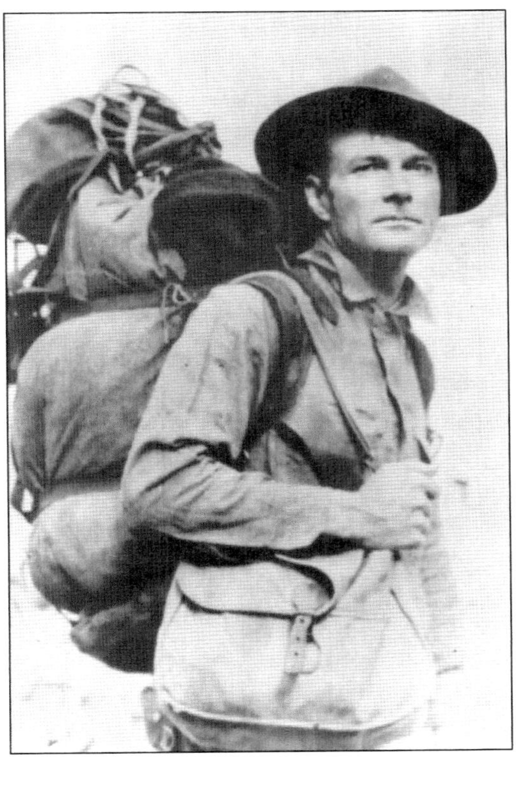

Norman Clyde writes carefully of his experiences on Sierra Nevada peaks in *Close-Ups of the High Sierra*. "In passing along the upper reaches of the trail one should not fail to observe the vivid blue clumps of alpine polemonium, and the pink and white clusters of mountain phlox. No where are these flowers finer than on Mount Whitney, and the former sometimes even survives at the extreme altitude of 14,000 feet." He was a teacher and a principal in the public school system, and reputedly would take no guff from high school students. His stern face reflects the necessary discipline he practiced in the mountains.

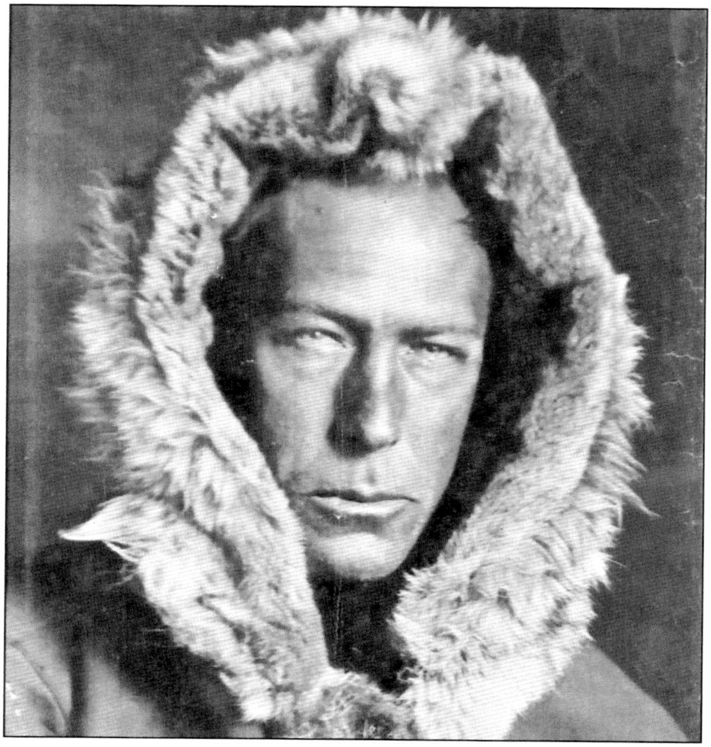

Orland Bartholomew (Bart) looks the part of winter explorer of Mount Whitney and the Muir trail in this photograph from 1929. (Howell North Books.)

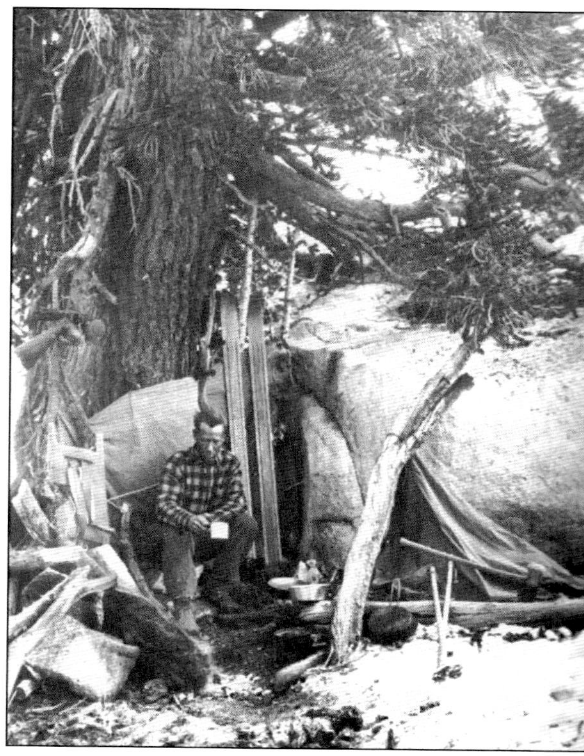

The hardships Bart endured in his winter assault on Mount Whitney in the late 1920s, as captured in *High Odyssey* by Eugene A. Rose, are quite obvious in this photograph of one of his camps. (Howell North Books.)

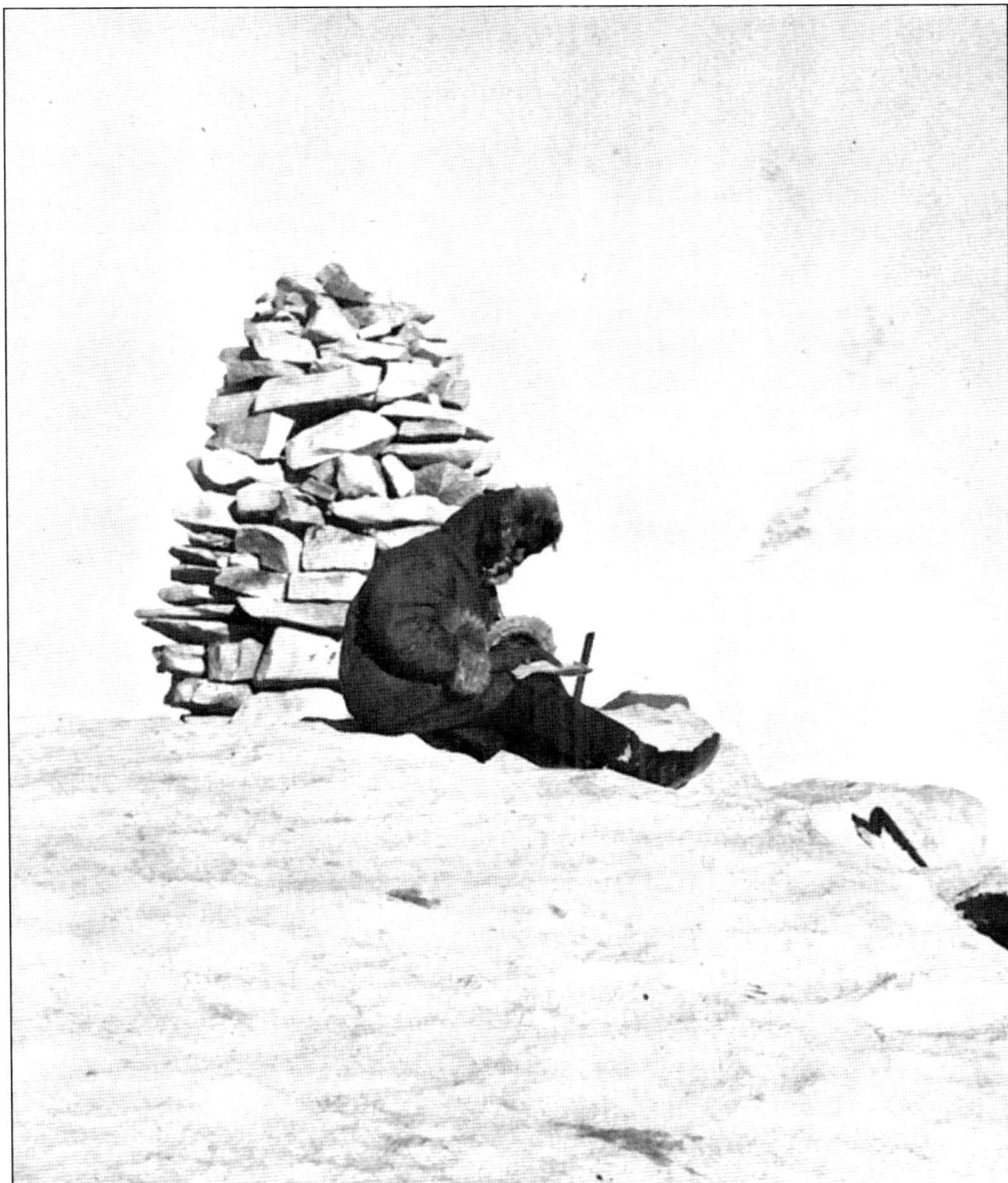

He had only a very short time on the summit of Whitney, but Bart determinedly set a camera and caught this image. When he finally made the summit, Bart later reflected, "but even thus fortified, how small the thrill of victory! Rather one is lost in the awe of forces and factors about him: the infinite solitude, the savage terrain, the weird dissonance of the wind. And the dangers of being trapped on the mountain by darkness." This photograph captures one mysterious aspect of man's relationship with mountains: getting to the top and overcoming all obstacles and challenges to be above all else. (Howell North Books.)

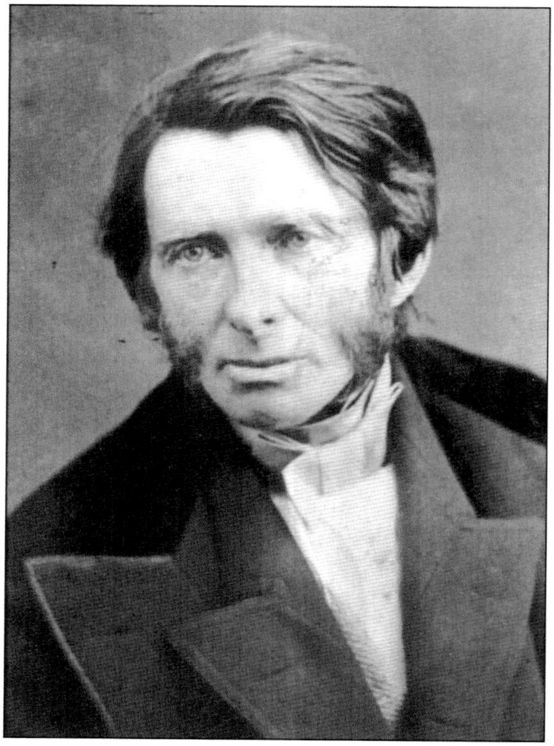

A British art critic, essayist, and poet, John Ruskin influenced both landscape artists and writers. His book *Modern Painters, Vol. IV: Of Mountain Beauty* describes mountain forms in great detail.

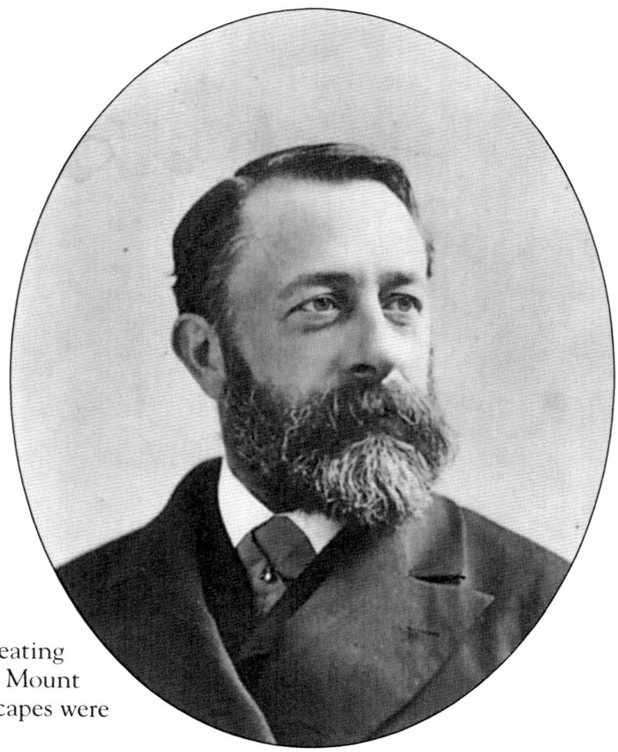

Albert Bierstadt travelled the West, creating large paintings of the Sierra Nevada, Mount Whitney, and Owens Lake. His landscapes were not exact duplicates of what he saw.

Six

SEEING IT

In an age of space, place, and landscape, where the dominant human sense is vision, ways of seeing and ultimately recording Mount Whitney and the Sierra Nevada are diverse in both style and medium.

Albert Bierstadt's name is foremost among painters who responded to Whitney and more generally the landscape of the West. Three paintings of Bierstadt are of particular interest to this text. They are *Mount Whitney* (1877), formerly titled *Sierra Nevada; Sunrise in the Sierras* (1872), and *Among the Sierra Nevada, California* (1868). Bierstadt had trouble with critical reception, which ultimately led to financial troubles in his life.

Today, watercolorist Dave Kirk works in Inyo County. Kirk explains his art:

> I like to contemplate landscapes especially. I imagine that the effects and play of light upon the shapes and surfaces of the Eastern Sierra are as dynamic and fascinating as anywhere in the world and hence the subject for the majority of my work. I believe that landscape shapes culture and when a landscape is negatively altered or defaced, the culture is impoverished on many levels.

If photography profoundly changed painting's role in the arts, two photographers have contributed significantly with their landscapes. Ansel Adams's name is synonymous with American landscape photography, and some of his most famous and familiar works are of and in the Sierra Nevada. In his book *Mountain Light: In Search of the Dynamic Landscape*, photographer Galen Rowell describes the experience of climbing both the 1,800-foot East Face of the Keeler Needle and the West Face of Mount Conness. It was during another attempt that Rowell photographed the alpenglow, creating the work he titled "Alpenglow on Mount Whitney, California: 1976." Rowell writes, "Dawn brought the most vivid alpenglow I had ever seen, and both Gordon (Wiltsie) and I scrambled for our cameras . . . I do know that Mount Whitney is an exceptional location for alpenglow when there is direct sunlight from the east at dawn."

David Muench is another contemporary photographer who has taken more than two dozen images of Whitney in her many moods. Muench is well aware of preserving the pristine nature of these landscapes and has been actively engaged in seeking protection for the land while preserving access for the many users of the area.

Since around 1915, Mount Whitney has appeared hundreds of times in various film projects. More recently, with the available new technologies, climbing Whitney has been the subject of many film projects produced by nonprofessionals posted on the Internet.

The Virginian (1923), made by Preferred Studios, worked in Lone Pine and the high country around Whitney and the Bishop area for several weeks in 1922. The Fox Company, making *Riders of the Purple Sage*, was in Lone Pine at the end of October 1924 for several weeks. No motion picture is more famous for filming on Whitney than the classic *High Sierra*, starring Humphrey Bogart and Ida Lupino and directed by Raoul Walsh. *Brigham Young* filmed in the area of Whitney and at Whitney Portal in 1939. Withe the Sierra standing in for Utah's Wasatch Range, it was from this setting that the Mormon refugees first cast their eyes on the "promised land," where ultimately they would build Salt Lake City. *Rawhide*, starring Tyrone Power and Susan Hayward, begins with footage shot at the Portal and on the road in several feet of snow. The film tells the story of the Jackass Mail, and this footage illustrates the ideas that "the mail must go through." A famous sequence shot on the Portal Road at the switchback turn just as the road turns into the canyon is the part of the film *The Long, Long Trailer* that people remember most vividly. Lucille Ball and Desi Arnaz are traveling in a trailer, and Lucy has loaded the trailer with souvenir rocks as they try to go over the mountains. Another film, *Man in the Saddle*, starring Randolph Scott and directed by Andre de Toth, has one of the very best stunt sequences made at the Whitney Portal at the frozen Portal waterfall.

Nonfiction or documentary films have been made since the 1920s and deserve mention as well. When Silas Christofferson flew over Mount Whitney on June 25, 1914, he was the first to fly above the mountain, and he also broke the existing American altitude record. The local paper reported, after the pilot's second attempt, which proved successful: "With a camera attached to the side of his seat, Christofferson took a photograph of the peak as he passed over." On February 24, 1925, the feat was duplicated but this time with a motion camera on board. On May 18, 1933, *The Inyo Independent* led with a story that stated, "Mount Whitney has been conquered by the movies and 1,500 feet of film showing scenes along the trail and on the summit of the nation's highest mountain will be released shortly through a prominent syndicate."

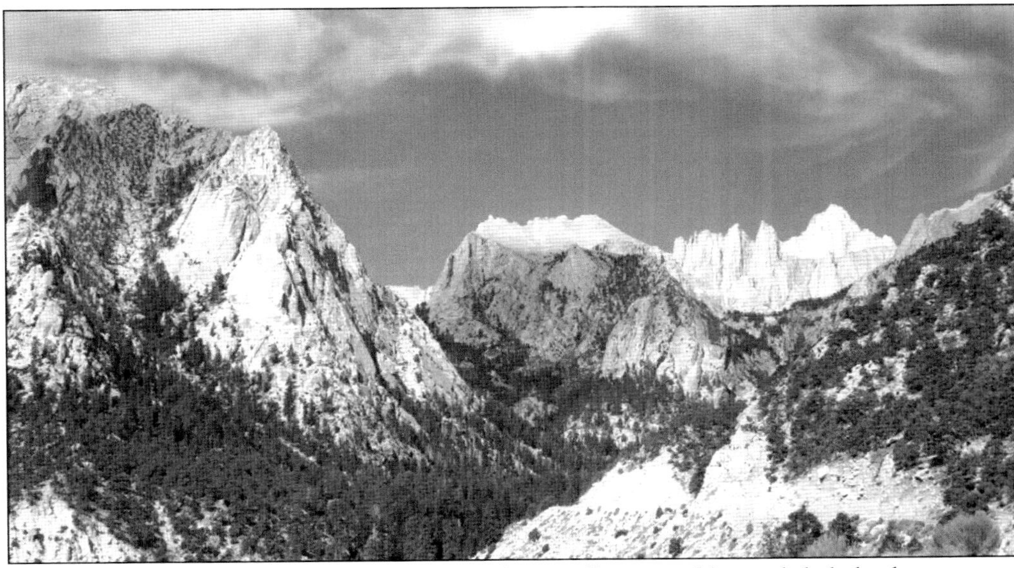

This photograph of the Sierra Nevada with Whitney illuminated by a subtle light demonstrates the inspiration that led Bierstadt to paint several pictures of the mountains. (Langley.)

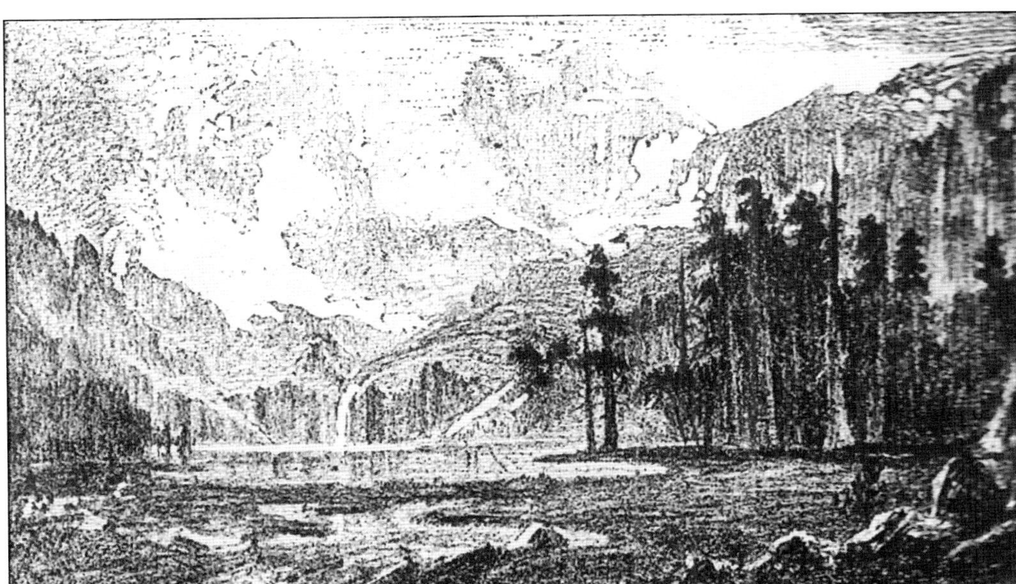

Many of Bierstadt's paintings were published in popular magazines, educating US citizens about the western regions of their country. His paintings were often romantic in nature. This etching of a Bierstadt painting is by an unidentified artist.

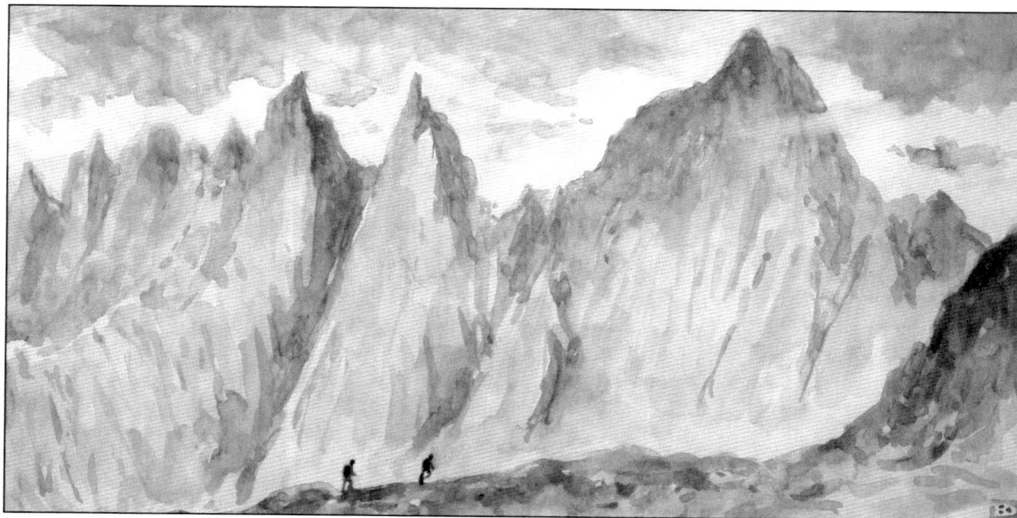

Kirk Study No. 1 compares the immensity of the mountain with two lone figures making their way to the top. (Dave Kirk.)

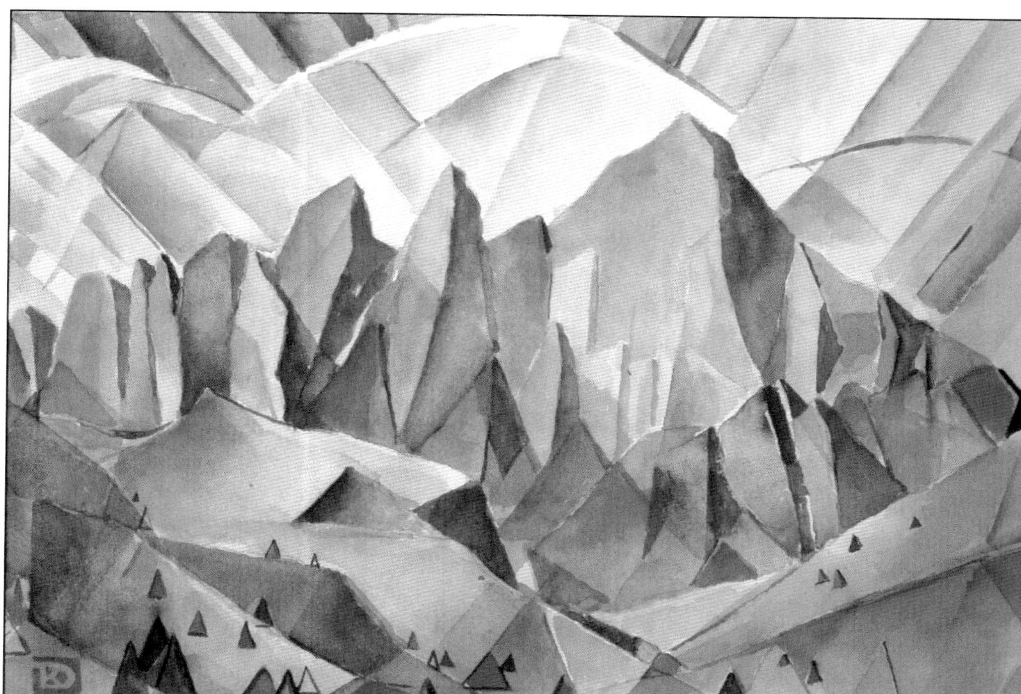

Kirk Study No. 3 isolates the crags and streaming light in cubist form, analyzing the complexity of the Sierra Nevada structure, a "wall of rock" from the east side. (Dave Kirk.)

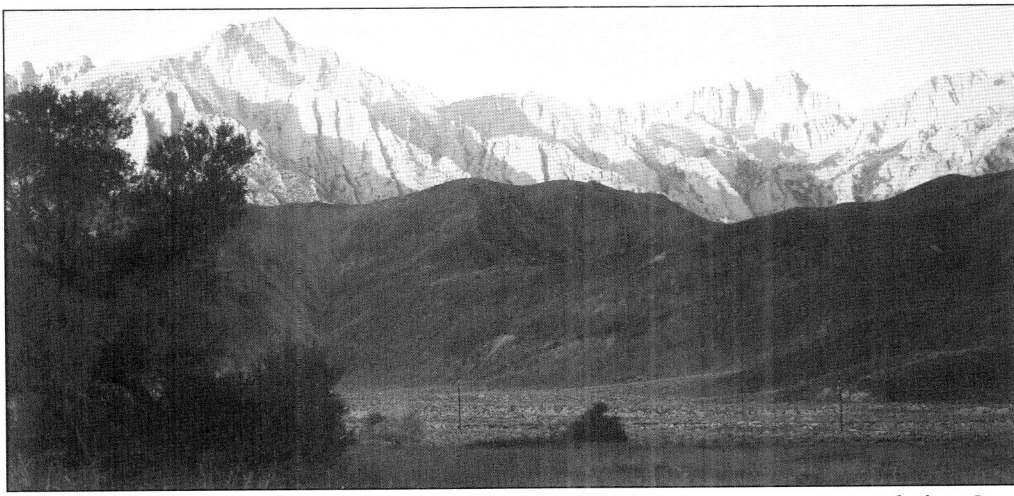

Students and enthusiasts try to recreate Adams's famous *Winter Sunrise, Sierra Nevada from Lone Pine, California*, but the challenge is with the light. The spot that the photograph was made is approximately west of the sheriff's substation on Highway 395 in Lone Pine. Adams describes the making of the exposure dramatically in his autobiography. "One very cold and very early morning in December of 1943, Virginia and I arose before dawn and drove to Lone Pine. I selected a spot not far from the main highway, parked the car, and set up my camera on the platform. We then huddled together in the car, gratefully sipping from a thermos of steaming coffee that Virginia had prepared. Soon, the sun rose above the Inyo Ranged behind us, glowing pinkly upon the Sierra summits. I scrambled up to my camera, knowing the time was close but feeling it was not quite right. Beams of light began highlighting the brushy trees in the foreground of my compositions; they also illuminated the rear end of a horse as it calmly grazed in front of the trees. Frustrated, I watched as the light appeared, just and I had hoped. Serendipitously, the horse momentarily turned to profile and I made the exposure. Within seconds, the tonal variety that created the mood of the scene was destroyed by a flood of even sunlight." (Langley.)

To the east of Lone Pine are several playas that often fill with water in the winter. Adams made several studies of this location. The cracked surfaces, after drying, have a subtle reflective quality, contrasted with the Sierra Nevada to the west. (Langley.)

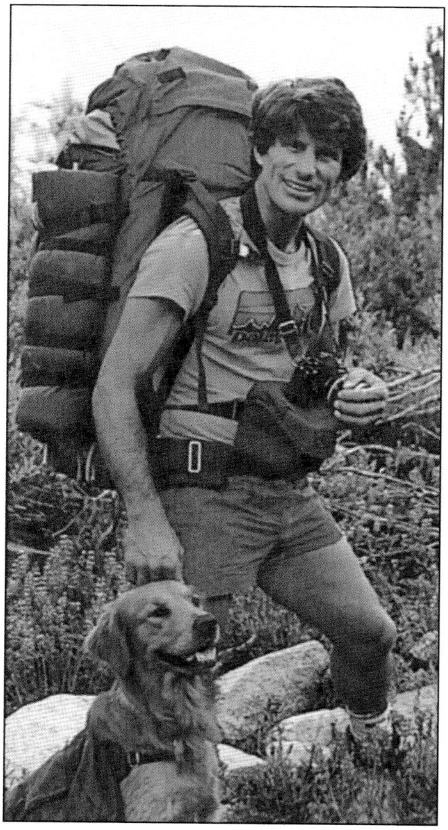

Galen Rowell traveled the world in search of spectacular images of mountains. His studies of Mount Whitney and the Sierra are some of his best and are contained in his book *Mountain Light: In Search of the Dynamic Landscape*. It was during another attempt that Rowell photographed the alpenglow creating the work he titled "Alpenglow on Mount Whitney, California: 1976." He wrote, "Because of the curvature of the earth, light rays that first hit Whitney's eastern ramparts have almost kissed the horizon far away in Nevada."

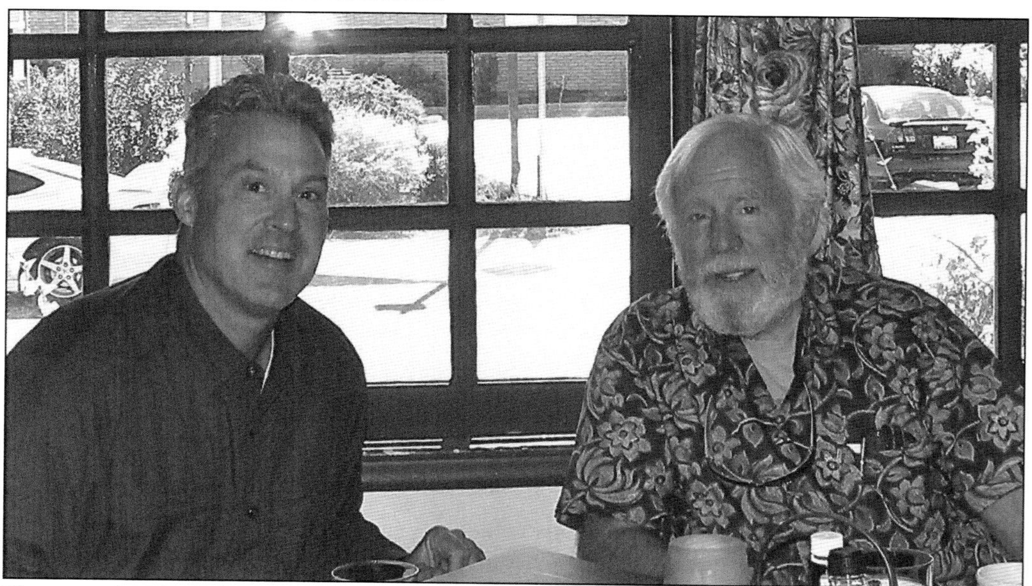

Photographer David Muench (right) has captured the many moods of the Sierra Nevada and Whitney in his work. Here, he meets with Kevin Mazzu of the Friends of the Alabama Hills about a National Scenic Area designation for this unique and stunning landscape. (Kevin Mazzu.)

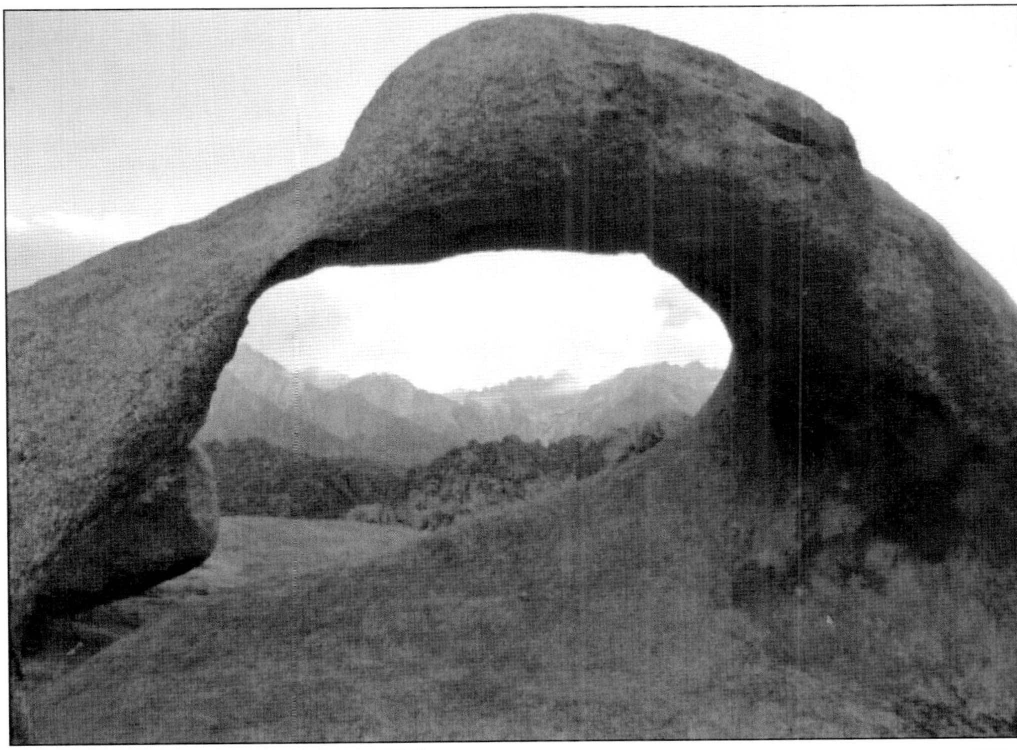

The Mobius Arch in the Alabama Hills found fame on the Land of Freedom Pass for tourists to the Alabama Hills. The visitors can line up the arch with Mount Whitney in a unique composition. (LPFHM.)

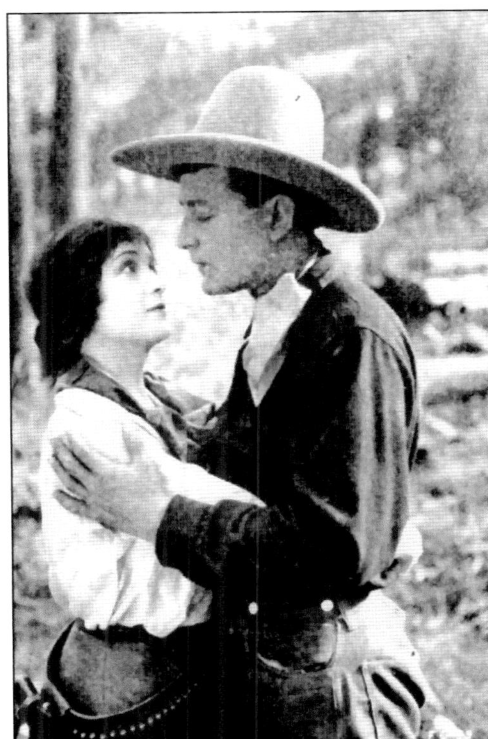

The popular Owen Wister novel *The Virginian* stands as the classic Western. It has been filmed many times, but in 1923, a version was made in Lone Pine and actually in the high country around Whitney, including cabins at Monache Meadows. Some of those are still there. (LPFHM.)

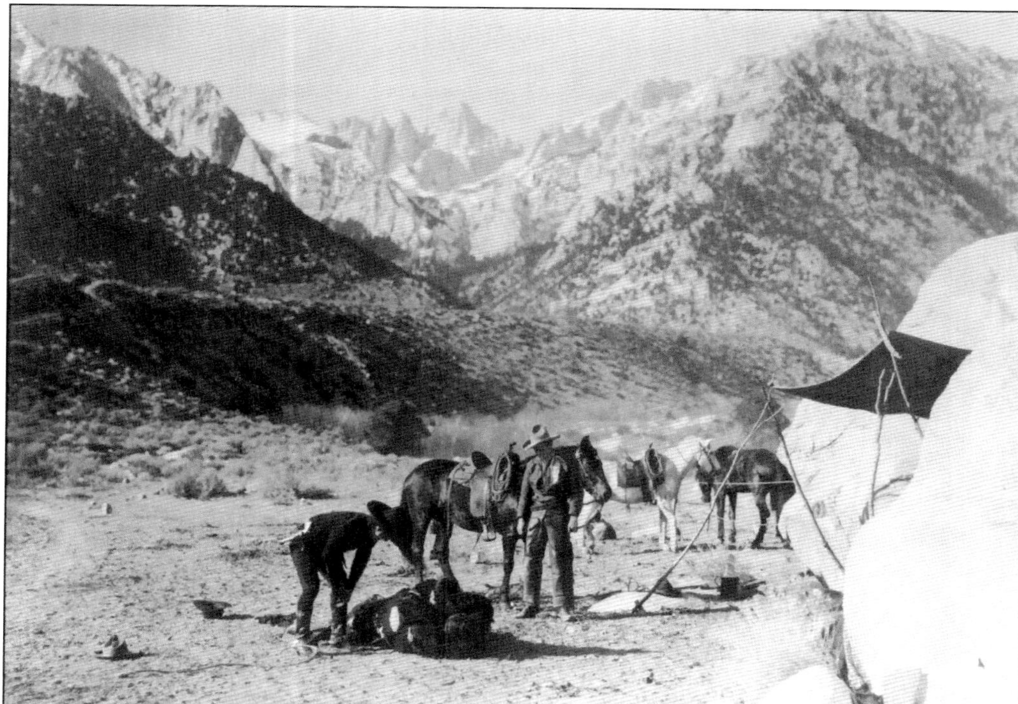

Filming in 1924, the Tom Mix classic silent film *Riders of the Purple Sage* shot in many hard-to-access areas around Mount Whitney. Here, they work near the future location of the CCC camp that would build Portal Road. (LPFHM.)

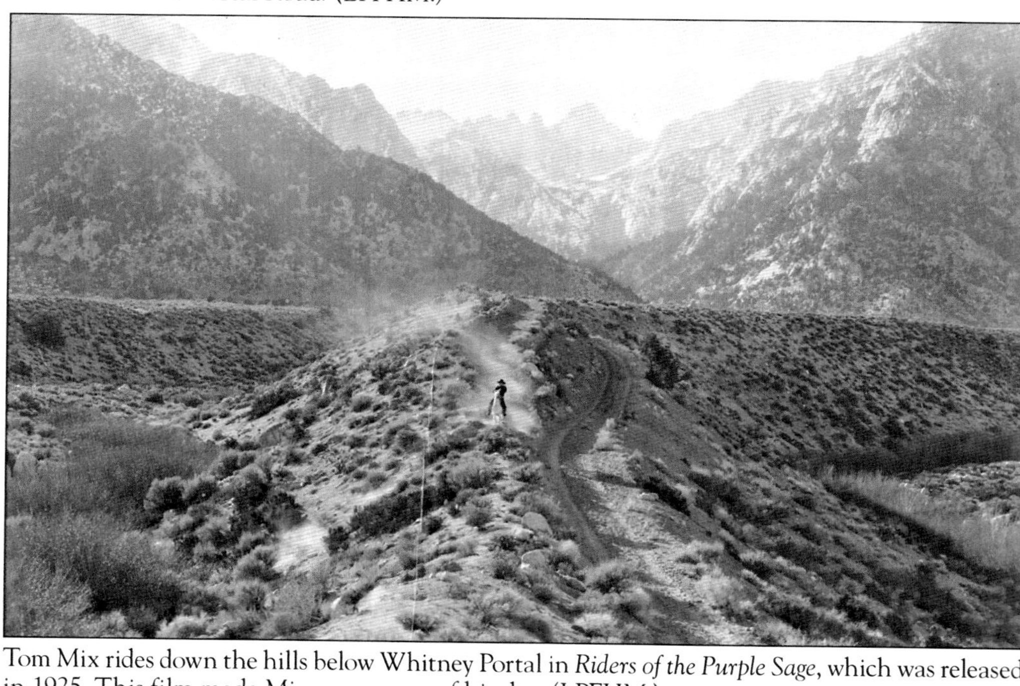

Tom Mix rides down the hills below Whitney Portal in *Riders of the Purple Sage*, which was released in 1925. This film made Mix a superstar of his day. (LPFHM.)

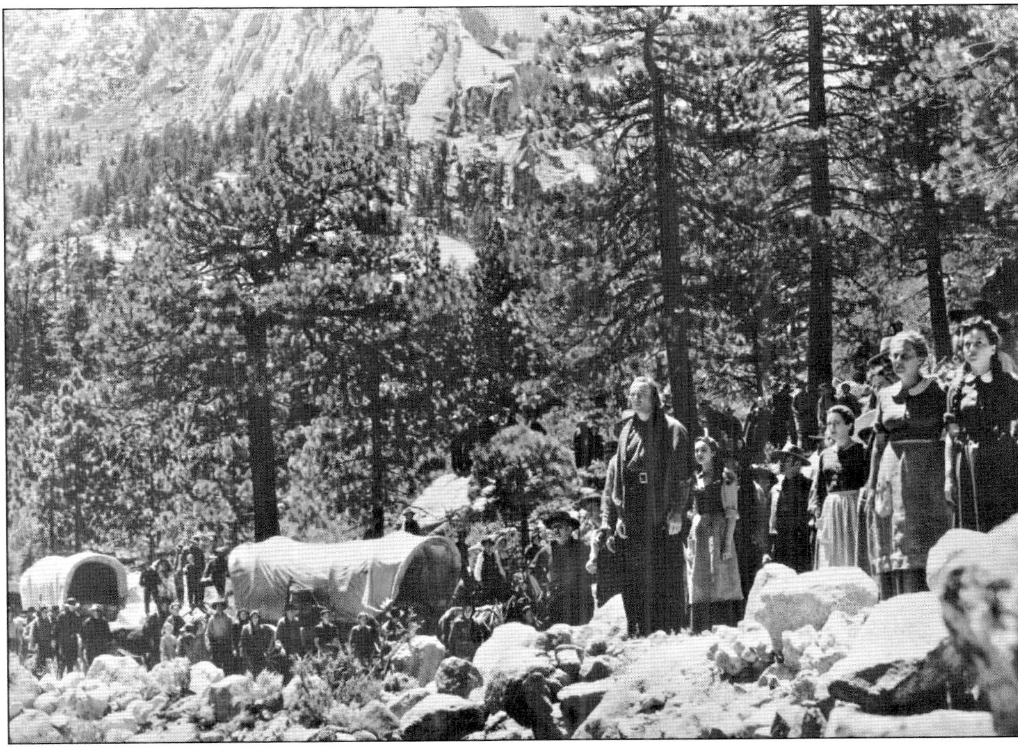

In 1940, a large Paramount production of *Brigham Young* is on location at the Whitney Portal area reenacting the Mormon pioneers' first view of the future location of Salt Lake City. (LPFHM.)

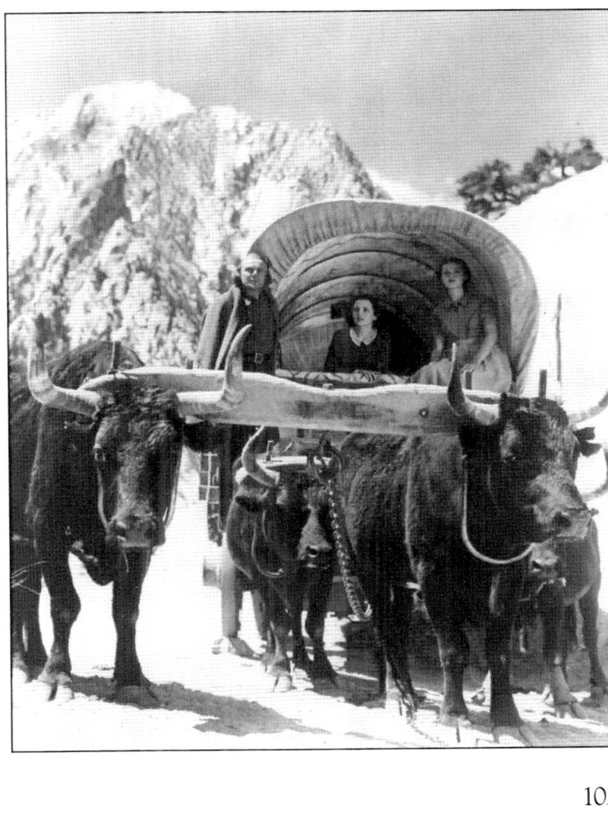

In a scene from *Brigham Young*, Pioneers Jonathan Kent (Tyrone Power) and Zina Webb (Linda Darnell) are in their covered wagon with the Wasatch Range (Sierra Nevada) rising behind them at the Whitney Portal area. (LPFHM.)

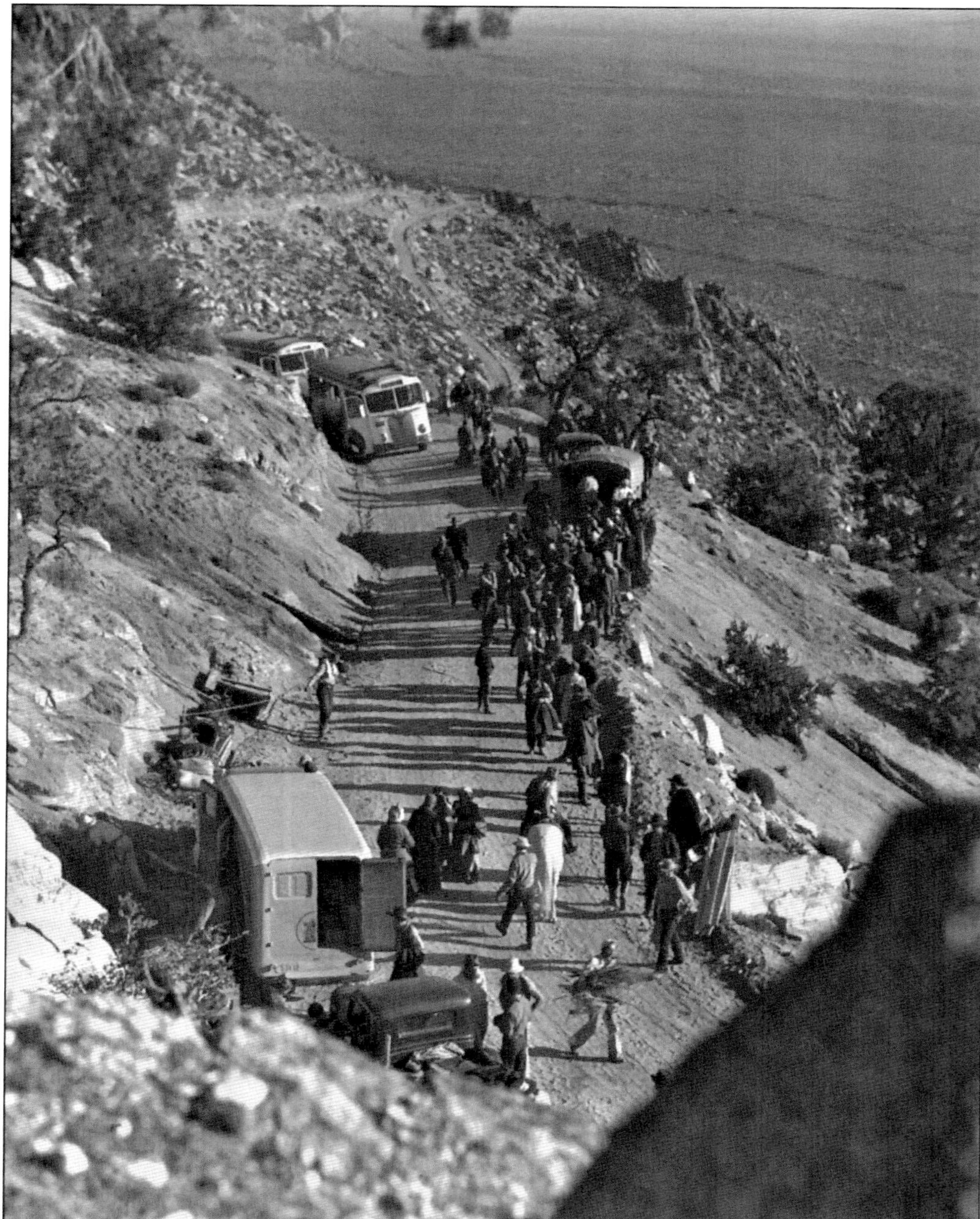

The *Brigham Young* cast and crew work on a shot on the recently built but unpaved Whitney Portal Road. (LPFHM.)

In the aptly named film noir of 1941, Humphrey Bogart, as pursued gangster Roy "Mad Dog" Earle, kneels high on the flank of Mount Whitney in *High Sierra*, directed by Raoul Walsh. (LPFHM.)

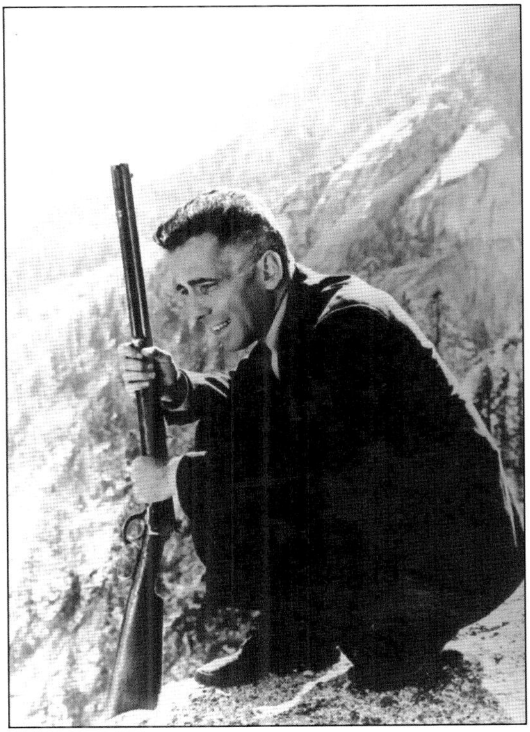

Earle has tumbled down the cliffs of Whitney here and landed at some boulders that are still visible today at Mount Whitney. Marie, played by actress Ida Lupino, mourns his death as police look on. For Bogart's final death scene on Mount Whitney, director Walsh and stuntman Buster Wiles scouted peaks high above Lone Pine. Of Walsh's first choice, Buster remarked he could do the fall, but would be dead by the end. Of a second crag, he boasted, "If I can't, I'll eat Mount Whitney." He did the dead man's careening tumble down the mountainside and missed the first two lifelines and just caught the third to keep from falling to his death. It is reported that Wiles was not totally happy with the fall although he had bounced five times, hit rocks, and was scraped. (LPFHM.)

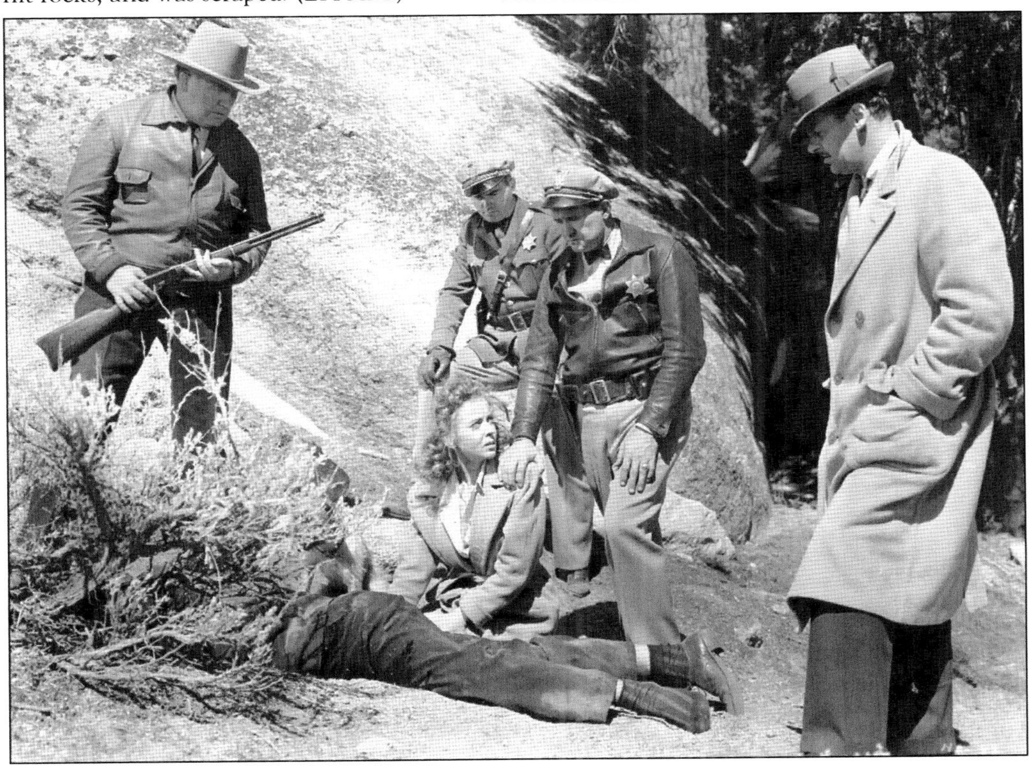

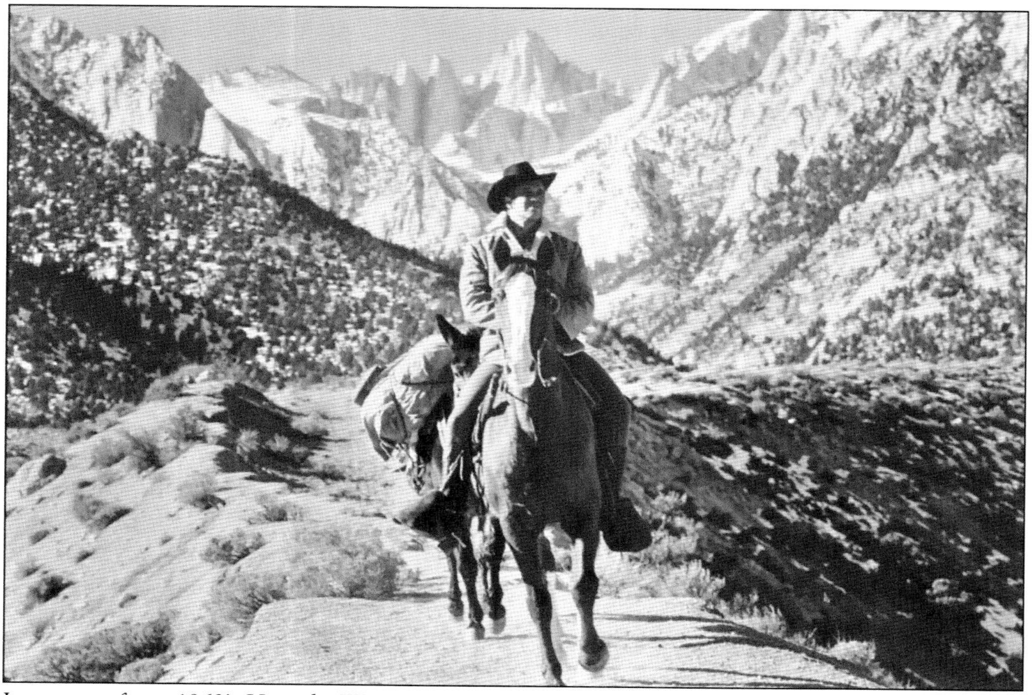

In a scene from 1962's *How the West Was Won,* actor George Peppard rides down the same trail followed by Tom Mix nearly 40 years earlier. (LPFHM.)

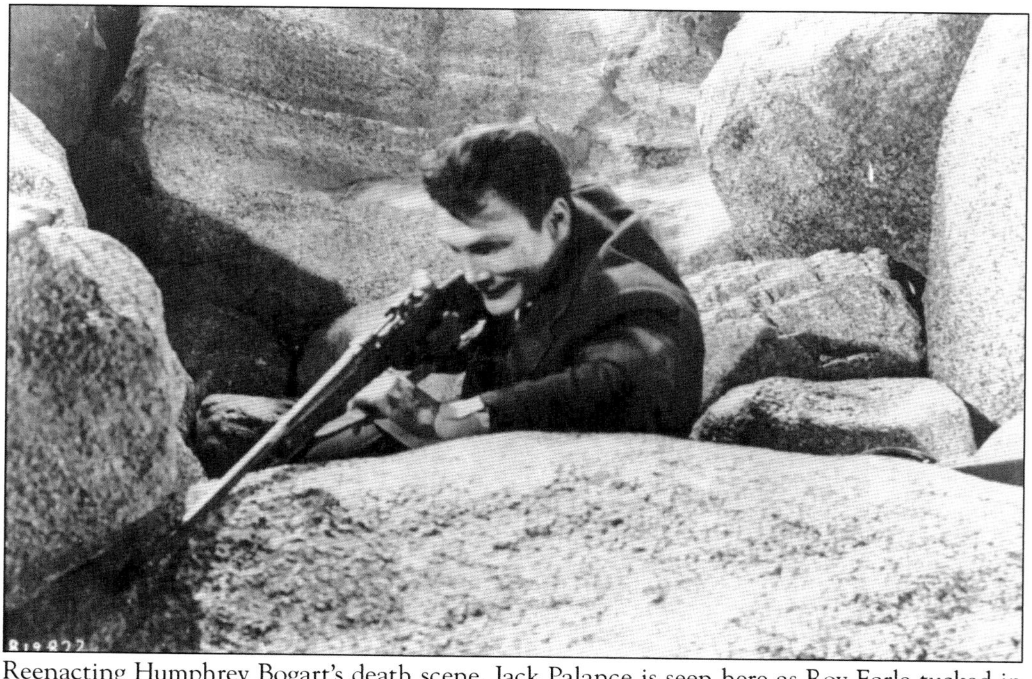

Reenacting Humphrey Bogart's death scene, Jack Palance is seen here as Roy Earle tucked in the boulders high up on the Whitney cliffs above the Portal. This image is from the 1955 film *I Died a Thousand Times.* (LPFHM.)

A character from the 1959 Paramount picture *Thunder in the Sun* celebrates the Basque wagon train's survival of an Indian attack staged at the Whitney Portal. (LPFHM.)

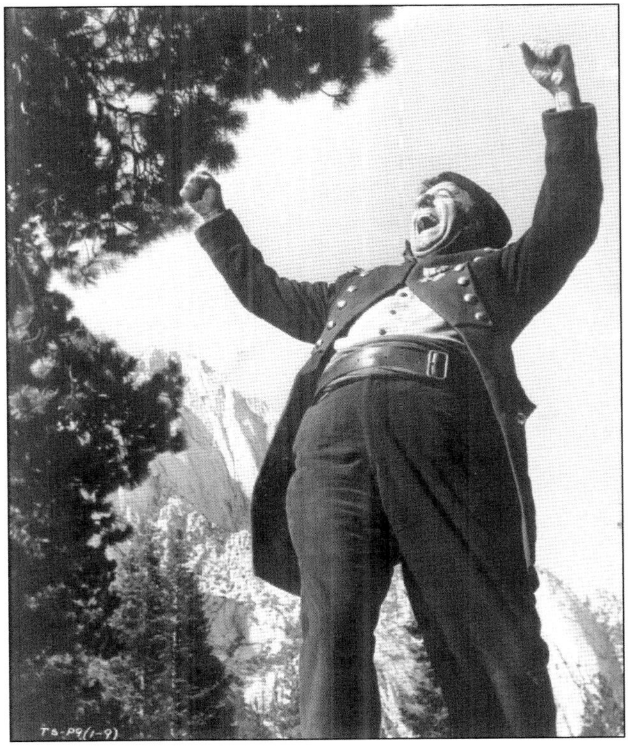

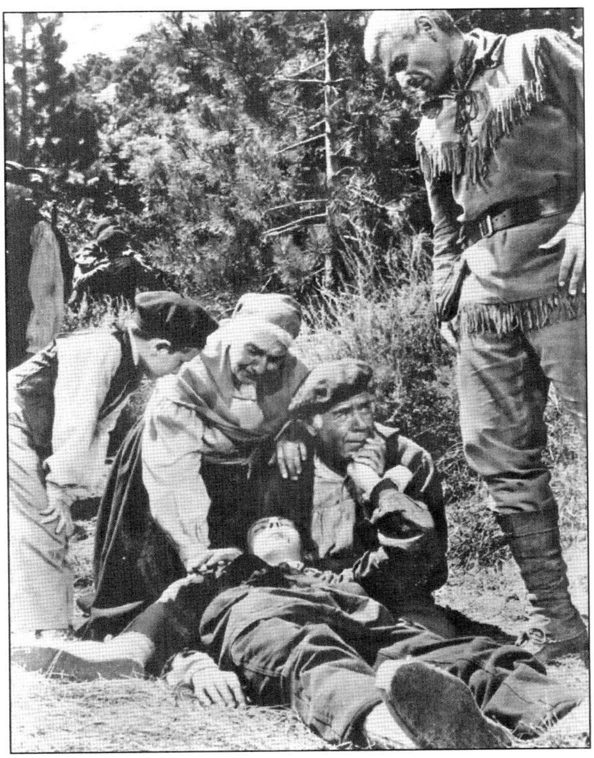

Scout Lon Bennett, played by Jeff Chandler (right), and Basque pioneers assist a victim in a scene made at the Whitney Portal area for *Thunder in the Sun*. The attack was staged by acrobatic stuntmen jumping on trampolines from behind the boulders there. (LPFHM.)

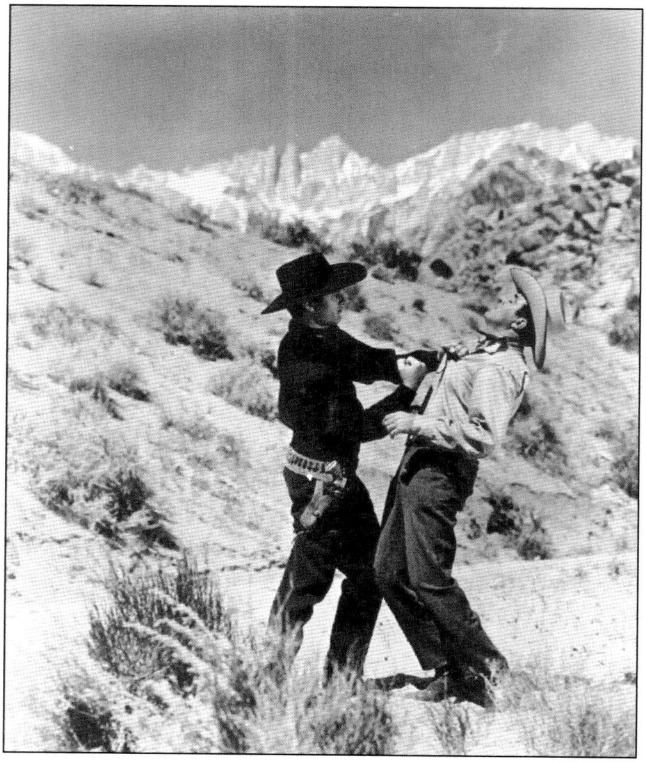

In a remake of *Riders of the Purple Sage* starring George Montgomery, Mount Whitney peeks above a hill in 1941. (LPFHM.)

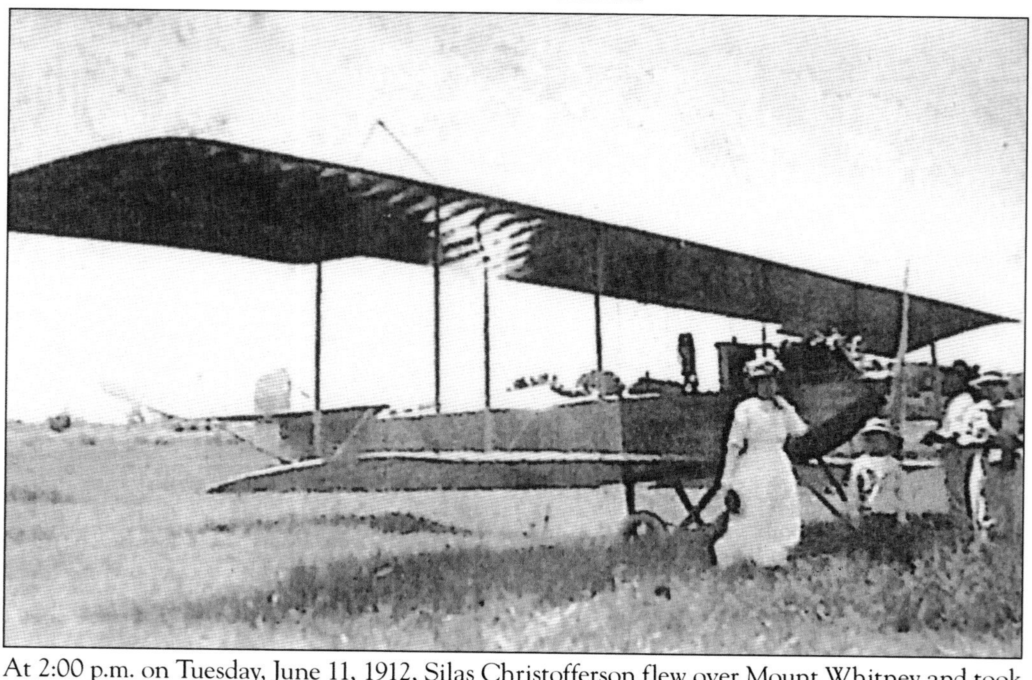

At 2:00 p.m. on Tuesday, June 11, 1912, Silas Christofferson flew over Mount Whitney and took photographs—the first ever from a plane—of his view looking down on its summit. He was only 23 years old at the time. (Branson collection.)

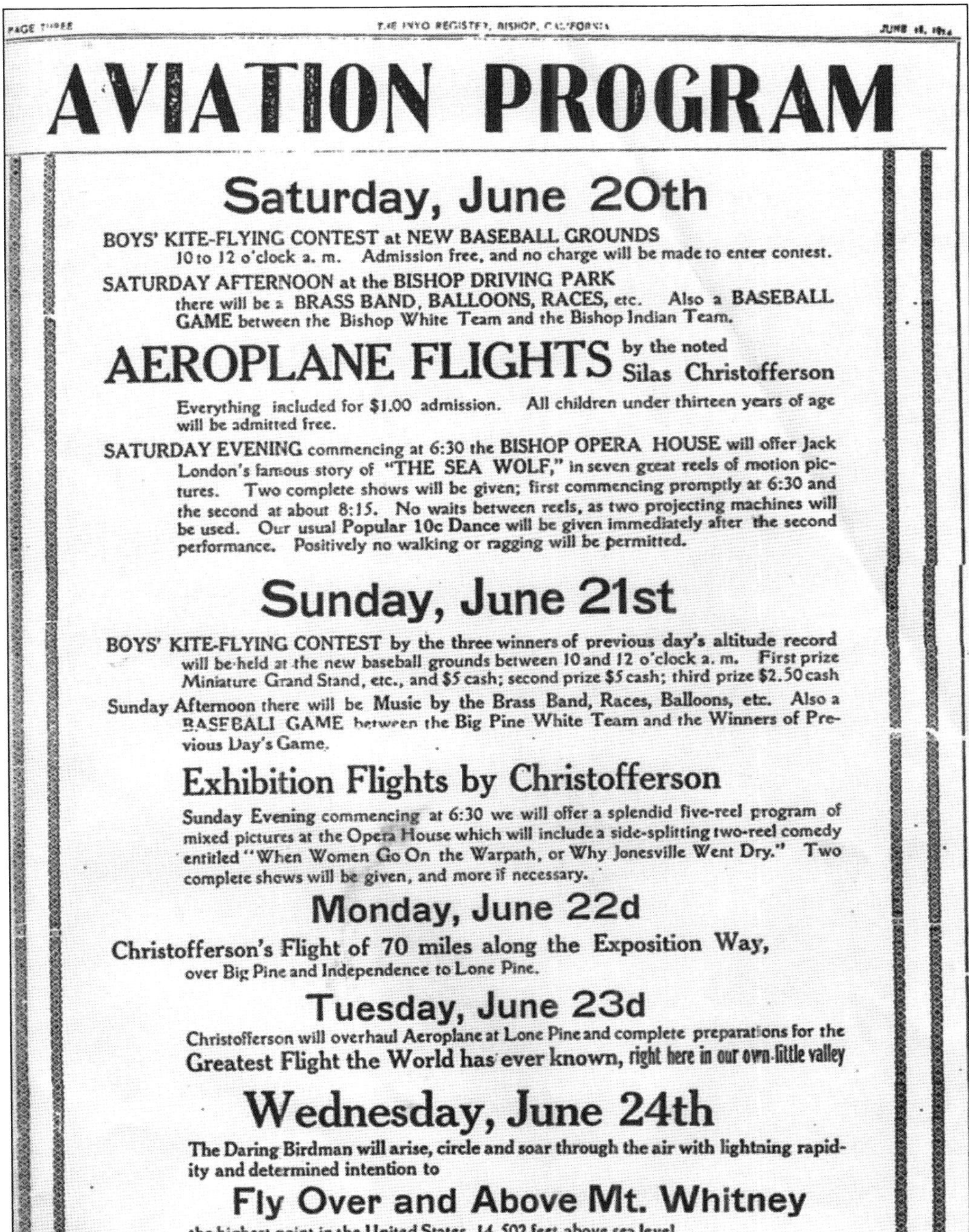

PAGE THREE — THE INYO REGISTER, BISHOP, CALIFORNIA — JUNE 18, 1914

AVIATION PROGRAM

Saturday, June 20th

BOYS' KITE-FLYING CONTEST at NEW BASEBALL GROUNDS
10 to 12 o'clock a. m. Admission free, and no charge will be made to enter contest.

SATURDAY AFTERNOON at the BISHOP DRIVING PARK
there will be a BRASS BAND, BALLOONS, RACES, etc. Also a BASEBALL GAME between the Bishop White Team and the Bishop Indian Team.

AEROPLANE FLIGHTS by the noted Silas Christofferson

Everything included for $1.00 admission. All children under thirteen years of age will be admitted free.

SATURDAY EVENING commencing at 6:30 the BISHOP OPERA HOUSE will offer Jack London's famous story of "THE SEA WOLF," in seven great reels of motion pictures. Two complete shows will be given; first commencing promptly at 6:30 and the second at about 8:15. No waits between reels, as two projecting machines will be used. Our usual Popular 10c Dance will be given immediately after the second performance. Positively no walking or ragging will be permitted.

Sunday, June 21st

BOYS' KITE-FLYING CONTEST by the three winners of previous day's altitude record will be held at the new baseball grounds between 10 and 12 o'clock a. m. First prize Miniature Grand Stand, etc., and $5 cash; second prize $5 cash; third prize $2.50 cash

Sunday Afternoon there will be Music by the Brass Band, Races, Balloons, etc. Also a BASEBALL GAME between the Big Pine White Team and the Winners of Previous Day's Game.

Exhibition Flights by Christofferson

Sunday Evening commencing at 6:30 we will offer a splendid five-reel program of mixed pictures at the Opera House which will include a side-splitting two-reel comedy entitled "When Women Go On the Warpath, or Why Jonesville Went Dry." Two complete shows will be given, and more if necessary.

Monday, June 22d

Christofferson's Flight of 70 miles along the Exposition Way,
over Big Pine and Independence to Lone Pine.

Tuesday, June 23d

Christofferson will overhaul Aeroplane at Lone Pine and complete preparations for the **Greatest Flight the World has ever known, right here in our own little valley**

Wednesday, June 24th

The Daring Birdman will arise, circle and soar through the air with lightning rapidity and determined intention to

Fly Over and Above Mt. Whitney

the highest point in the United States, 14,502 feet above sea level.

Christofferson flew down the Owens Valley before his flight over Whitney, demonstrating heavier-than-air flight to citizens, many of whom had never witnessed it. Kite flying was a diversion for the witnesses to the flight. The event became an excuse for an "all day lark." (*The Inyo Independent.*)

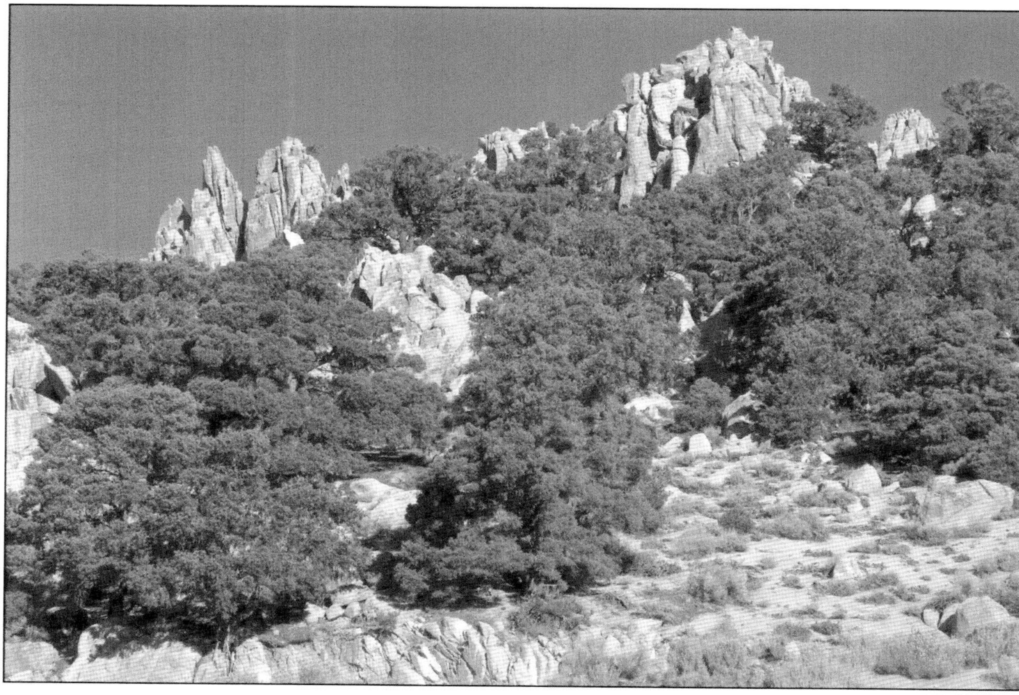

The first forest entered on the east side is a short, dispersed piñon forest. Pinyons produce pine nuts in the fall for wildlife and people, too. (Mike Prather.)

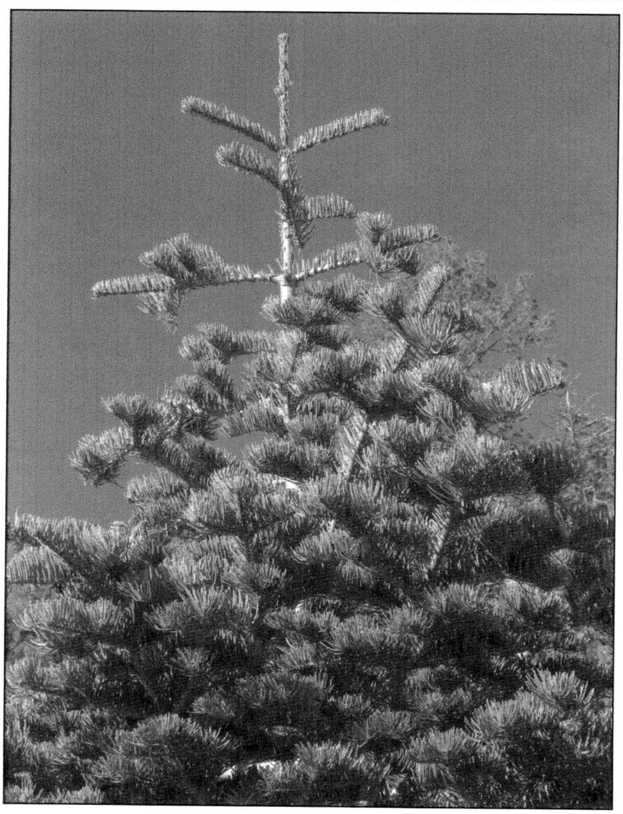

White fir grows in protected canyons and on shaded slopes. (Mike Prather.)

Seven

Natural History Along the Trail

Hiking up the rocky trail to the summit of Mount Whitney, one passes through several varied life zones. There is subtlety here, as nature does not create these zones with hard-and-fast edges. She places them across the landscape using elevation, slope, light, moisture, and temperature as guides. The variation in these factors creates the plant communities that are seen, which in turn influence the distribution of the animals. Look and listen carefully.

The road to Whitney Portal from Lone Pine begins at 3,700 feet of elevation in the Sonoran Zone (high desert) and arrives in the Montane Zone at 8,500 feet. The Montane Zone extends from roughly 7,500 to 9,000 feet in elevation. It is most obviously represented by two pines—singleleaf pinyon and Jeffrey pine. White fir mixes in as well. The lower edge of the singleleaf pinyon forest is coincidently the lower edge of the snow after winter storms. The Jeffrey pine and white fir grow mostly on the north-facing slopes and the canyon bottom, while the singleleaf pinyon prefers the south-facing slopes and full sun. The large, rich seed of the short singleleaf pinyon was a staple of the Paiute-Shoshone. It was a critical winter survival food and was traded with tribes on the Sierra's west side along with obsidian, salt, and brine fly pupae from Owens Lake. Jeffrey pine, the close cousin of the ponderosa pine, is a large tree with vanilla-scented, jigsaw-puzzle bark, and three long needles in each bundle. White fir has the classic Christmas tree appearance. All are evergreens.

Between 9,500 and 11,000 feet in elevation is the Subalpine Zone. Two pines dominate—foxtail and lodgepole. The lodgepole pine can grow in a variety of sites, but it is mostly found near the canyon bottom and water. It has cornflake bark, rather small cones, and two needles in each bundle. The foxtail pine, a close relative of the bristlecone pine of the Great Basin, prefers the upper slopes of the canyons and the ridge tops. It has warm colored, thick, alligator hide—like bark and short needles in a bundle of five. Their appearance is much like a baby bottle cleaning brush. Foxtail pines are the oldest trees in the Mount Whitney area, where they can live as long as 2,500 years. Its extremely hard wood weathers slowly, leaving beautiful blond-colored snags set against hard-blue skies. In addition, limber pine, an often multi-trunked pine, grows in scattered locations at higher elevations where it is buffeted by hurricane-force winds. It has five 3-inch pale green needles in each bundle. The western or Sierra juniper grows here as well, although it is less frequently seen. It favors sunny, exposed rock slopes.

The Alpine Zone begins around 11,000 feet in elevation, depending on whether it is a shaded or sunny slope—north- or south-facing. Colder, north-facing slopes force the tree line down; while the sunny, warmer south-facing slopes allow the timberline to creep higher. But generally, leaving the trees behind, the hiker enters a zone of small shrubs, grasses, and cushion plants. The growing season is measured in weeks, freezing temperatures can occur during any month, and ultraviolet light—unhindered by the thicker atmosphere at lower elevations—can damage plant cells. Plants grow as flat cushions on the soil to absorb soil warmth and avoid desiccating winds. Flowers are often protected from ultraviolet radiation by red pigments. The arctic willow crawls along the ground barely three inches tall in the Alpine Zone. Shrubs like alpine gooseberry seek protection by huddling close to boulders and are shaped by hurricane-force winds in winter. Most plants of the mountains are perennials rather than annuals. A perennial has life insurance and does not need to gamble with year-to-year vagaries of weather and conditions. The risk for annuals is by placing everything on the success of each year's germination, and growth is great; adapt or perish is the rule.

Whether in the past, present, or future, changes in climate place stress on plant and animal populations. Variations in moisture and temperature can decrease or increase native flora and fauna. Animals have mobility within limits that might allow movement up or down the mountains, but plants do not have the advantage of mobility and are less able to spread to higher or lower elevations in response to change. The relationship of plants and animals means neither can realistically adapt without the other. Animals depend on plants for food, shelter, and reproduction. Many plants depend on animals to move their seeds. Changes in climate and adaptation may be gradual or sudden. Time will tell.

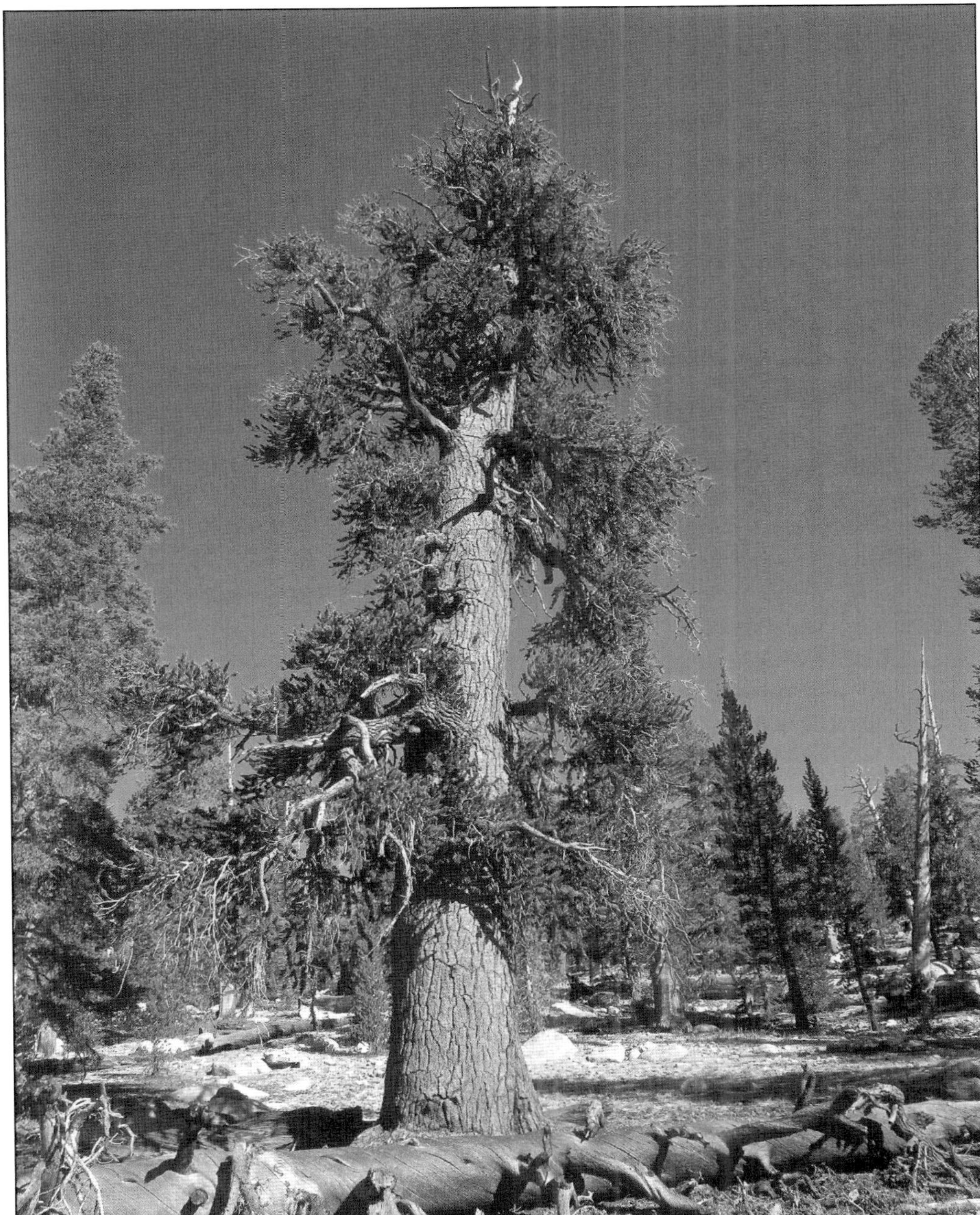

Foxtail pines grow high in the Southern Sierra. With short needles growing along their branches, they have a foxtail appearance. These trees can live for more than 2,000 years. (Mike Prather.)

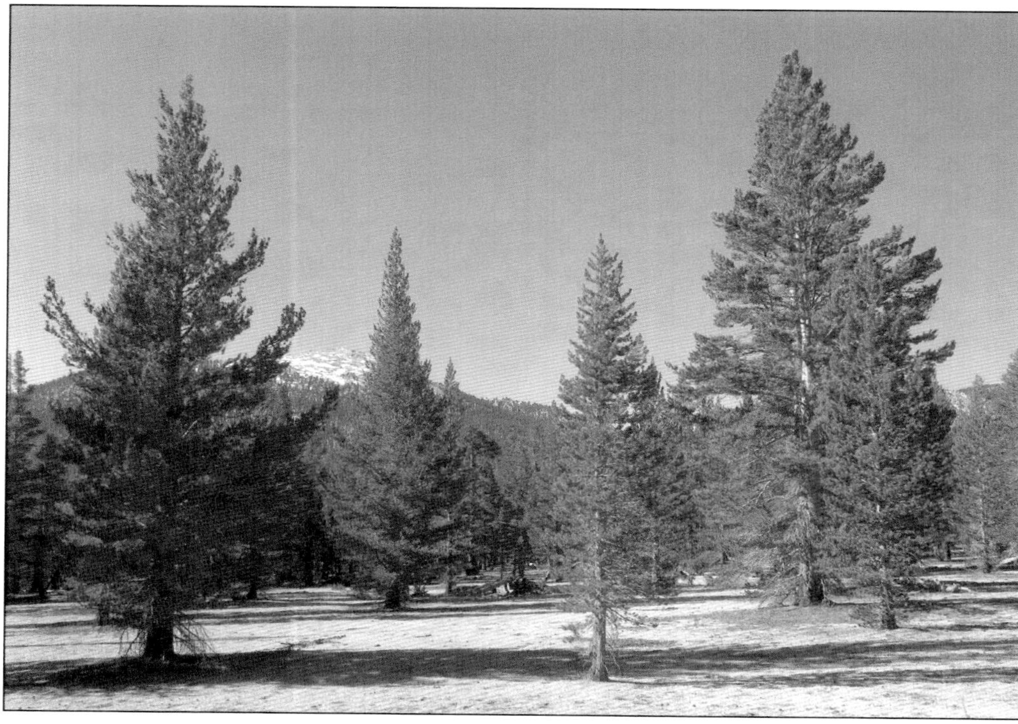

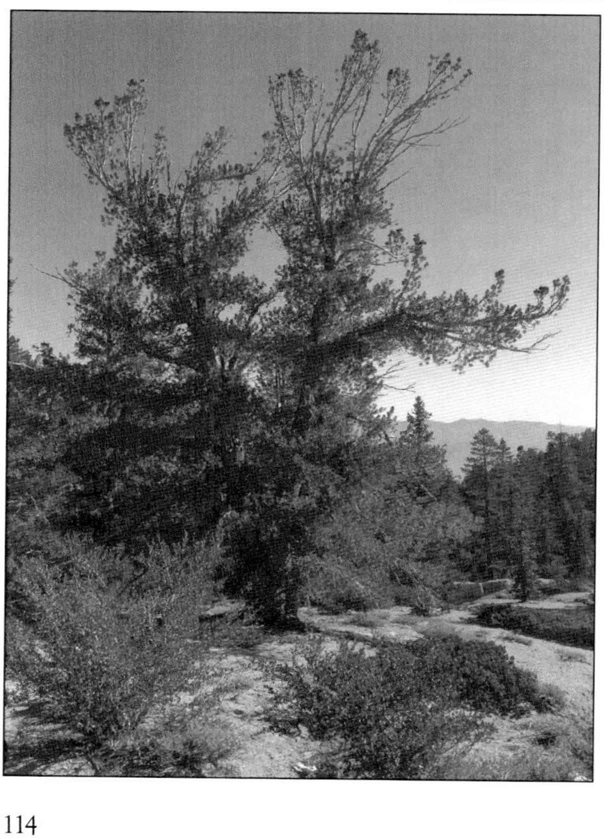

The lodgepole pine grows in varied locations, both wet and dry. IT has straight trunks, cornflake bark, small cones, and two needles in a bundle. (Mike Prather.)

Limber pines are indeed limber and do well along windy slopes and ridges. The scientific name is *Pinus flexilis*. Winter storms bring hurricane-force winds of over 100 miles per hour to passes and ridge tops. Being flexible helps; the trees bend, but do not break. (Mike Prather.)

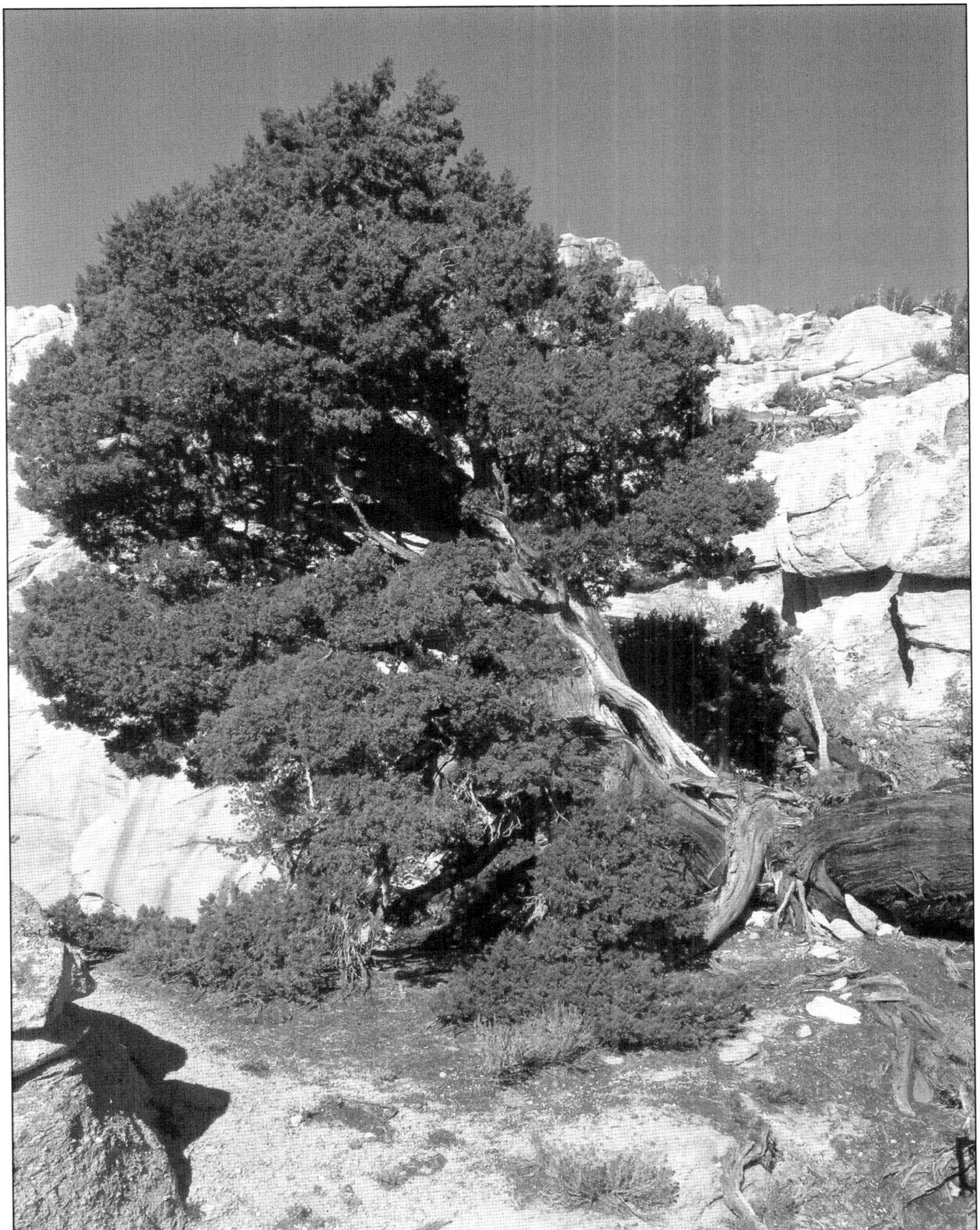

Western or Sierra juniper prefers exposed, rocky locations. It grows higher than other junipers. These trees have warm, soft, fibrous bark. (Mike Prather.)

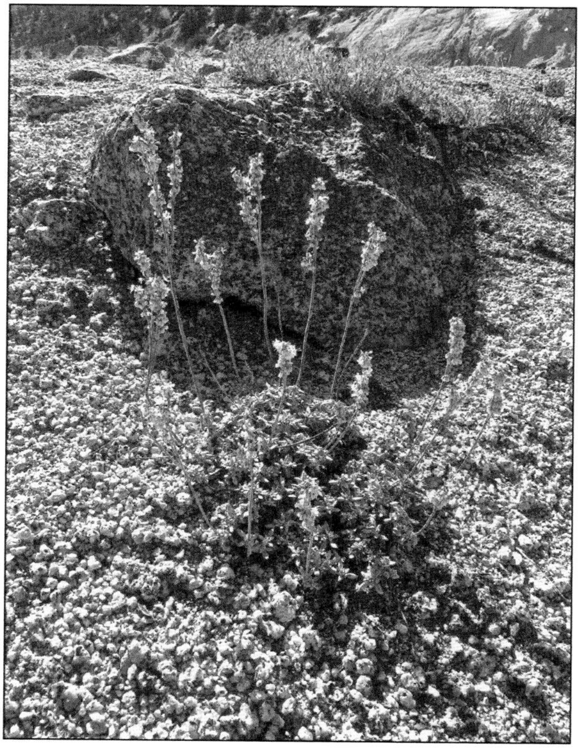

A plant adaptation for surviving in the mountains is to grow as a cushion—flat on the ground. These cushion plants avoid strong winds and gain warmth from hugging the soil. (Mike Prather.)

The arctic willow is found growing in wet meadows and along the edges of high lakes. Its catkins (flowers) are taller than its creeping, woody branches. (Mike Prather.)

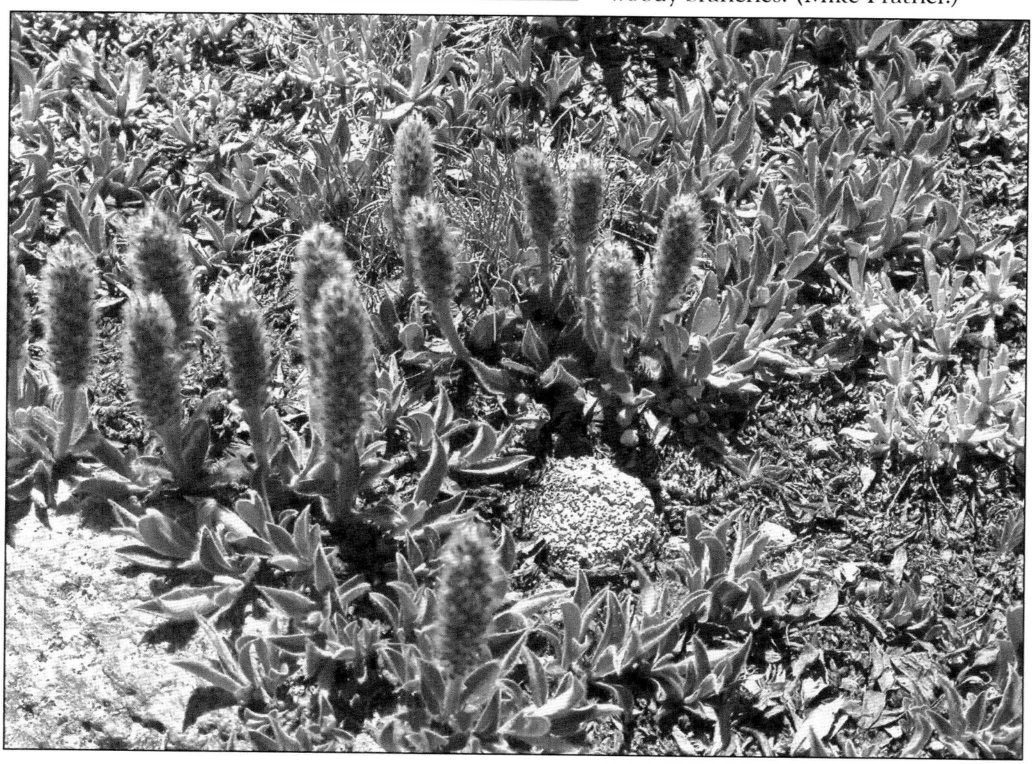

Sierra Primrose is found near the tree line and is higher growing along the margins of boulders. It flowers soon after the snow melts away.

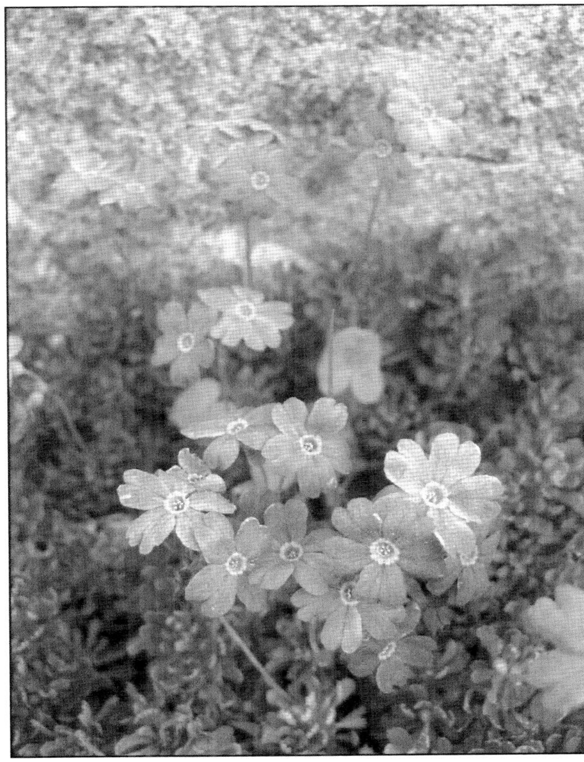

Alpine gold often grows from small depressions in the decomposed granite soil near the tree line. Its seeds drift and are caught in a footstep, where they germinate the next year. The flowers have long hairs with a pineapple scent. (Mike Prather.)

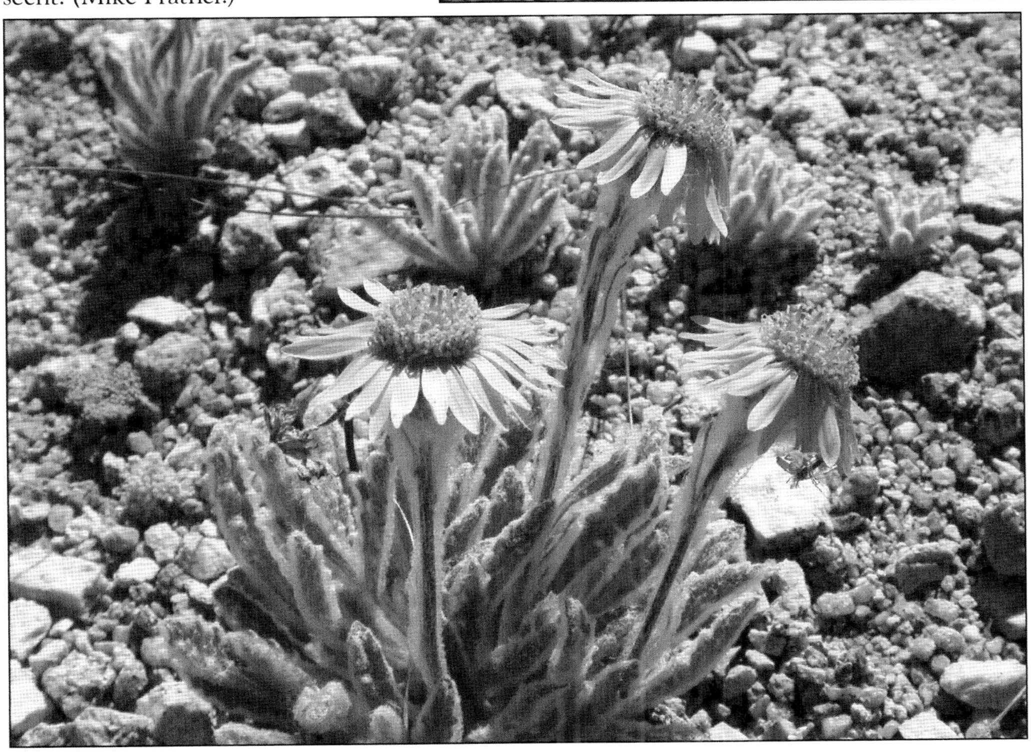

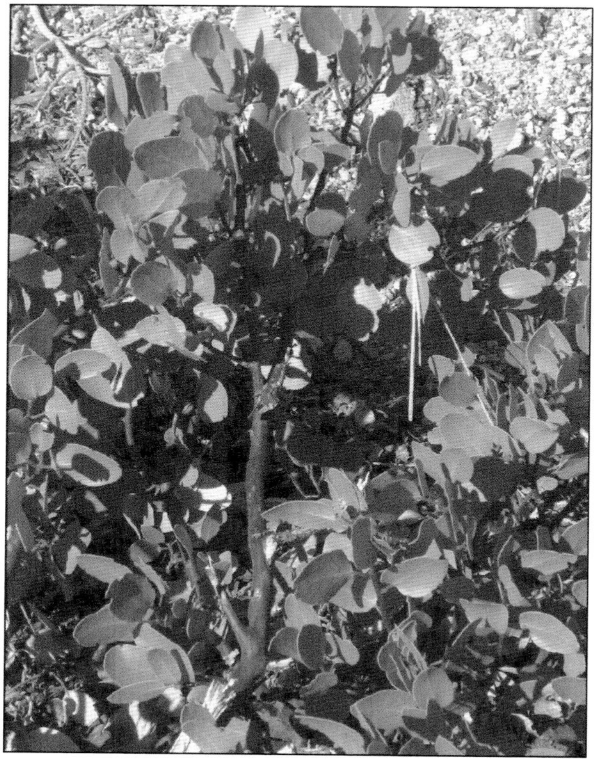

This dense, rounded shrub with smooth brick-red branches called manzanita is found on dry, sunny slopes in the Montane Zone. It can be spotted near the trailhead at Whitney Portal. (Mike Prather.)

This low-growing shrub called chinquapin often seeks shelter by hugging boulders. The spiny husks enclosing the seeds are easily seen. (Mike Prather.)

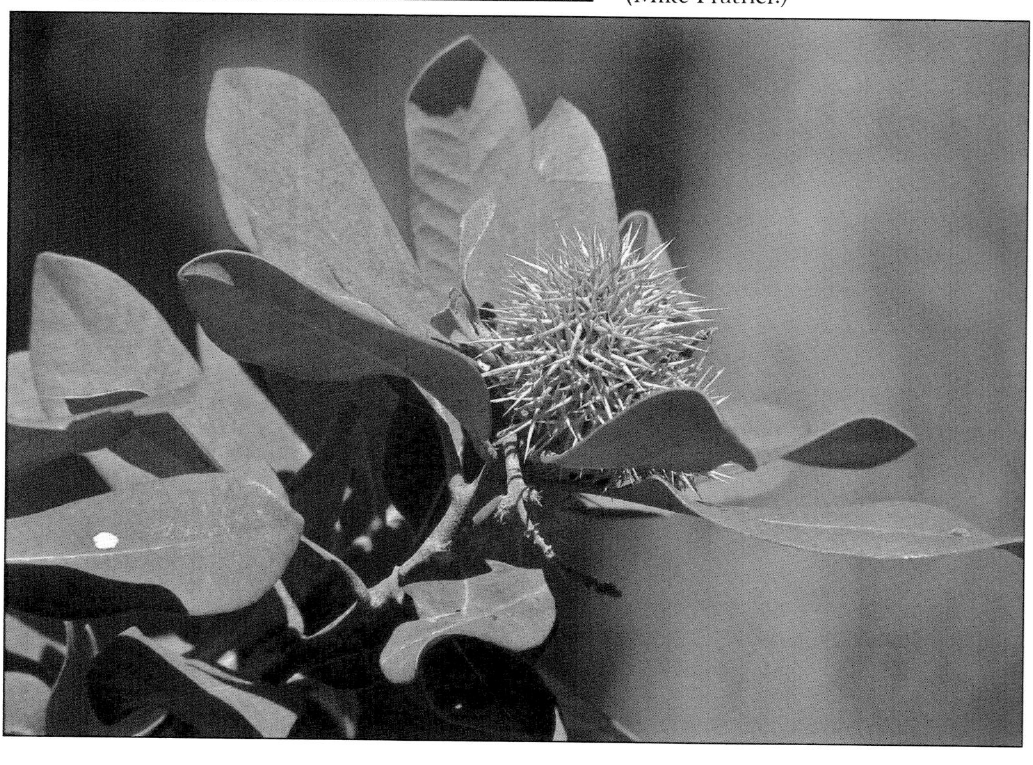

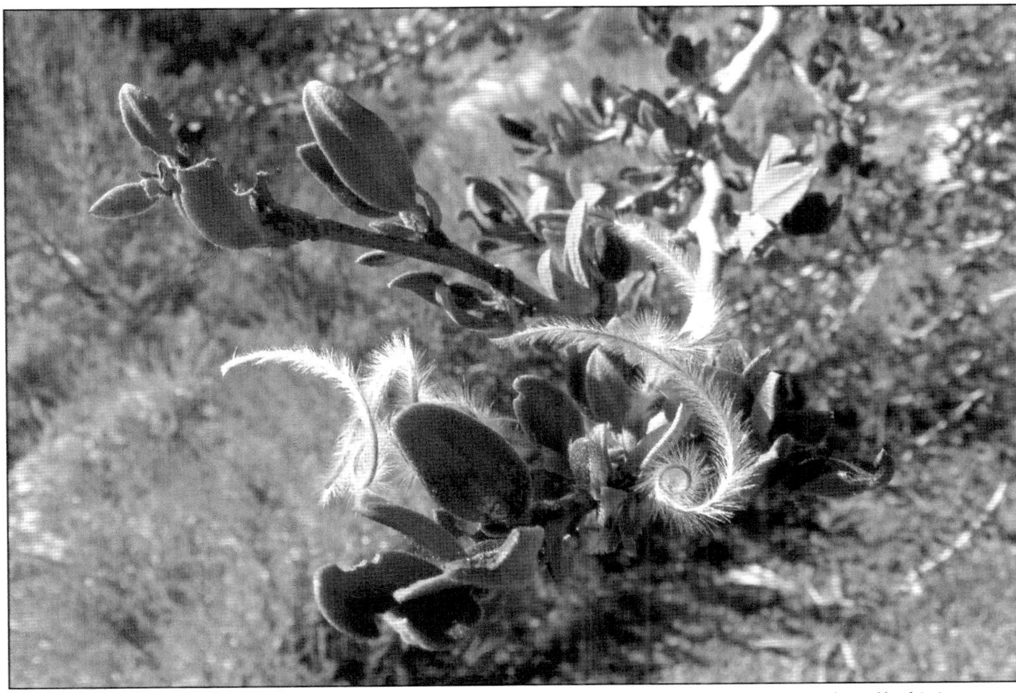

Gray, upright branches bearing seeds having long fuzzy tails identifies this shrub called Mountain Mahogany. It prefers dry, south-facing slopes. (Mike Prather.)

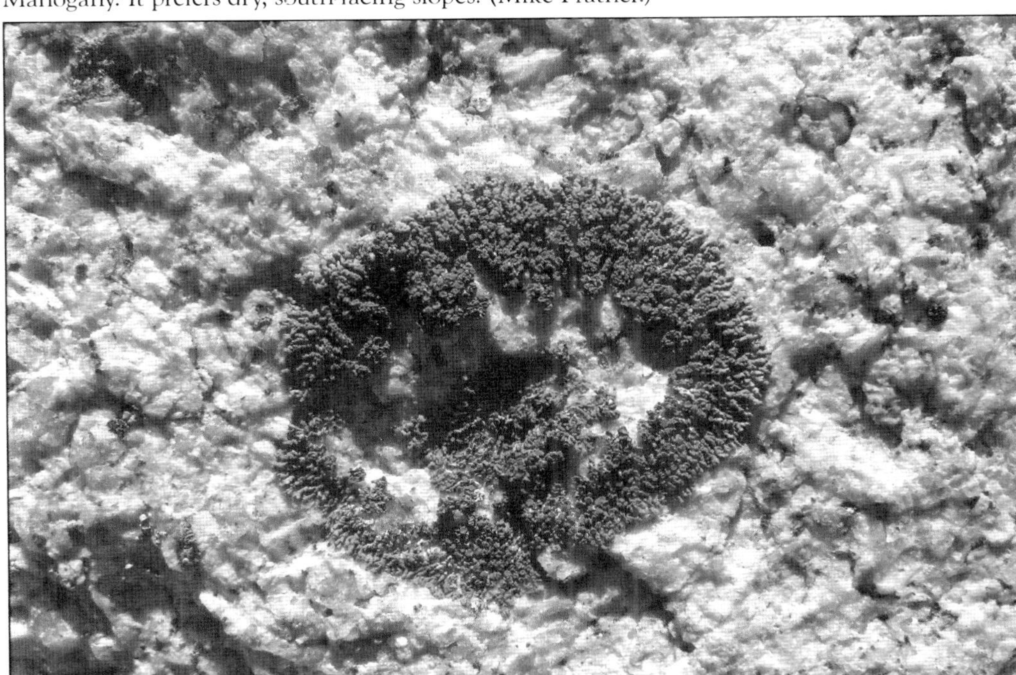

Lichens are the first soil formers producing acids that dissolve solid rock Their varied colors of orange, yellow, and brown decorate rock surfaces. (Mike Prather.)

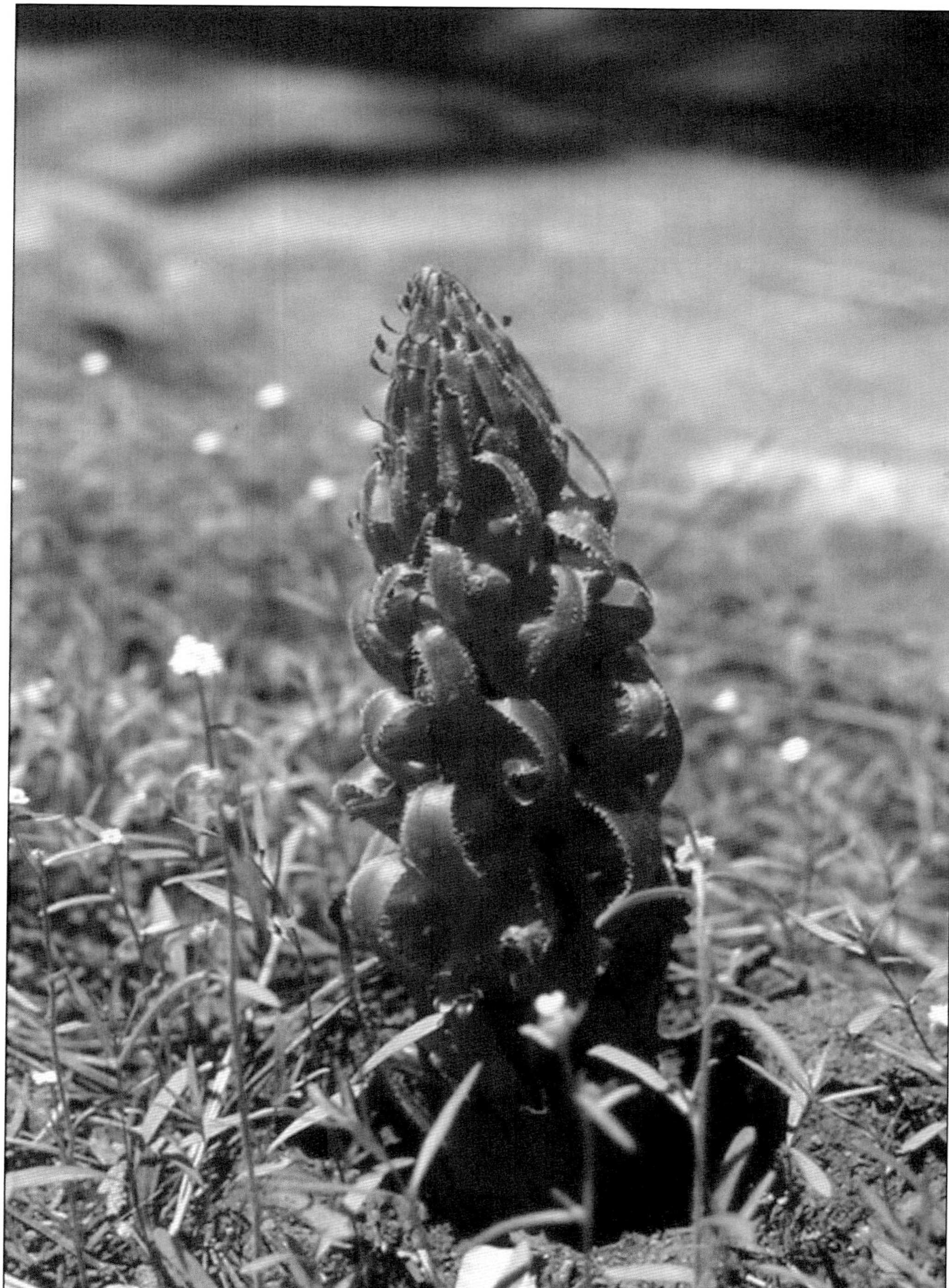

In early summer, this strange parasitic plant called snow plant emerges from the duff in the Whitney Portal area. Lacking chlorophyll, it attaches to the root of its host.

This bright magenta-purple flower known as shooting star grows in wet areas. (Mike Prather.)

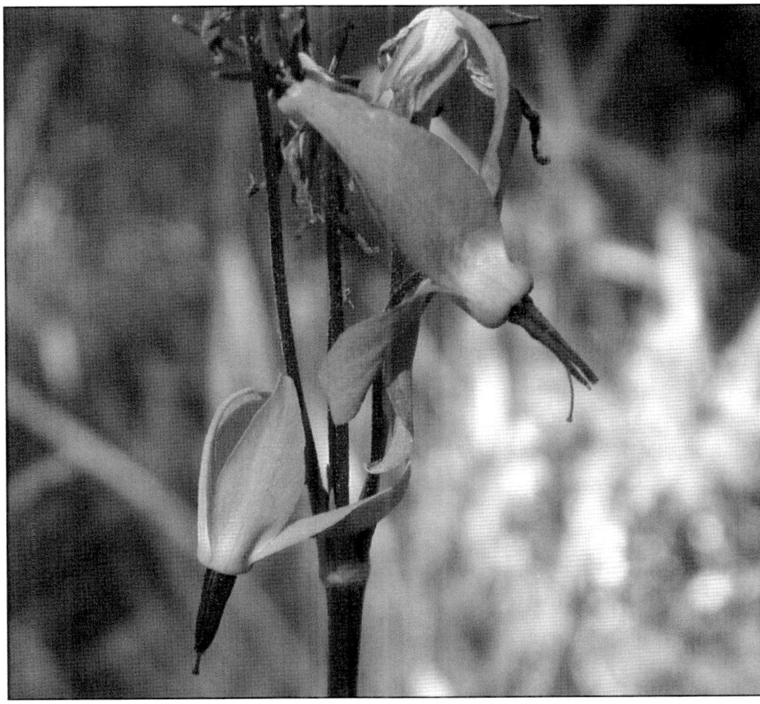

Water-loving, the orange columbine lines the banks of brooks and streams.

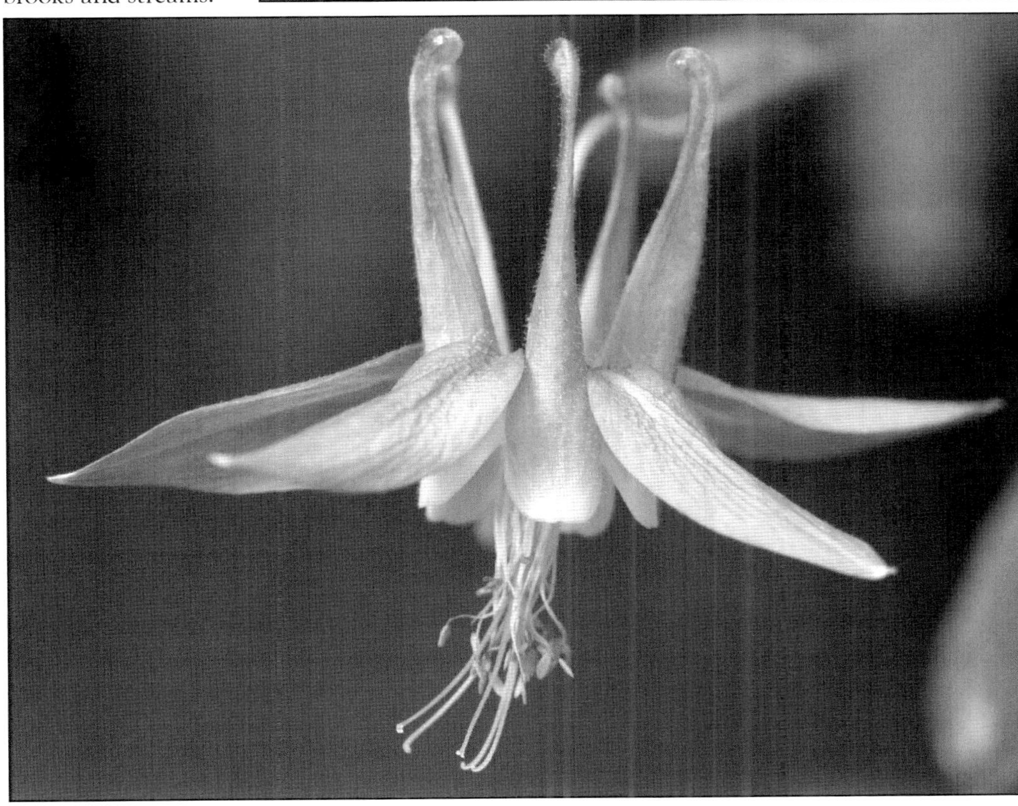

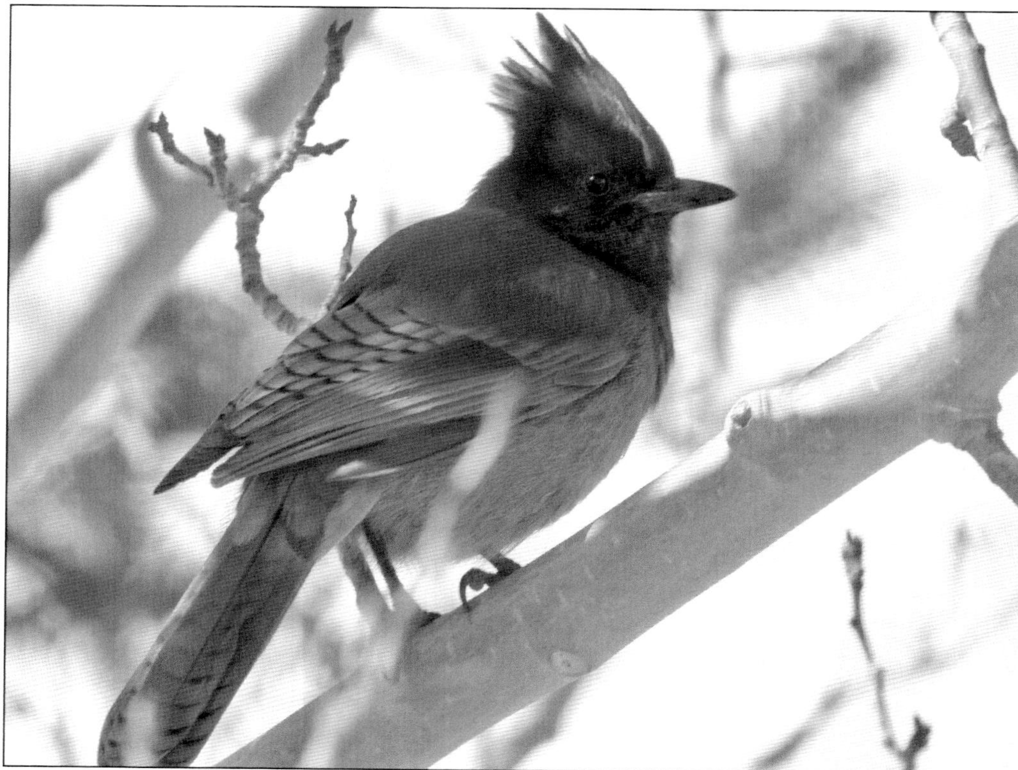

If one is eating in the mountains, then he or she will be visited by the Steller's jay. Its crest is raised or lowered based on excitement levels. (Alison Sheehey at Nature Ali.)

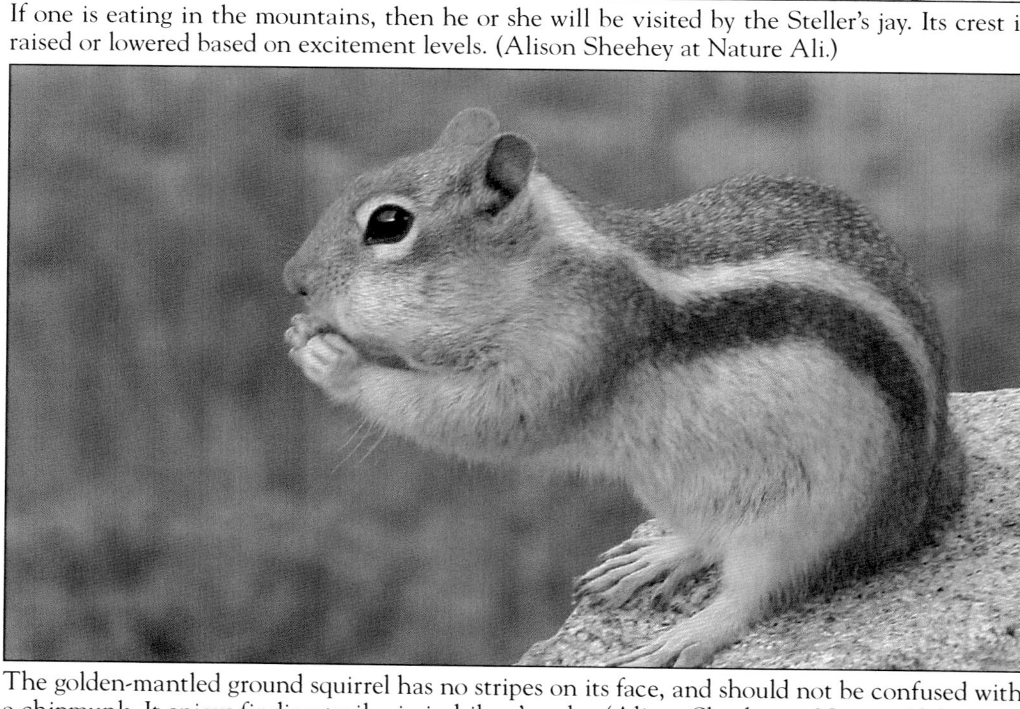

The golden-mantled ground squirrel has no stripes on its face, and should not be confused with a chipmunk. It enjoys finding trail mix in hikers' packs. (Alison Sheehey at Nature Ali.)

Chickarees are a beautiful tree squirrel. Dark above and light below, they spend most of their time in trees. Piles of pinecone scales and cores can be found at the chickarees' favorite feeding stations. (Alison Sheehey at Nature Ali.)

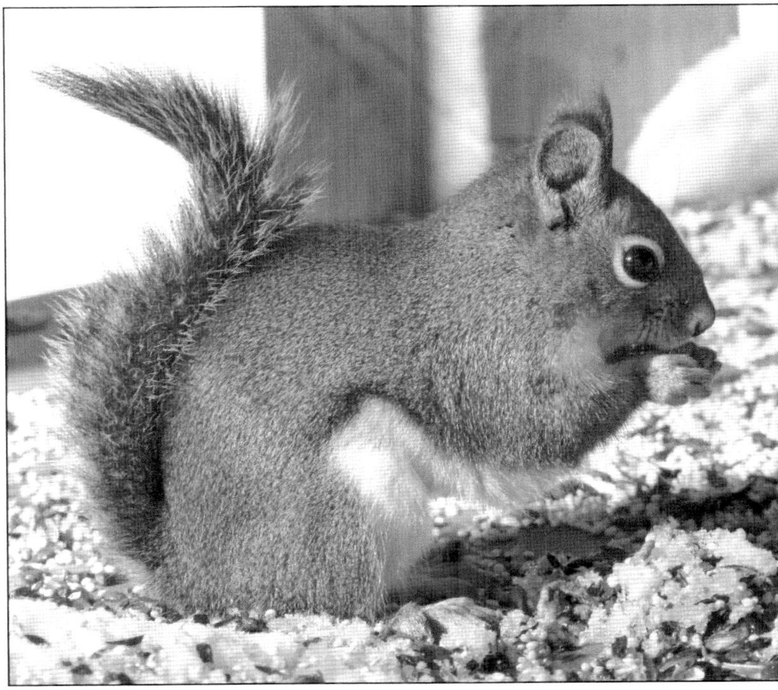

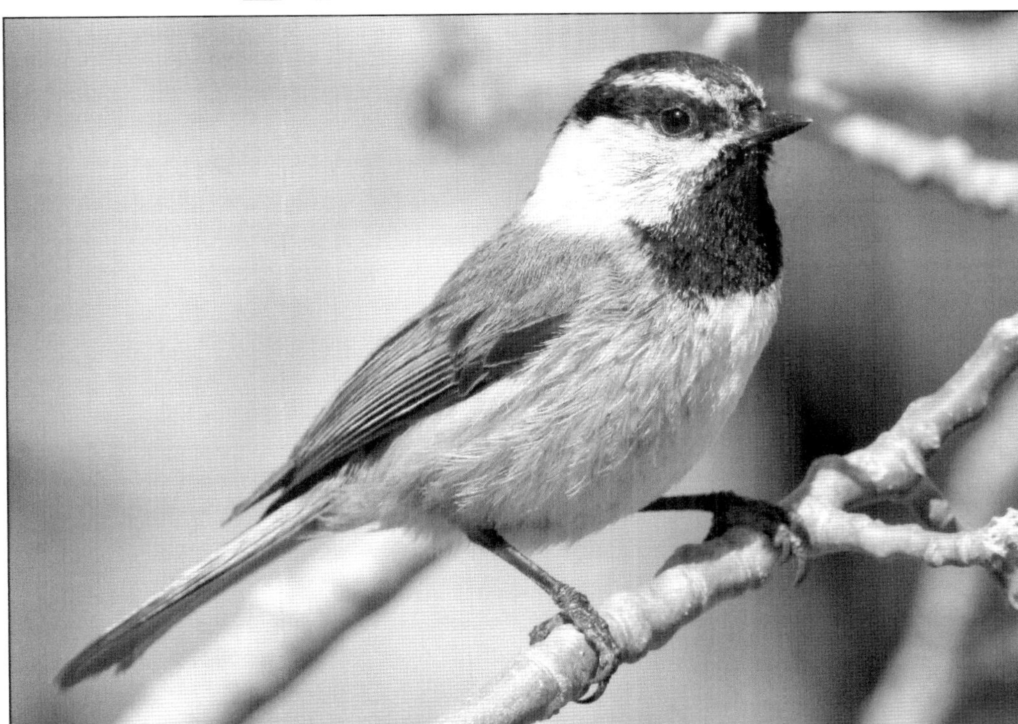

Mountain chickadees are great company in the woods. Their constant song "chick-a-dee, chick-a-dee-dee" announces them. (Alison Sheehey at Nature Ali.)

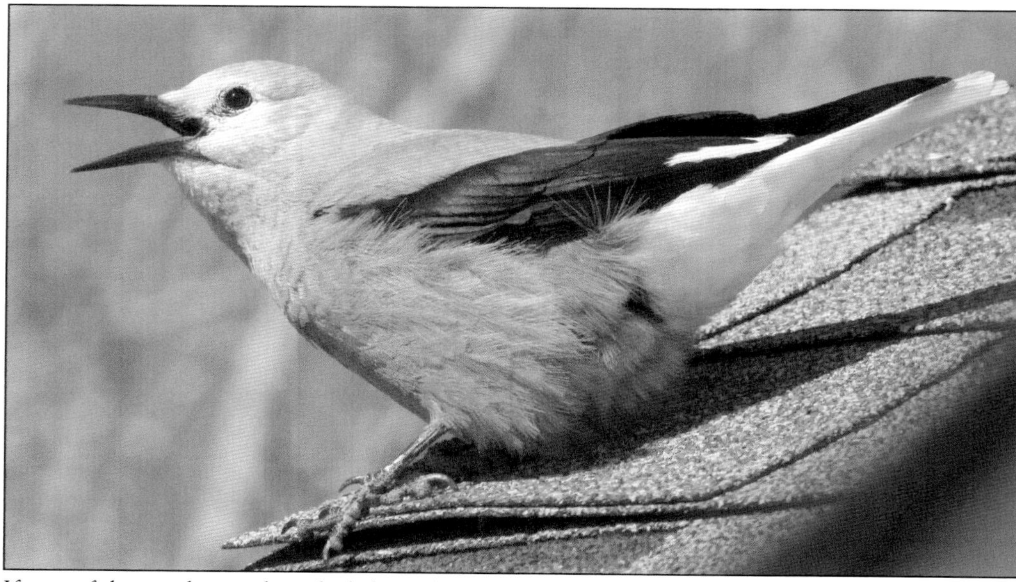

If an awful screeching is heard while in the mountains, it may be a Clark's nutcracker. Related to crows and jays, they use their strong bills to open green cones for seeds that other birds cannot get to. (Alison Sheehey at Nature Ali.)

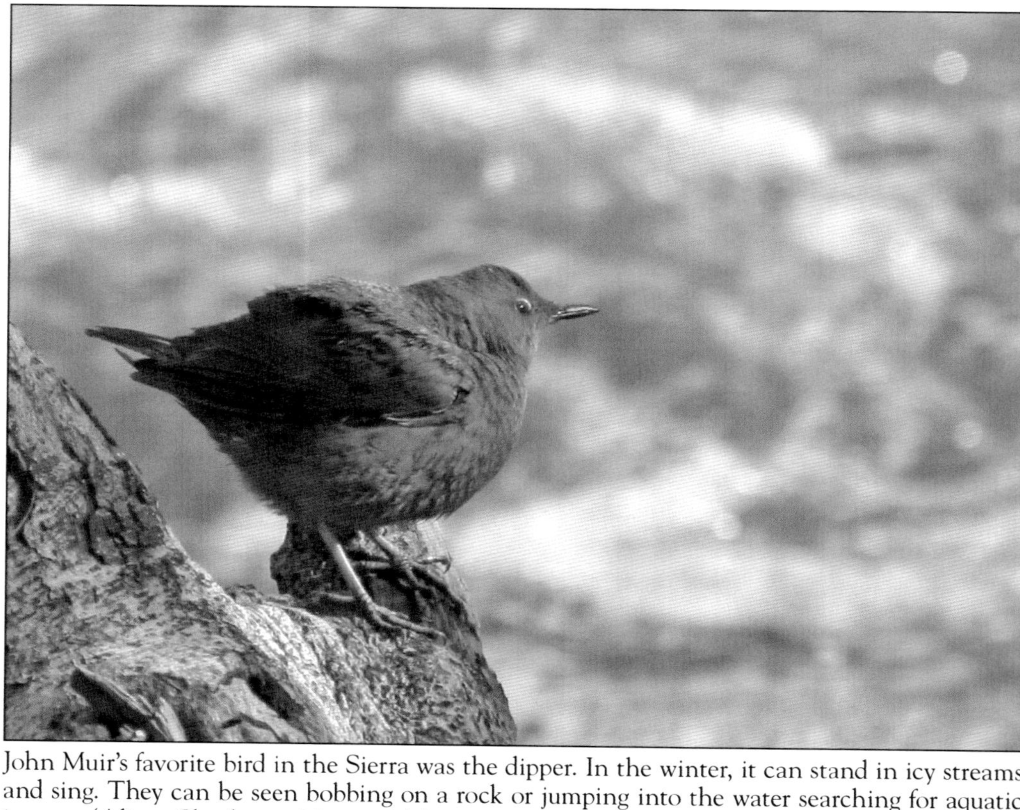

John Muir's favorite bird in the Sierra was the dipper. In the winter, it can stand in icy streams and sing. They can be seen bobbing on a rock or jumping into the water searching for aquatic insects. (Alison Sheehey at Nature Ali.)

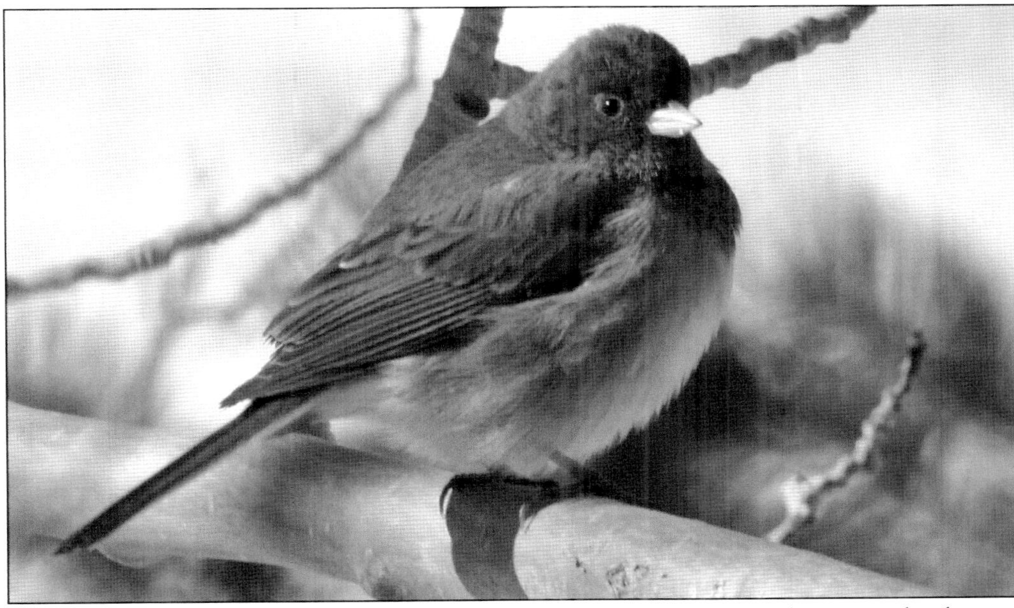

The most common bird in the Sierra is the dark-eyed junco. They are seed-eaters and only go up into the mountains during the snow-free seasons. Juncos nest on the ground and can be quite tame. (Alison Sheehey at Nature Ali.)

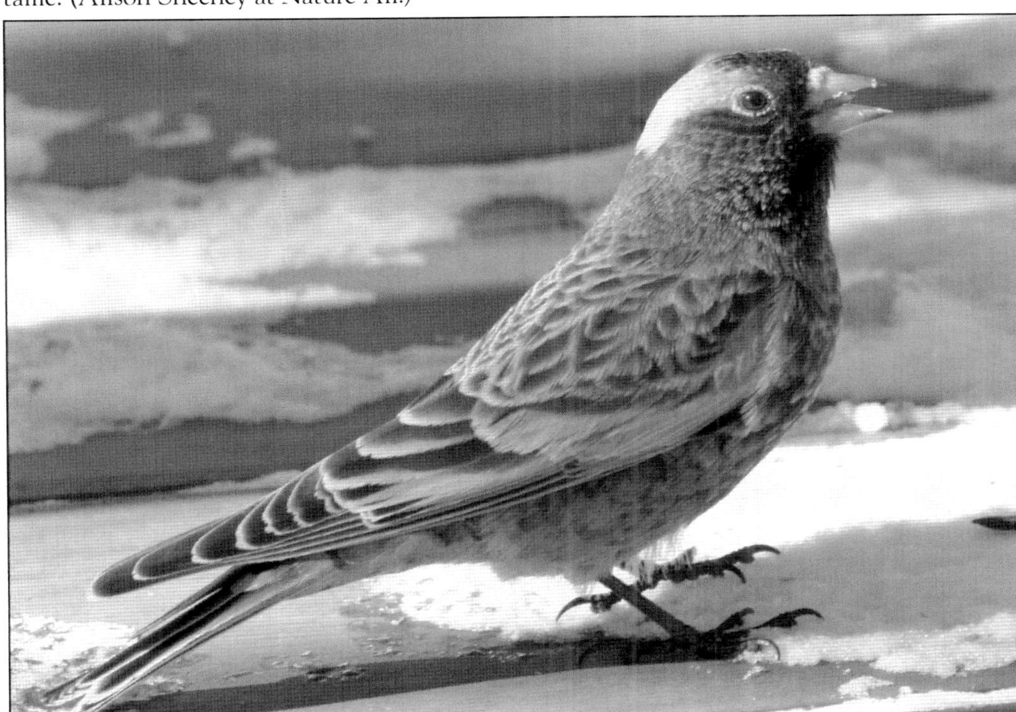

Hikers traveling along the highest ridges and peaks will see the gray-crowned rosy finch feeding on or near snowfields picking at seeds and insects. On the summit, these hearty alpiners may hop around one's feet with little care. (Alison Sheehey at Nature Ali.)

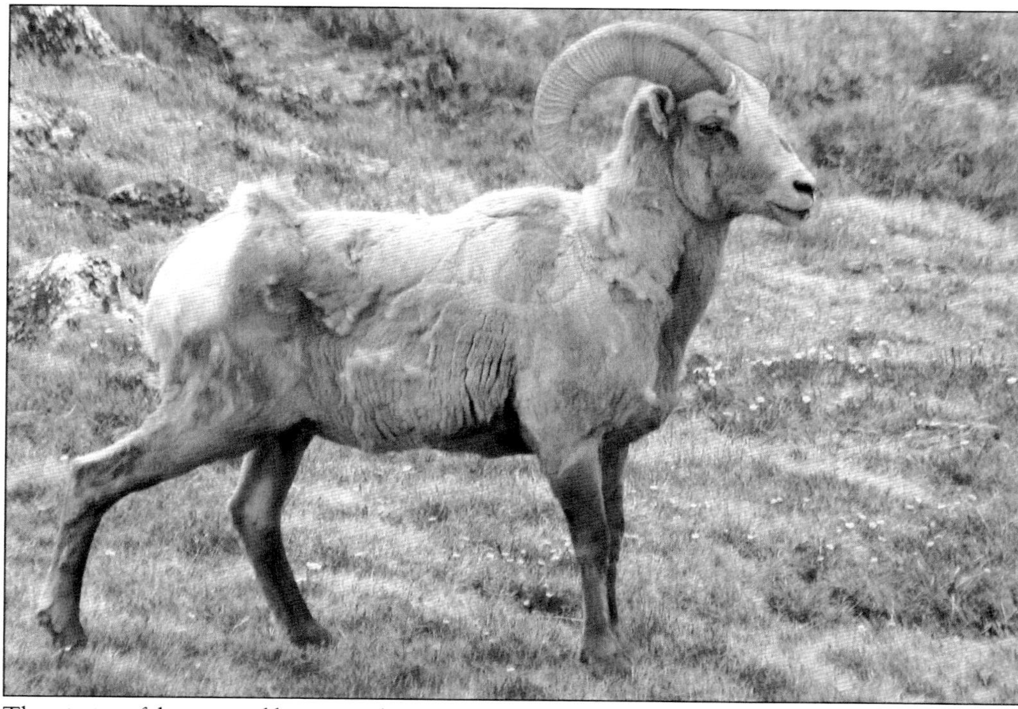

The victim of disease and hunting, the Sierra bighorn was extirpated from the Whitney Crest area years ago. They have been reintroduced in the Mount Langley area just south of Mount Whitney and once again run the cliffs of the High Sierra. (Alison Sheehey at Nature Ali.)

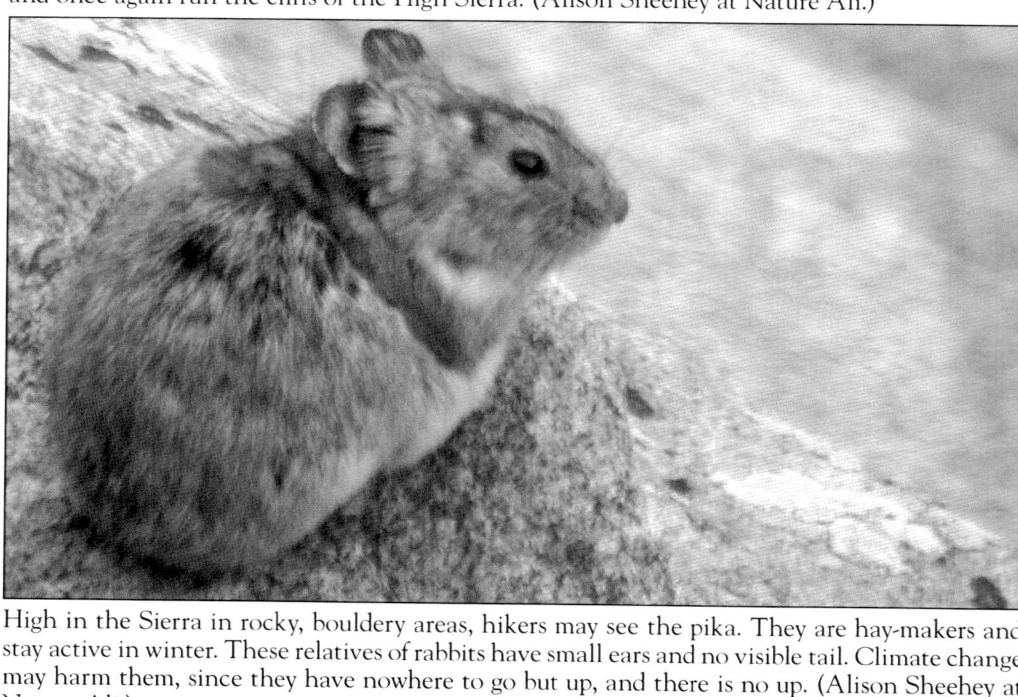

High in the Sierra in rocky, bouldery areas, hikers may see the pika. They are hay-makers and stay active in winter. These relatives of rabbits have small ears and no visible tail. Climate change may harm them, since they have nowhere to go but up, and there is no up. (Alison Sheehey at Nature Ali.)

Foxtail pines heavily damaged by lightning can survive on thin strips of living bark for centuries. In the high exposed environments of these pines, lightning strikes are common. Their needles can remain on the tree for 30 years or more. (Mike Prather.)

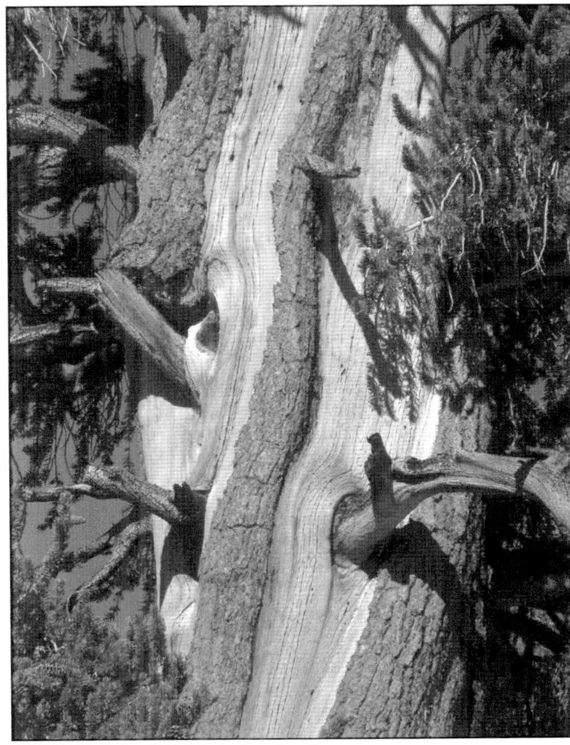

Foxtail pine needles look like a foxtail. Their cones lack the spines of their cousin, the bristlecone pine, which is found in the Inyo Mountains across the Owens Valley to the east. (Mike Prather.)

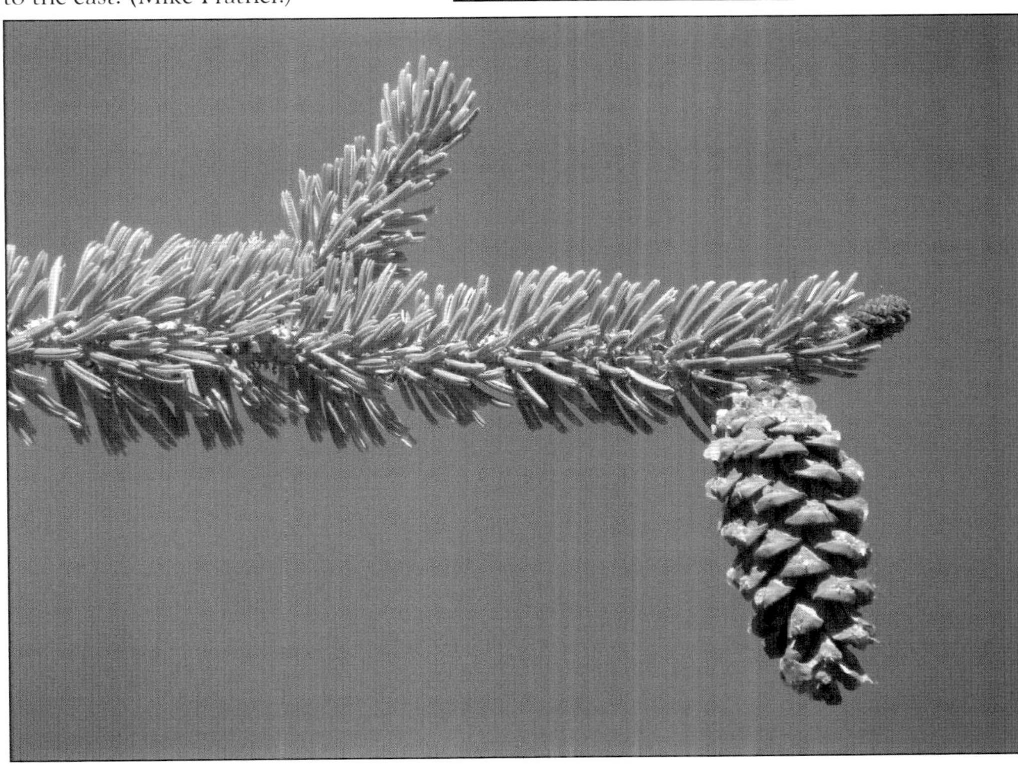